ABOUT ISLAND PRESS

From
Abundance
to Scarcity

Dear Lee,
Thanks for sharing
your knowledge and
experiences.

[signature]

From
Abundance
ᵗᵒ Scarcity

A History of
U.S. Marine Fisheries Policy

Michael L. Weber

ISLAND PRESS

Washington • Covelo • London

ISLAND PRESS is a trademark of the Center for Resource Economics.

Weber, Michael (Michael L.)
    From abundance to scarcity : a history of federal marine fisheries policy / by Michael L. Weber.
        p. cm.
Includes bibliographical references (p.)
    ISBN 1-55963-705-6 (cloth : alk. paper) — ISBN (1-55963-706-4) (paper : alk. paper)
    1. Fisheries—Government policy—United States—History. I. Title.
SH221 .W424 2001
333.95'6'0973—dc21

British Cataloguing-in-Publication Data available.

Printed on recycled, acid-free paper ⊛

Manufactured in the United States of America
10 9 8 7 6 5 4 3 2 1

For my father,
who taught me to persevere,
and for my brother,
who taught me to care

For my father,
who taught me to persevere,
and for my brother,
who taught me to care

Contents

Preface

In 1995, Peter Fricke of the National Marine Fisheries Service (NMFS) asked if I would be interested in writing a history of the agency and its predecessors back to 1940. This history was to accompany a similar history by Theodore Whaley Cart, whose thesis described federal involvement in marine fisheries between 1870 and 1940. Taken together, the two histories were to help the NMFS celebrate the 125 years that had passed since the U.S. Fish and Fisheries Commission was formed in 1870. I accepted the challenge and set about compiling background materials.

It is difficult for me to explain the pleasure I derived from reading annual reports in the Department of the Interior's library. Agency annual reports sound like dull stuff, but for me, they offered a glimpse into the way that political leaders then portrayed their world to the public and to other political leaders. There were times that an annual report startled me, as when I first read of Interior Secretary Stewart Udall's dream of powering coastal upwellings of nutrients with power from submerged nuclear power plants! Much of what I read helped in explaining how we have come to where we are in managing uses of marine wildlife.

Reconstructing the history of the NMFS, created by presidential order in 1970, was somewhat more difficult, for a simple reason: In the early 1980s, the agency ceased issuing annual reports. I do not know what paltry budget savings were generated from stopping the preparation and printing of those reports, but halting a tradition that stretched back more than century presented real difficulties for me as a historian. Fortunately, my career inside and outside the NMFS over the previous two decades gave me some advantage in reconstructing the period after the agency's annual reports ceased.

When I realized that the NMFS was not going to publish my history, I approached Island Press in 1997. About that time, Island Press was showing greater concern about marine issues. Dan Sayre was interested in my proposal, but asked that I reorganize the material thematically rather than chronologically. I happily agreed to do so.

As I set about reorganizing the material I had collected, I became more curious about the people behind the decisions that I read about in reports. So, I began a new line of research. By the time I completed my second round of research, I had interviewed dozens of people both inside and outside government who had been involved in key turning points pertaining to government policy on marine wildlife. I owe a special debt of gratitude to the following people who took the time to share with me their experiences and their insights: Lee Alverson, Lee Anderson, Henry Beasley, E. Curtis Bohlen, Gene Buck, Ken Coons, David Crestin, Lee Crockett, Jim Crutchfield, Scott Dickerson, Roland Finch, William Fox Jr., Peter Fricke, Spencer Garrett, Congressman Wayne Gilchrest, William Gordon, John Grandy, Eldon Greenberg, C. Wolcott Henry III, Ken Hinman, Suzanne Iudicello, Bob Jones, Milton Kaufman, Andy Mager, Roger McManus, Rod Moore, Bruce Morehead, Bill Mott, Paul Paradis, Frank Potter, G. Carleton Ray, Lewis Regenstein, Wendy Rhodes, Richard Roe, Carl Safina, Christine Stevens, Michael Sutton, Lee Talbot, John Twiss Jr., Stanley Wang, Jack Wise, Missy Wittler, and Nina Young.

I should note that I have worked with many of the people whom I interviewed for this book. While at the Center for Marine Conservation from 1980 to 1990, I worked closely with staff there and in other conservation organizations. I also worked with several people at the NMFS, in other agencies, in Congress, and in the fishing industry. From 1990 to 1994, I served as a special assistant to Bill Fox when he was director of the NMFS. In that position, I worked with agency staff, some of whom I interviewed for this book.

Both while at the Center for Marine Conservation and after I began working as a freelance writer in 1994, I worked under contract to some of those I interviewed and received funding for projects from the Munson Foundation and the David and Lucile Packard Foundation, among others. I neither sought nor received funding for writing this book other than the modest amount provided by Island Press.

I did not personally know many other interviewees, whom I contacted based on referrals by others or on my own research. It is fair to say that all my interviewees were authorities in their areas. Whether or not I had tangled with them in the past on this or that policy issue, they all were gracious and open in expressing their views and their recollections. Remarkably, only a few people from whom I requested an interview did not respond.

Many of those whom I interviewed also provided me with materials from their personal files that were enormously helpful. Others who provided information include W.T. Olds, Kate Naughten, and staff at the libraries of the

National Oceanic and Atmospheric Administration and the Department of the Interior.

I also benefited from comments on early drafts of individual chapters. For this, I wish to thank Henry Beasley, Bill Mott, Suzanne Iudicello, Terry Young, and William Schrank. Midway through the project, Peter Fricke generously reviewed the entire manuscript. Finally, Todd Baldwin at Island Press provided me with comments that were concise, challenging, and a sure guide for revising the manuscript. Todd's suggestions on reorganizing the manuscript were particularly valuable in establishing the book's themes. Whatever errors or causes of confusion may remain are entirely my responsibility.

MLW
Redondo Beach, California

Introduction

There is a new fish just beginning to appear in the markets around where I live. That is to say, it's not a new fish at all, but one that's been nosing about in Atlantic waters from New Foundland [sic] to North Carolina ever since fish began. However, we had not paid it any mind until the price of our usual fish became so astronomical that our fishery people began looking more carefully at their catch.

. . . Its looks are against it, however, and that is probably the reason we've not seen it in our markets here. The trouble is with its head, which is enormous, with a wide mouth full of vicious teeth, and it has a body that tapers abruptly from neck to tail. So dreadful is its appearance thought to be that even in France the fish is always sold without its head. . . .

At any rate, monkfish is what I saw the other day at my fish market—for the first time ever, and so very much cheaper than cod, haddock, sole, swordfish. Not many people know it around here, I was told by the proprietor. . . . As soon as word gets around, though, there will be demands for it, and it will be shipped all over the country, not just to Europe.

Thus did Julia Child introduce monkfish (*Lophius americanus*) to American cooks in a May 1979 article published in *McCall's* magazine. The path-breaking chef, who revolutionized American eating and cooking habits in the 1960s and 1970s, later cooked a 25-pound monkfish on her television program.

"By mentioning monkfish on her show, she introduced it to America. *Time* took a picture, and that's her power. She could take an underused item and after one show, monkfish takes off and it's still popular 20 years later," George Berkowitz of Boston's Legal Sea Foods commented to a Boston Globe reporter in 1997. French restaurants and home cooks in the United States took Julia Child's advice, and market demand for monkfish grew in the late 1970s and early 1980s. The average price that New England fishermen received for monkfish jumped from 35¢ per pound in 1978 to 60¢ in 1981.

As in other marine fisheries in the United States and elsewhere, catching and marketing monkfish soon outstripped understanding and management of the fishery.[1] Within 15 years of Child's article, monkfish populations off New England joined a growing list of overexploited marine wildlife populations.

For many years, New England scallop dredgers and trawlers had caught monkfish, but discarded most of them because there was no market for them. Although Atlantic coast fish markets sometimes sold monkfish as "the poor man's lobster," most monkfish landed in New England were exported to Europe where chefs considered it a delicacy. Government programs helped U.S. fishermen enter European markets for monkfish, as they had done earlier with other species such as skates and dogfish, which had attracted little interest among U.S. consumers.

The rise in monkfish prices, the decline in catches of cod, haddock, and several flounder species, and the National Marine Fisheries Service's (NMFS) promotion of monkfish as an "underutilized" alternative to groundfish caused New England fishermen to take a second look at monkfish in the late 1980s. Trawl fishermen, scallop dredgers, and gillnetters began targeting monkfish. The fishery caught fire in 1987, the year after exvessel prices in New England reached a peak of $1.29 per pound, more than twice the level just two years before. New England landings of monkfish alone nearly tripled from 2,053 metric tons in 1986 to 5,928 metric tons a year later.

In the late 1980s, average prices paid to fishermen for monkfish received another boost when exporters began supplying Japanese sushi bars with monkfish livers. By 1992, fishermen caught enough monkfish to supply processors with 322 tons of monkfish livers, for which they were paid an average of $3.66 per pound. During the winter months, fishermen could receive as much as $13.56 per pound for the pinkish-orange organs. The rise in prices for livers made it financially sensible for fishermen to land monkfish that dealers would have rejected before the market in livers developed.

The fishery might have cooled in the 1990s had the U.S. government not successfully removed trade barriers to South Korean imports of monkfish from the United States. Working through the World Trade Organization, trade representatives from the NMFS, the lead federal agency for marine fisheries management, received approval for the import of frozen monkfish by container load without the involvement of intermediaries. In 1995, Korean importers paid U.S. exporters $2.5 million for 734 metric tons of monkfish.

The growing foreign demand for monkfish kept prices strong and attracted heavier fishing effort. By 1997, landings of monkfish from Maine to the Carolinas reached their peak of 27,967 metric tons, more than $2\frac{1}{2}$ times the 10,000 metric tons of catch that scientists believed the fishery could take over the long term. Between its 1979 American debut and 1999, monkfish catapulted from 21st in value to 3rd in value among New England fisheries.

But the expansion of the monkfish fishery came at a tremendous biological cost. By 1996, monkfish populations had dropped to their lowest levels since NMFS annual trawl surveys had begun in 1963. Younger and smaller fish dominated catches, as larger, older fish were removed. In some years, the appearance of large groups of young monkfish from successful spawns encouraged more exploitation. The idea of allowing populations to rebuild themselves never caught on.

Part of the problem was that the decision to increase fishing required no justification other than market prices, but the decision to manage, in contrast, required a crisis. Until 1996, the burden of proof fell on those proposing restraints on the growth of fisheries. The presumption that fisheries were sustainable reflected a widespread belief in the limitless bounty of the oceans that found broad support in the scientific community as late as the 1970s. In comparison, little attention was paid to the numerous cases in which individual fisheries were fished out in a race to capitalize on new markets.

The monkfish fishery was under the jurisdiction of the NMFS, but the real power to manage it rested with regional fishery management councils. The lack of unequivocal scientific evidence of decline discouraged fisheries managers at the New England and Mid-Atlantic Fishery Management Councils from beginning to develop a management plan for the monkfish fishery until 1991. By 1994, a working group formed by the New England Fishery Management Council had developed alternative management schemes that proposed more management than fishermen wanted, but that would not end overfishing.

In 1996, after many meetings and public hearings, the councils proposed an amendment to the groundfish management plan intended to bring the monkfish fishery under some control by early 1998. But the complexity of the fishery led to great complexity in the management measures. Not only did some fishermen use different kinds of fishing gear to catch monkfish for market, but also, other fishermen incidentally caught monkfish that they might sell or discard. Each group of fishermen would have to be managed somewhat differently. Equitably allocating catch among these different types was fraught with controversy.

In this sad but common saga, developers, processors, marketers, and fishermen influenced the growth of the fishery far more than fishery managers. Managers adapted slowly to the growing threat of overfishing, while marketers responded with frightening speed and ingenuity. As NMFS administrators and members of the New England and Mid-Atlantic Fishery Management Councils wrestled with conflicting interests, viewpoints, proposals, and legal requirements, marketers sensed an opportunity in the pending restrictions on monkfish catches. In March 1999, a major supermarket chain in California devoted an entire page in an advertising supplement to monkfish. The advertisement noted that monkfish had become so popular that "catches have to be sharply limited."[2] For this supermarket chain, which distinguished itself by offering "rare tastes," the pending restrictions on monkfish catches were good news, since consumers were likely to pay more for a fish that apparently was becoming rarer every day.

The Management Paradox

In the last several decades of the twentieth century, in response to such catastrophes as befell the monkfish, Congress amended the country's principal marine fisheries law, the Magnuson-Stevens Fishery Conservation and Management Act, to require that each of eight regional fishery management councils overseen by the NMFS adopt definitions of overfished populations and overfishing in each of their fishery management plans. Based upon those definitions, the NMFS was required to determine in which fisheries the rate of exploitation jeopardized the capacity of a fishery "to produce the maximum sustainable yield on a continuing basis."[3]

In its report for 2000, the NMFS was unable to determine the status of more than 600 of the 905 fish populations within the geographical areas of the eight regional fishery management councils. Some of these species were the targets of major fisheries. For example, of 47 rockfish species caught by groundfish fishermen along the Pacific coast, the status of 37 was unknown. More generally, of the 287 fish populations that accounted for the vast majority of landings in the United States, 56 were overfished. In some overfished fisheries, excessive levels of exploitation continued, including yellowtail flounder (*Limanda fertuginea*) and summer flounder (*Paralicathys dentatus*) in the mid-Atlantic, queen conch (*Strombus ginas*) in the Caribbean, snappers and groupers in the South Atlantic, reef fish in the Gulf of Mexico, and several species of tuna, billfish, sharks, and swordfish in the Atlantic, as well as monkfish in New England and the mid-Atlantic.

Some overfished fisheries developed differently than the monkfish fishery.

For instance, some grew without the involvement of some participants mentioned earlier. Sometimes, it was the government (not chefs or retailers) that triggered the growth of a fishery. In other cases, the development of new fishing gear allowed fishermen to catch species that previously could not be caught economically. But with few exceptions, fishery managers became involved in fisheries well after investment, product development, marketing, and other activities were under way.

Thus, the story of the monkfish is not an isolated one. In fact, it is in many ways emblematic of the paradoxical nature of U.S. fisheries management agencies because they work to conserve fisheries even as (and usually after) they encourage their expansion. The pattern could first be seen as early as the nineteenth century, when the U.S. Fish and Fisheries Commission was founded by Spencer Fullerton Baird under the auspices of the Smithsonian Institution to resolve scientific issues surrounding a dispute over groundfish catches. The original functions of the fish commission (and its successor agencies) were to study the fish in U.S. waters, study fishing methods, compile statistics, and propagate food fish.

After Baird's death in 1887, Congress turned the fish commission into an independent agency and severed most of its ties with the Smithsonian Institution. In February 1914, the functions of the commission were placed in the Bureau of Fisheries in the new Department of Commerce and Labor. Management of the fur seal hunt on the Pribilof Islands in the Bering Sea also was transferred to the new Bureau of Fisheries from the Department of the Treasury. In April 1939, the Bureau of Fisheries, together with the Department of Agriculture's Bureau of the Biological Survey, was transferred to the U.S. Department of the Interior as part of Presidential Reorganization Plan No. II.

Under Reorganization Plan No. III of June 1940, the Bureau of Fisheries was merged with the Bureau of the Biological Survey to form the Fish and Wildlife Service in the Department of the Interior. This organization of federal fisheries activities persisted until Congress passed the Fish and Wildlife Act in 1956, which established the U.S. Fish and Wildlife Service with two bureaus: the Bureau of Commercial Fisheries and the Bureau of Sport Fisheries and Wildlife. Management responsibility for cetaceans and pinnipeds was given to the Bureau of Commercial Fisheries, while the Bureau of Sport Fisheries and Wildlife received responsibility for sea otters, manatees, and walrus.

Concern over the competitiveness of U.S. maritime industries and marine research capabilities grew in the 1960s, culminating in the formation of a commission on U.S. ocean policy and government programs. In 1969, the Commission on Marine Science, Engineering, and Resources, which came to be called the Stratton Commission after its chairman (Julius Stratton) issued a report called *Our Nation and the Sea*. Besides thoroughly reviewing U.S. ocean activities, the report made dozens of recommendations. Among the most significant of these recommendations, the Stratton Commission called for the consolidation of most federal ocean activities in an independent agency, modeled somewhat after the National Aeronautics and Space Administration. When the Nixon administration acted in 1970, it did not entirely accept the commission's recommendation. Instead of creating an independent agency, Executive Order 11564 established the National Oceanic and Atmospheric Administration (NOAA) in the Department of Commerce. Most functions of the Interior Department's Bureau of Commercial Fisheries and marine programs of the Bureau of Sport Fisheries and Wildlife were transferred to NOAA's National Marine Fisheries Service (NMFS).

This reorganization of ocean agencies resulted in separate federal management systems for marine, freshwater, and anadromous wildlife. The NMFS was given responsibility for marine fish and shellfish, while the U.S. Fish and Wildlife Service in the Department of the Interior was made responsible for federal management of freshwater fish and shellfish. The two agencies were to share management of anadromous species of fish.

The executive order also divided jurisdiction over marine mammals between the NMFS and the U.S. Fish and Wildlife Service. Under the executive order, the Bureau of Sport Fisheries and Wildlife, which had been responsible for the conservation and management of sea otters, Pacific walrus, polar bears, manatees, and dugongs, remained in the U.S. Fish and Wildlife Service. The Bureau of Commercial Fisheries, which had been responsible for other marine mammal species, was moved to the NMFS. This split jurisdiction was intended to be a temporary arrangement, but plans by the Nixon administration to create a single Department of Natural Resources that would have included all wildlife management were never fulfilled.[4] The temporary arrangement became permanent, and the conflict between conservation and commercial exploitation was thus left unresolved.

The Geography of Jurisdiction

Geographical jurisdiction of the various levels of government over marine wildlife was more stable than the organization of government agencies, although it presented a different set of tensions. Until the 1970s, state governments held jurisdiction over marine wildlife within state waters, which extended 3 miles offshore, except off the Gulf coasts of Florida and Texas, where the seaward boundary was 3 marine leagues (9 nautical miles) offshore. Beyond territorial waters lay the high seas, where nations were free to do as they wished, except as international agreements might constrain them.

Until passage of the Magnuson-Stevens Act, the only marine fisheries that the federal government actually managed were in the territories, principally Alaska and Hawaii. Otherwise, management of fishing was left in the hands of the individual states or of international commissions such as the International Pacific Halibut Commission and the International Whaling Commission.

Lack of coordination was a persistent problem in the management of fisheries that straddled state boundaries. In an attempt to address this problem, Congress established a compact among Atlantic coast states under the Atlantic States Marine Fisheries Commission in 1940. Congress granted similar authority for a compact among Pacific coast states in 1947 and among Gulf of Mexico states in 1949. In 1962, Alaska and Hawaii were added to the Pacific States Marine Fisheries Commission. In the 1980s, failure of middle-Atlantic states to adopt measures for the conservation of striped bass led Congress to authorize the federal government's imposition of a moratorium on fishing for striped bass in the territorial waters of any state that did not adopt the measures proposed by the Atlantic States Marine Fisheries Commission. This authority was later broadened to other shared fisheries in territorial waters.

Fisheries management also was influenced by international competition. In an early effort to protect domestic fishermen from foreign vessels, President Harry S. Truman issued a proclamation in 1945, claiming that the United States had the right to establish special conservation zones on the high seas adjacent to the territorial sea. In these zones, the United States would unilaterally adopt conservation measures if negotiations with foreign nations fishing there failed to reach an agreement.

In 1966, growing concern about the activities of large foreign fishing vessels just beyond state waters led Congress to extend U.S. fisheries management jurisdiction in a so-called contiguous zone between the territorial sea and 12 miles offshore. This action created a management vacuum since Congress did not extend state jurisdiction into the contiguous zone, nor did it provide clear authority for federal agencies to manage fishing in this zone.

By the early 1970s, when the United Nations launched negotiations for a new Law of the Sea, many countries were pressing for international sanction of

xxii   Introduction

fisheries jurisdictions to 200 miles offshore. In 1976, long before the United Nations negotiations concluded in 1982, Congress passed the Fishery Conservation and Management Act. (Later, this legislation became better known as the Magnuson-Stevens Act, reflecting the important roles that Alaska Senator Ted Stevens and Washington Senator Warren Magnuson played in the legislation.) The legislation asserted U.S. jurisdiction over marine fisheries in a fishery conservation zone that extended from territorial waters to 200 miles offshore. By an executive order issued in 1982, President Ronald Reagan renamed this zone the Exclusive Economic Zone, or EEZ, making U.S. terminology consistent with international practice under the United Nations Law of the Sea.

Today, the overlapping of jurisdictions is stable, but still offers the possibility of conflict. As with the tension between conservation and exploitation, the differing agendas of local, national, and international interests have profoundly shaped U.S. marine fisheries policy.

From Abundance to Scarcity

Since the establishment of the U.S. Fish and Fisheries Commission in 1870, federal policy on marine fisheries has reflected prevailing assumptions about the predictability and abundance of marine wildlife populations. Until the 1990s, federal policy and practice were generally based on the belief that the ocean's productivity was almost limitless and could be manipulated for maximum production and utilization. The chief goal of policy was to increase the capacity of U.S. fishing fleets to exploit this abundance. Fishing was assumed to be sustainable in the absence of significant evidence that it was not.

Although passage of the Magnuson-Stevens Fisheries Conservation and Management Act of 1976 marked a federal policy departure in other respects, it continued previous policies that promoted the expansion of exploitation. Indeed, the first 15 years after passage of the Magnuson-Stevens Act saw an unprecedented expansion of fishing capacity and catches by U.S. fleets.

By the 1990s, the collapse of the New England groundfish fishery and the decline of other fisheries in the United States and abroad reinforced shifts in assumptions that had first emerged in the 1970s regarding marine mammals and endangered species. Scientists no longer predicted that the oceans would yield 400–500 million metric tons annually. (Global catches had never exceeded 90 million metric tons.) Rather than viewing the ocean as endlessly productive and predictable, many scientists saw limits and uncertainties that traditional management had regularly ignored. Rather than using uncertainty as a license to expand exploitation, they insisted that the benefit of any doubt should go to conservation. Policy makers began to recognize that, rather than being limited by the size of fishing fleets, catches now were limited by the amount of fish.

Rather than abundance and predictability, marine wildlife populations seemed to be characterized by scarcity and uncertainty. This history of federal fisheries policy revolves around these two themes of abundance and scarcity.[5]

As described in chapter 1, scientific research was at the root of federal involvement in marine fisheries, although research that could aid in management of fisheries seldom received much support. Rather, the focus of research became location of new fish populations for U.S. fishing fleets. In the 1960s, predictions of almost limitless catches and scientific management of fisheries laid the basis for three decades of government effort to boost the exploitation level of the country's marine wildlife.

Increased catches were prevented by an absence of consumer demand and a lack of capacity to catch and process fish, as described in chapter 2. With passage of the Fish and Wildlife Act in 1956, the federal government launched consistent efforts to assist the fishing industry in overcoming these obstacles through product and technology development, marketing, and financial assistance.

The prevailing belief that humans could manipulate natural systems for maximum production precipitated the burst of dam construction in the Pacific Northwest that began in the 1930s. Chapter 3 describes how the construction of dams and the decline of salmon runs were hastened by assurances from aquaculturists and engineers that the damage from dams could be overcome through technology. In the 1950s and later, less dramatic forms of habitat destruction attracted the government's attention, but federal fisheries agencies were given little leverage to combat those losses.

In the first decade after World War II, the United States entered into several international agreements that aimed at promoting conservation and maximum utilization of marine fisheries. Like most other such agreements, the International Commission for Northwest Atlantic Fisheries (ICNAF), designed to manage fisheries in the northwest Atlantic, suffered major shortcomings. Chapter 4 describes the failure of ICNAF to control foreign fishing off New England in the 1960s and the failure of United Nations negotiations to arrive at a new international law of the sea. These failures contributed to passage of the Magnuson-Stevens Fishery Conservation and Management Act in 1976.

Chapter 5 reviews the federal government's limited role in the management of marine fisheries before the Magnuson-Stevens Act. Until 1976, the federal government's role was largely advisory to the states. Passage of the Magnuson-Stevens Act marked a major change in policy. The complexity of the management system created by the act, weak conservation standards, a pervasive lack of critical information, and the focus of government and industry on expansion of domestic fishing led to weak management of domestic fisheries. By the late 1980s, the New England groundfish fishery was showing unmistakable signs of overfishing.

While some scientists were predicting virtually limitless catches from the oceans in the 1960s, other scientists began urging greater caution and reliance on an ecosystem perspective. At the same time, animal rights activists and others began campaigning to end commercial whaling, which had decimated several great whale populations. As described in chapter 6, U.S. policy on whaling changed rapidly in the late 1960s, leading to the end of U.S. commercial whaling and a campaign for a global moratorium.

Chapter 7 describes the growing concerns of both government and the general public regarding the environment in the late 1960s and early 1970s. Although federal fisheries agencies were concerned about the impacts of pollution, Congress provided them with little authority to counteract the growing problem. At the same time, a campaign by animal rights activists overcame opposition in government agencies and the scientific community and led to passage of the Marine Mammal Protection Act (MMPA) in 1972. In a strong expression of the precautionary approach, which calls for erring on the side of conservation when faced with uncertainty, the MMPA prohibited "taking" marine mammals, with a few exceptions, unless it could be demonstrated that no harm would be done to a population. The legislation placed the NMFS at odds with its traditional constituents—the fishing industry.

In the 1980s, continued campaigning by animal rights advocates and conservationists led to the end of the United States's own fur seal hunt and to a global moratorium on commercial whaling. Chapter 8 describes how activists also pressed a reluctant NMFS to reduce both the drowning of dolphins in tuna nets and the drowning of endangered and threatened sea turtles in shrimp trawls.

Chapter 9 describes the growing recognition of the consequences arising from having to rely on poor information in managing fisheries and their impacts on ecosystems. After a lawsuit by conservation organizations nearly halted many U.S. fisheries, Congress adopted a mechanism for applying the precautionary approach to restrictions on the capture of marine mammals in fisheries. Internationally, the United Nations applied the precautionary approach in calling for an end to high seas drift net fishing, and explicitly included the approach in a treaty on international fisheries adopted in 1995.

The decade after passage of the Magnuson-Stevens Act was marked by rapid expansion of U.S. fleets, growing numbers of overfished fisheries, and economic decline and destructive competition among fishermen. With varying degrees of commitment and success, fishery management councils struggled to overcome these threats to fisheries. As described in Chapter 10, the decline of the New England groundfish fishery in the late 1980s triggered the involvement of conservation organizations that had formed their views in campaigns for marine mammals and endangered species. In 1996, these organizations and some fishermen's organizations succeeded in forcing a major reform of federal fisheries policy through the Sustainable Fisheries Act.

The book's conclusion begins by revisiting management of the Atlantic monkfish fishery, and then reviews the performance of the NMFS, the fishery management councils, and Congress in implementation of the Magnuson-Stevens Act. It discusses the introduction of new values into federal marine fisheries policy by the conservation community, and describes the emergence of international trade and the use of economic sanctions and consumer boycotts in influencing global standards of conduct. Finally, the conclusion reviews recent efforts to reduce fleets that expanded after passage of the Magnuson-Stevens Act and argues that reduction of fleets is the single most important challenge facing reformers.

Notes

1. As used in this book, the word fishery sometimes refers to an exploited population of fish. At other times, it refers to "the interaction between some kind(s) of fishermen using some kind(s) of fishing gear to catch some kind(s) of fish in a certain area during a certain time," in the words of Jack Wise. Fishery management has to do with the latter definition.
2. From a March 1999 advertising supplement of Pavillions supermarkets.
3. 16 U.S.C. 1802 (29).
4. More confusing was the situation with sea turtles. Hours of negotiations led to an agreement that the NMFS would be responsible for sea turtles while in the water. The Fish and Wildlife Service retained authority over management activities while sea turtles were nesting or hatching on land.
5. This book focuses upon fisheries policies and practices that the NMFS and its predecessors carried out, particularly since World War II. Little is said about policies and programs regarding freshwater fisheries, which NMFS's predecessors pursued. Furthermore, the following discussions emphasize policies and practices regarding commercial fisheries, since these dominated the concerns of federal agencies throughout the history of federal involvement in marine fisheries.

Part I | Abundance

*Albatross.
at Washington
navy yard*

1870–1940   In 1882, the U.S. Commission of Fish and Fisheries established its first permanent research station at Woods Hole, Massachusetts. In 1902, a second station was established at Beaufort, North Carolina, at a federal cost of less than $13,000. By 1941, the federal government had constructed 110 fish hatcheries around the country, at an average cost of $513,000, adjusted for inflation.

During its first decade, the commission had to rely upon vessels loaned or transferred from other agencies. In 1882, however, the commission completed the construction of two research vessels: the 200-foot Albatross *and the 146-foot* Fish Hawk. *Between 1870 and 1940, artificial propagation of fish and shellfish dominated federal funding for fisheries, accounting for 65% of the total. Federal funding for biological research averaged 8% of the entire budget for fisheries activities. Funding for industry services averaged 3% of the total.*

In 1940, Presidential Reorganization Plan III merged the Interior Department's Bureau of Fisheries with the Agriculture Department's Biological Survey to form the Fish and Wildlife Service in the Department of the Interior with four divisions: fishery biology, fish culture, fishery industries, and Alaska fisheries.

Chapter 1 | The Sciences

Traditional groundfish fishermen who worked the nearshore waters of Massachusetts and Rhode Island with handheld longlines had endured enough. Newfangled fish traps seemed to be robbing them of their catch and threatening their future. But the fishermen who tended the traps charged the longliners with interfering in their livelihood. In the winter of 1869–1870, the controversy spilled into the state legislatures of Rhode Island and Massachusetts. The Massachusetts legislature refused to intervene in the controversy, while the Rhode Island legislature considered complete and immediate removal of the traps. The lack of knowledge about fish off New England fueled the controversy.

Combining his stature as a scientist with uncanny political instincts, an ambitious young naturalist at the Smithsonian Institution in Washington, D.C., by the name of Spencer Fullerton Baird transformed the controversy into a platform for committing the federal government to investigating marine life off New England. Baird, who was born in Reading, Pennsylvania, in 1823, had joined the staff of the Smithsonian Institution in 1850, after a brief career as a professor of natural history at Dickinson College.

During summer collecting expeditions in New England, Baird had gained firsthand experience with fishermen's complaints about declining fish populations. Baird believed that resolving the controversy depended upon greater understanding of the fishes themselves. With $100 from the Smithsonian and a 30-foot Treasury Department sloop, Baird continued his own investigations in 1870. By the end of the year, he had prepared a proposal for an expanded inquiry that would require a larger budget and its own institution.

On January 23, 1871, Congressman Henry Dawes of Massachusetts introduced Baird's proposal as a joint resolution of Congress. In urging support for the proposal, Congressman Dawes quoted a supporting letter from Baird: "Before intelligent legislation can be initiated, however, and measures taken that will not unduly oppress or interfere with interests already established, it is necessary that a careful, scientific research be entered upon, for the purpose of determining what really should be done; since any action presupposes a knowledge of the history and habits of the fish of our coast, that, I am sorry to say, we do not at present possess."[1]

Less than three weeks later, President Ulysses S. Grant signed a joint congressional resolution requiring the appointment of a Commissioner of Fish and Fisheries. The unsalaried fisheries commissioner was to undertake an inquiry aimed at "ascertaining whether any . . . diminution in the number of the food-fishes [sic] of the coast and the lakes of the United States has taken place; and, if so, to what causes the same is due; and also whether any and what protective, prohibitory, or precautionary measures should be adopted."[2]

The U.S. Fish and Fisheries Commission was a commission of one, and Baird the first fisheries commissioner. Baird successfully argued for insulating the office from political interference by making the position unsalaried and by insisting on scientific training. Because the work of the commission was expected to take just a few years, Congress provided no office space. Instead, Baird operated the commission out of his home.

Baird never resolved the controversy that gave rise to the commission. Like the many later controversies that engulfed the New England groundfish fishery, and many other fisheries, the conflict between fishermen using different gears had more to do with the fishermen than with the fish. It was unlikely that groundfish populations were in any danger of overfishing, given the rudimentary techniques that fishermen used, but the competition between fishermen was quite real. No fisherman owned the fish until he caught it. Once several fishermen began targeting the same fish populations or fish in the same area, each fisherman felt compelled to race to catch fish before a competitor could. This "race for the fish" generally produced conflicts between fishermen but did little damage to fish populations. The race did, however, have the unexpected consequence of putting science at the center of controversy surrounding marine fisheries, a place it would never relinquish.

The U.S. Fish and Fisheries Commission and its successors in the Departments of Interior and of Commerce were not charged specifically with resolving controversy, but with conducting and sponsoring research to increase knowledge generally, to assist the fishing industry, and to promote scientific management of fisheries. Especially after World War II, the federal government expanded its role in locating new fisheries off the United States and abroad as a means of increasing the economic viability of the fishing industry and to maintain U.S. leadership in the world. At the same time, the demand for data on fish populations and on fishing grew as governments at all levels attempted to manage conflicts among fishing fleets and extract maximum yield from fisheries. Through the 1950s and 1960s, confidence grew in the ability of scientists to manage fisheries for maximum sustainable yield. Together with estimates of potential catches that proved wildly generous, this confidence in scientific management encouraged a drive to increase catches that continued for the next 25 years.

Exploration

The birth of the U.S. Fish and Fisheries Commission is one of several emblematic events in the rise of marine biology in the 1860s and 1870s. Naturalists and oceanographers expanded their explorations of the oceans' depths, once thought to be entirely lifeless. Until 1860, scientists believed that the oceans' deepest waters never moved and, as a result, never received life-giving nutrients. The recovery of a cable encrusted with sea life from waters off Sardinia in the Mediterranean Sea brought an end to the theory and a beginning to one of the richest periods of ocean exploration in history. In December 1872, the HMS *Challenger* began its four-year, 69,000-mile voyage of exploration that collected 13,000 specimens of plants and animals from the oceans.

Although the immediate pretext for research by the fish commission was to investigate the causes for an alleged decline in New England food fishes, the institutional stature of the commission allowed Spencer Fullerton Baird to pursue his principal interest as a biologist: to assemble a portrait of marine wildlife in New England waters. Baird faced the daunting task of funding his research in the face of congressional skepticism about the practical benefits of field research. Instead of seeking direct funding from Congress for the commission's work, Baird used the status of the fish commission as a government agency to secure support from other government agencies. In the first summer of research under the auspices of the commission, Baird set up his research headquarters in a building at Woods Hole, Massachusetts, owned by the Light House Board. In 1873, Baird talked the Navy into lending the fish commission an 80-ton steamer to explore the waters off Maine.

Baird had no staff, but with offers of collecting gear, small boats, and lab tables, he was able to recruit other biologists. While their tools were rudimentary, these biologists enjoyed the enormous advantage of waters within shouting distance of shore that had never been explored. In the first summer of research, 106 different species of finfish were collected, and Baird began preparing life histories for scup (*Stenotomus chrysops*) and bluefish (*Pomatomus saltatrix*). By the end of the commission's first decade, researchers had identified 1,000 new species in New England waters.

Baird desperately wanted the fish commission to establish a permanent research station. Rather than looking first to Congress, Baird sought out and obtained private funding. Between private support and later, congressional appropriations, the fish commission was able to open its first permanent facility at Woods Hole in 1885. Baird also secured funding for the USS *Albatross,* the country's first research vessel dedicated to oceanographic and fisheries research. Launched in 1882, the *Albatross* later sailed to the Pacific, where it explored the waters off the Pacific coast, Alaska, and as far west as the Philippines and Formosa (Taiwan).

Although Baird had greater interest in a general understanding of the fish off American shores, he and the fish commission did carry out research into fisheries problems. In 1871, for example, Baird conducted public hearings at ports in southern New England regarding the controversial decline of food fishes that had been a primary reason to create the fish commission. Baird used testimony from these hearings and results of his expeditions to prepare the commission's first report, which was issued in 1873.

Baird also set a precedent for linking research to benefit scientific understanding with research to benefit fishermen. In instructing the captain of the *Albatross* before an expedition in New England waters in 1883, Baird directed that the distribution of fish should be noted. Baird then suggested the following: "Should you deem it expedient you will cruise off the coast a sufficient distance to determine the outward line of motion of the fish, and you will communicate to such fishing vessels as you may meet any information that may enable them the more successfully to prosecute their labors."

Baird may simply have been showing his characteristic good political sense in seeking to benefit commercial fishermen while fulfilling his own desire for knowledge about the distribution of fishes off southern New England. Decades later, however, the link between science and commerce was made explicit when Congress began to direct the Bureau of Fisheries to seek out new species for commercial fishermen. In 1940, for instance, Congress appropriated $100,000 for a survey of king crabs in waters off Alaska, which led to a booming fishery by the end of the decade.

As in Baird's day, the task of locating new fish populations after World War II was left to the government. The fishing industry itself invested very little in exploring new fishing grounds. For federal fisheries biologists, this was just as well. Research cruises aimed at locating commercially valuable fish populations enabled them to continue their basic biological work.

During the late 1950s and early 1960s, the Bureau of Commercial Fisheries enlarged its fleet of research vessels. With these vessels and chartered commercial fishing vessels, the bureau expanded its exploratory cruises into deeper water and to waters off other countries. In New England, the R/V *Delaware* discovered new fishing grounds for ocean perch (*Sebastes marinus*) in 1956. The R/V *Oregon* located concentrations of deepwater red shrimp (*Hymenopenaeus robustus*) and yellowfin tuna (*Thunnus albacares*) in the Gulf of Mexico. The *Oregon* later located large concentrations of pink shrimp (*Penaeus duorarum*) and brown shrimp (*Penaeus aztecus*) off French Guiana. Off Washington, the R/V *John N. Cobb* used an echo sounder to locate areas suitable for trawling for Petrale sole (*Eopsetta jordani*), Dover sole (*Microstomus pacificus*), and Pacific ocean perch (*Sebastodes alutus*). Other vessels explored the western Pacific for tuna and the waters off West Africa.

"It was the neatest job a young graduate student could have," says Richard Roe about exploratory cruises in the Gulf of Mexico conducted by the Bureau of Commercial Fisheries during the 1960s. Roe later served in several senior positions at the NMFS, including regional director in New England.

"Surprisingly, there was very little known about the biota of the Gulf of Mexico and the Caribbean," Roe says. "We did things that today you wouldn't be able to do. We dragged all the way out to 2,000 fathoms, collecting and studying deepwater animals. We shipped stuff off wholesale to the Smithsonian, all of which was new, lots of new species and genera."

"In the 1960s, we started doing some longline research in the Gulf and Caribbean because the Japanese were operating down there with longlines fishing for yellowfin tuna," says Roe. "We would get access to their published reports, and noticed there were some billfish being taken, particularly swordfish. So we started doing our own exploratory long-lining, and we found swordfish."

The Bureau of Commercial Fisheries made a point of quickly disseminating the results of such cruises to the commercial fishing industry. In some cases, commercial fishing awaited further government research on fishing gear, processing equipment, or marketing. In the mid-1950s, for example, the *Delaware* tested the effectiveness of different types of fishing gear for exploiting newly discovered Atlantic bluefin tuna (*Thunnus thynnus*).

The federal government sometimes intervened even more strongly in the development of fisheries. A year after the R/V *John N. Cobb* first located large schools of Pacific hake (*Merluccius productus*) off the state of Washington in 1964, the federal government chartered the commercial fishing vessel *St. Michael* to continue this research. At the end of its charter, the *St. Michael* began fishing commercially for hake, becoming the first U.S. commercial vessel to do so. The federal government was so anxious to develop this fishery that it also provided trawls and depth finders to several other fishing vessels. With this assistance, fishing effort grew, as did landings. In 1966, the small fleet landed 1,800 metric tons of hake, which was processed into fish meal and cat food. Offshore, an even larger fleet of factory trawlers from the Soviet Union began fishing for hake as well, landing 100,000 metric tons.

The expansion of the Gulf of Mexico longline fishery for swordfish (*Xiphias gladius*) followed a similar pattern of government research cruises and encouragement fostering increased exploitation by U.S. fishing fleets.

"We convinced a couple of long-liners to come down from Maine, about 1965 or 1966, and they came down and made absolutely bonanza trips, because the fishery was unexploited," says Roe. "They were large fish. Once that fishery began to open up and people started making bucks, down came the long-liners. And of course, in those days, there were no regulations. They started pounding on that resource, as well as marlin and sharks and a lot of the other species you catch on longlines."

In the absence of effective controls, landings of swordfish from the Gulf of Mexico grew to 157 metric tons in 1970 and reached a peak of 957 metric tons in 1989.

"Our swordfish fishery has been banged to hell and gone," says Roe. "It all started in many ways back in those days, because we moved all the way up the East Coast with our exploratory efforts and essentially opened that whole area up to the fishing industry, [which] had not bothered to come down there because they didn't think that there was much there."

"It was something that started out with good intentions, but because of the lack of controls, it really got out of hand."

The Race for Data

Whether directly managing fisheries or advising state and international organizations, federal fisheries agencies needed to know how marine wildlife populations might respond to different levels and types of fishing. Although theories and population models changed over the years, there was little change in the kinds of hard data required by the models. The distribution of ages among fish in a population, size and age at sexual maturity, and natural mortality rates were among the most common types of information that had to be assembled.

Some of this data could be obtained by examining what fishermen caught and brought to land. In collecting statistics on fisheries, as in collecting specimens off Woods Hole, the fish commission enlisted the help of other agencies. In collaboration with the Bureau of the Census, the fish commission launched the first comprehensive survey of U.S. fisheries as part of the 1880 census. Specialists gathered information on the number of fishermen, vessels, and catch in all areas of the country except the Mississippi River and Alaska. The resulting seven-volume survey, *The Fisheries and the Fishery Industries of the United States,* became the standard reference for two decades.

The physical limitations on collecting fisheries information were enormous. For decades, the standard equipment of a government "canvasser" included no more than a typewriter, a briefcase, and a portable file box. In 1938, some agents had their tasks lightened, if not their luggage, with the addition of an adding machine that could not subtract.

Until 1928, when canvassers began using agency automobiles, transportation was by railroad or street trolley, horse, or buggy, when it was not by "shank's mare." An agent might begin a survey of South Atlantic fisheries during January in Key West, Florida, then proceed north, county by county, until reaching North Carolina in the fall. Turnover in agents compromised the quality of the information, and the extensive travels reduced the frequency of surveys. Discrepancies in the ways that fishermen, processors, and state agencies reported landings of different species further undermined the reliability of these statistics.

In 1940, the statistical section in the branch of Commercial Fisheries set out to solve this problem by assigning agents to field offices in the Atlantic, Gulf, and Central States regions. It was only in 1950, however, that a sufficient number of agents were available to survey all states. Until then, comprehensive surveys of landings, vessels, and other data were sporadic in some regions, such as the Gulf of Mexico and the South Atlantic.

For most fisheries, landing statistics were the only systematic, long-term data available. They often provided evidence of growing fishing effort and always served as an illuminating historical record. Landings statistics, however, had weaknesses. Among other things, intentional and unintentional misreporting often undermined their reliability. Landings statistics also excluded whatever marine wildlife was caught and discarded because, for example, it had no market value or was under legal size limits.

In some fisheries, the federal government tried to fill this gap partly by requiring fishermen to record all that they caught in a logbook. The reliability of this information was also open to question for several reasons. Tallying and logging such information was time-consuming, and as a result, logbooks often were incomplete. In some fisheries, the identification of species could be very difficult.

To increase the accuracy and reliability of such fishery-dependent data, the NMFS sometimes placed trained observers on a small group of fishing vessels, as fisheries agencies did elsewhere in the world. These observers recorded critical information about catches and sometimes took samples for later analysis, for example, of age and health. Information collected by observers also provided a standard for judging the reliability of information collected in logbooks.

Placing observers on domestic fishing vessels was problematic. Besides concerns about liability for the accidental injury of a government observer, fishermen feared that the use of information collected by observers would be used for enforcement purposes. Placing observers on foreign vessels proved far easier. As foreign fishing effort grew off the United States in the 1960s, the federal government negotiated agreements with foreign governments that included requirements for U.S. observers on their vessels in certain areas.[3]

Thus, even the most reliable of such fishery-dependent data suffered from serious flaws. Most significantly, the information generally was not collected in a statistically valid fashion. Commercial fishing vessels sampled marine wildlife communities only in those areas that they fished. Also, commercial fishing gear often failed to capture important parts of a marine wildlife community, such as young fish that escaped through the meshes of commercial trawls. Finally, comparing catches in commercial fishing gear between years became highly unreliable, as fishermen changed their gear and practices.

The only way of gathering information on marine wildlife populations that met the standards of statistical models was through surveys that operated independently of fishing activities. By sampling from randomly selected areas with standard gear over a period of years, surveys begun in the 1960s provided a much more reliable, if still imperfect, picture of trends in marine wildlife populations. Compared to the investment in exploratory cruises, the federal investment in research aimed at managing fisheries was spotty and often driven by crises in commercial fisheries.

Scientifically designed surveys enjoyed little support among fishermen, politicians, or even federal fisheries managers, for several reasons. Sending vessels offshore to sample marine wildlife over large areas was an expensive form of research that often did not yield clear, unequivocal answers to controversial questions. Also, the methodology of randomly selecting sampling areas led to sampling in areas that were not fished. This appeared to fly in the face of observations by fishermen, who claimed that they could find fish when scientists could not.

The apparent irrelevance of statistically valid surveys was further aggravated by the seemingly small number of samples upon which estimates were based. Research surveys also did not provide the kind of quick economic and political payoff that attracted support to other types of research, such as product development or surveys to locate unexploited fish populations. Indeed, the results from resource assessment surveys sometimes ran counter to the short-term interests of fishermen. Finally, scientists and research program managers did little to encourage better understanding of surveys or to engage fishermen in identifying issues that surveys might illuminate.

In several fisheries, resource assessment surveys were carried out for several decades. In 1963, in response to a quadrupling of foreign fishing effort in New England waters, the Bureau of Commercial Fisheries launched the longest-running program of bottom trawl surveys in the world. During the fall, and in later years during the spring, Bureau of Commercial Fisheries research vessels used trawls to sample bottom-dwelling fish and shellfish at hundreds of randomly selected sites in waters of 2 to 200 fathoms deep from Maine to Cape Hatteras. These surveys, which were coordinated through the International Commission for the Northwest Atlantic Fisheries (ICNAF), demonstrated that foreign fleets were overfishing groundfish, and led to increasingly strict quotas in the early 1970s.

As the controversy over foreign fishing off the Atlantic coast built in the late 1960s, the demand for scientific advice grew. Between 1963 and 1977, the United States and seven other countries carried out more than 200 joint research projects on 40 different vessels. Scientists in the United States and elsewhere scrambled to develop models that could portray the impact of fishing on the marine wildlife communities off New England.

In 1976, passage of the Magnuson-Stevens Act, which required that the federal government manage fisheries in federal waters, generated an immediate demand for all kinds of fisheries data. In some regions, the demand for information spurred a commitment to annual surveys, such as those conducted in New England. In 1979, for instance, NMFS scientists began annual bottom trawl surveys of the enormous groundfish and crab populations within the 200-mile limits off Alaska established by the Magnuson-Stevens Act. As domestic fish-

ing effort off Alaska grew in the 1980s, Alaska scientists undertook other surveys, including surveys of pollock (*Theragra chalcogrammus*) on their winter
spawning grounds.

In most areas of the country, however, annual systematic surveys continued to take a back seat to other pressing demands and political agendas. During the 1980s, the Reagan administration's cuts in the NMFS budget, including research and data collection, combined with competing demands on the
aging and faltering federal research fleet to reduce the capacity for biological
surveys. Regular surveys were carried out only where there was a long tradition,
as in New England, or strong political support, as in Alaska. Elsewhere, surveys
were irregular, undermining their usefulness in managing fisheries.

The Rise of Maximum Sustainable Yield

The desire to match fishing effort with the biological productivity of fish populations spurred not only the collection of biological data but also the development of theories about the causes for fluctuations in exploited fish populations. In the 1890s, E. W. Holt suggested that overfishing was caused by taking
spawning fish out of an ecosystem. According to a rival theory of Petersen, who
was the first to place fisheries within an economic context, overall profitability
would be greater if fish were allowed to grow to a larger size. In 1918, Baranov
developed a quantitative explanation that equated fishing effort with changes
in key biological parameters, such as mortality and growth rates.

By the 1930s, government biologists could claim some success in the management of Alaska salmon runs, where the federal government did have authority to apply its research directly to the management of fisheries. Likewise,
scientific advice contributed to successful efforts by the Pacific Halibut Commission to rebuild depleted halibut populations off Alaska. With some justification, then, government and academic biologists argued that science could not
only avert overexploitation but ensure that the country received maximum benefit from its fisheries. In his 1941 annual report, the first director of the Fish
and Wildlife Service, Ira N. Gabrielson, ventured the following claim about the
benefits of scientific management: "Estimates based upon biological and statistical research have disclosed that the annual yield of the commercial fisheries
can be increased within a few years by as much as 46 percent. Management procedures would result in a moderate curtailment of catch during the first year,
but an increasing yield would become possible during succeeding years until
maximum productivity is attained."[4]

In the next year, Director Gabrielson confidently referred to fishery biology as "an exact science" that should guide the use of marine resources. The success of the Allies in World War II and the accompanying technological and economic achievements greatly enhanced confidence in the capacity of quantitative science to extract maximum benefit from living marine resources.

In the early 1950s, the theory of fisheries management took a dramatic turn with the development and adoption of maximum sustainable yield (MSY) as the gold standard for modern fisheries management. Drawing upon work by Milner Schaefer at the Bureau of Commercial Fisheries and Michael Graham in Britain, William Herrington, a biologist in the State Department, successfully promoted adoption of MSY as the standard for U.S. fisheries management, beginning with the ICNAF.

MSY was defined as the largest annual catch or yield in terms of weight of fish caught by both commercial and recreational fishermen that could be taken continuously from a population of fish under existing environmental conditions. The MSY standard was based on a sound observation that up to a point, and for some species, catching fish increased the amount of fish that could be caught. According to the theory, removing fish made more food available for remaining fish that thereby grew faster. For practical purposes, scientists and fishery managers assumed that a population of fish would produce the most fish at about half its unexploited size. In this way, the theory of MSY provided a scientific rationale for reducing fish populations as a matter of priority.

Economists built upon the theory of MSY in developing another model that aimed at determining the size of population or rate of fishing that would generate maximum economic yield, or MEY. Writing in 1956, Interior Secretary Fred A. Seaton confidently put the case for economically efficient management of fish populations: "With fuller understanding through research will come fuller realization of true conservation. For many species it will be possible to direct fishing to take fish at the time in their lives—considering growth rates and mortality rates—when the yield is greatest, and to deploy fishing time to encourage the most profitable and productive balance among fish stocks."[5]

Like other, later scientific formulations that were incorporated in fisheries policy, the limitations of MSY and MEY were largely ignored by decision makers and often by scientists. Among other shortcomings, these models assumed that the environment itself did not fluctuate and that interactions among fish populations had minimal effect. Neither assumption was borne out in reality.

Because fisheries generally developed far faster than information about them, necessary biological information was often scarce. The lack of information and knowledge about the dynamics of individual populations meant that half of the time, scientists best estimates of MSY for a population were above actual MSY. By using such estimates of MSY for setting annual quotas, decision makers tended to set quotas at unsustainable levels. The logical, but pernicious outcome of keeping catches at levels equal to or above actual MSY was that a population would be driven toward extinction at an accelerating rate as was observed by Sidney Holt, one of the founders of the MSY approach, in 1997. Even when government scientists warned that fishing at the same or increased levels would jeopardize future catches, decision makers often exploited the imprecision of the advice and allowed unsustainable levels of catch to continue.

The shortcomings of basing management of individual fisheries on MSY were also obscured by more general views of the oceans and of scientists's ability to manipulate their productivity. In 1970, the Department of the Interior's annual report captured the tenor of the times. "Now fisheries experts speculate on the possibility and the probability of literally 'farming the ocean.' These experts talk of huge undersea fish 'ranches' where fish are herded like cattle and fenced in by curtains of air-bubbles, and of artificial water-circulation techniques being used to increase plankton productivity. It takes only a lively imagination to envision whole cities under the sea."[6]

While farming the seas remained largely a matter of the imagination, the government's commitment to expanded, scientifically managed exploitation of fish populations grew as surely as scientists increased their estimates of potential catches. Even before the end of World War II, federal fisheries managers were convinced that there were plenty of fish to catch off U.S. shores. In 1944, Fish and Wildlife Service director Ira N. Gabrielson called for a government program to help the commercial fishing industry expand its catches to a potential 3.2 million metric tons—well above previous catches that averaged 2.0 million metric tons. Two decades later, in 1964, the Bureau of Commercial Fisheries estimated potential U.S. catches at 10 million metric tons—five times the highest previous catch. In 1975, even these estimates were nearly doubled, when the NMFS suggested that catches off the United States could grow to as much as 18 million metric tons. (Commercial landings at U.S. ports never exceeded 5 million metric tons.)

The generous estimates of possible U.S. catches reflected similar trends in estimates for world catches. "Many marine experts believe that about 90 to 95 percent of the ocean's productivity presently is unused and that utilization can be increased at least tenfold without endangering aquatic stocks,"[7] the Interior Department reported in 1964. "If so, under sound conservation management the world's ocean could produce at least 500 million tons of fish and seafood products annually, as opposed to 50 million tons today." In 1967, the Department of the Interior's estimates grew to between 1 and 2 billion tons annually, out of the 700 billion tons of living matter that scientists estimated the oceans produced each year. The department boasted that this was ten times the food necessary to feed the world's 3 billion people.

The rush of higher and higher estimates of potential catches culminated in 1969 with the findings of the distinguished panel of scientists and policy makers who made up the Stratton Commission.[8] In its report, the commission concluded: "It is, therefore, more realistic to expect total annual production of marine food products (exclusive of aquaculture) to grow to 400 to 500 million metric tons before expansion costs become excessive. Even this estimate may be too conservative if significant technological breakthroughs are achieved in the ability to detect, concentrate, and harvest fish on the high seas and in the deep ocean." Besides briefly encouraging investment in marine research, the Stratton Commission report reinvigorated the centuries-old belief in the boundless wealth of the oceans.

Other scientists offered less generous estimates, and many of the most optimistic qualified their estimates. The distinguished fisheries scientist and director of the Scripps Institute of Oceanography, Milner Schaefer, estimated that conventional fishing methods could conservatively produce 200 million metric tons of fish.[9] (Through the 1990s, world catches never exceeded 90 million metric tons.) There were dissenting voices within the federal government as well. In a blistering rejection of the Bureau of Commercial Fisheries's budget proposal for fiscal year 1970, the assistant director of the Bureau of the Budget, James Schlesinger, questioned the fisheries agency's estimate that the oceans would yield between 240 million and 1.2 billion tons of fish and shellfish.

"[I]t seems unlikely that the potential sustained yield of fish to man is appreciably greater than 100 million tons," Schlesinger quoted an advisor. "It is clear that, while the yield can be still further increased, the resource is not vast. At the present rate, the industry can continue to expand for no more than a decade."

A later report, developed by the National Oceanic and Atmospheric Administration (NOAA) as the Magnuson-Stevens Act was being drafted, warned that estimates of potential catches should be used with caution. The report also noted that increasing overall catches depended on increased catches of unfamiliar species, for which processing and marketing remained questionable. The NOAA also warned that catches of these species would reduce catches of more desirable species higher on the food chain.

The desire to reverse the decline of the domestic fishing industry's global stature overwhelmed this measured reasoning. "In that era, everyone believed that there was a whole wealth of resources out there," said Lee Alverson in 2000, who participated in many of the discussions about the potential of fish catches in the 1960s. "You had people like Wib Chapman suggesting a thousand million metric tons, but nobody bothered to look at the caveats. He was talking about biological productivity down on the planktonic level. Of course, he knew you couldn't harvest it at that time. But everybody took his numbers and ignored the various limitations that were set on them."

The implications of ignoring the warnings were enormous. If fisheries were for all practical matters limitless, there was little need for caution. Rather than managing exploitation to stay within biological limits, governments and fishing fleets soon were striving to expand exploitation as quickly as possible to satisfy public and private desires for cheap food and economic growth. The policies that guided the federal government's involvement in marine fisheries for the rest of the century were founded upon these assumptions of abundant living marine resources and of the capacity of science to guide their maximum sustainable use.

Summary

From the beginning, scientific research was at the root of federal involvement in marine fisheries. Besides providing information and advice to policy makers, federal scientists also assisted the fishing industry in locating fish populations. In the 1950s and 1960s, exploratory fishing blossomed as the federal government sought to encourage the growth of the domestic industry.

Although the federal government systematically collected information on commercial landings of marine wildlife, it did not regularly collect information on marine wildlife that was caught but not landed. With a few exceptions, the government did not sponsor research surveys that could gather information on fish populations independently of the activities of fishing fleets.

In the 1940s, federal policy makers emphasized their ability to manage commercial fisheries in a scientific manner. A decade later, a general theory of fisheries management, which aimed at producing a maximum sustainable yield, came to dominate thinking about fisheries. For the most part, the shortcomings of this model were ignored. At the same time, estimates of the oceans' productivity grew, fostering continued belief in the limitless capacity of marine wildlife populations to sustain exploitation. Government policy makers believed that commercial landings of marine wildlife were limited principally by the lack of capacity to catch them.

Notes

1. Quoted in Cart, T. W. 1968. "The Federal Fisheries Service, 1871–1940." A thesis submitted to the faculty of the University of North Carolina at Chapel Hill in partial fulfillment of the requirements for the degree of Master of Arts in the Department of History.
2. Ibid.
3. Later bilateral agreements required by the Magnuson-Stevens Act of 1976 included provisions for placing U.S. observers on foreign vessels fishing in the U.S. Exclusive Economic Zone. In contrast to the domestic fishing vessels, foreign fishing vessels thereby became a rich source of information on fish populations off U.S. coasts. By the late 1980s, however, this source of information vanished with the full Americanization of fisheries in U.S. waters and the exclusion of foreign fishing vessels from waters within 200 miles of U.S. shores.
4. U.S. Department of the Interior. 1941. *Annual Report of the Secretary of the Interior: Fiscal Year Ended June 30, 1941.* U.S. Government Printing Office, Washington, D.C.
5. U.S. Department of the Interior. 1956. *Annual Report of the Secretary of the Interior: Fiscal Year Ended June 30, 1956.* U.S. Government Printing Office, Washington, D.C.
6. U.S. Department of the Interior. 1972. *River of Life, Water: The Environmental Challenge.* U.S. Government Printing Office, Washington, D.C.
7. U.S. Department of the Interior. 1965. *Quest for Quality: U.S. Department of the Interior Conservation Year Book.* U.S. Government Printing Office, Washington, D.C.
8. The Stratton Commission was formally known as the Commission on Marine Science, Engineering and Resources.
9. From Warner, William W. 1983. *Distant Water.* Little, Brown and Company, Boston, Massachusetts.

1940–1945   During World War II, the federal government reorganized many of its programs to meet the need for food and supplies in the war effort. The Fish and Wildlife Service found itself thrust into managing part of a wartime economy rather than simply acting as a manager of wildlife.

The service's biological research focused upon increasing production from existing fisheries and discovering new ones. In 1940, for example, Congress appropriated $100,000 for a one-year study of king crab in waters off Alaska.

The service also served as the official advocate for industry in finding materials for constructing and operating fishing vessels. In 1942, commercial landings of fish declined partly as a result of the requisitioning of hundreds of fishing vessels by the armed services. By the end of the war, the U.S. fleet had been modernized with more than 2,000 new fishing vessels. The service declared that the industry had "the largest and most efficient fleet in its history."

The Office of the Fisheries Coordinator also consolidated fish processing plants for salmon and Pacific sardines, which had been declared to be of military importance.

Chapter 2 | Industry's Partner

By the end of the American War of Independence, political leaders openly embraced the New England fishing industry as the country's premier industry. The wealth that the fish trade with Europe had brought the colonies supported the war effort and irritated the British. In his first message to Congress in 1791, Secretary of State Thomas Jefferson decried the damage done by the war to the domestic fleet. Citing subsidized foreign fisheries, trade barriers, and discriminatory taxes, Jefferson called upon Congress to provide fishermen with tax relief, impose tariffs on foreign products, and promote free markets abroad. Speaking of the cod fishery, Jefferson wrote that "it is too poor a business to be left to itself, even with the nation the most advantageously situated." Congress obliged.

Ever since, federal marine fisheries agencies have assisted the fishing industry in a variety of ways, generally with the active, even insistent support of Congress and the industry itself. The end of World War II brought dreams of redirecting the government's capacity to marshal resources for waging war toward building the American economy, and rebuilding the U.S. fishing industry. In 1945, Fish and Wildlife Service director Ira N. Gabrielson proposed a "postwar program of public works" to assist the fishing industry.[1]

Little new support actually materialized. As government funding for replacing vessels all but vanished after World War II and prices slackened with the end of military purchases, the fishing industry in many parts of the country declined once again. Despite new government programs to develop new markets, products, and technology, catches remained at World War II levels. The United States slipped in its ranking among major fishing nations, and imports exploded, further weakening the balance sheets of domestic fleets. Both industry leaders and government officials began talking of the need to rehabilitate the fishing industry—a refrain that would be repeated for decades.

Marketing

The government's desire to modernize the commercial fishing industry after
World War II faced two fundamental challenges: lack of consumer demand for
seafood and lack of capacity to catch and process fish. Increasing demand would
raise prices fishermen received for their catches, thereby improving their financial condition and their ability to invest in new technology. At the same
time, increasing the capacity of fishing fleets would increase supplies of seafood,
reducing prices to consumers. Improvements in technology might also reduce
fishermen's costs. Growth in consumption was discouraged by the comparative
difficulty of cooking fish well, the seasonality of many kinds of fish, and the
poor quality of much of the fish offered on the market. Furthermore, beef and
chicken were more familiar to the majority of Americans who had been born
and raised in rural areas where farming was the dominant way of life and source
of food. Beef and poultry producers also gained an advantage by tapping growing interest in consumer convenience, which became a common promotional
theme in the 1950s and 1960s. Finally, both government and the cattle industry used effective marketing to build consumer preference for their products.

Beef and poultry producers also were able to increase production levels, which
reduced consumer prices. The federal government's agricultural support programs, which had blossomed under President Roosevelt's New Deal, grew in
size after World War II. New agricultural technology, much of it developed at
government expense, yielded new seeds, fertilizers, pesticides, animal breeding methods, and machinery. These new tools enabled American farmers to
produce surplus crops that were the envy of the world. Between 1950 and 1970,
domestic production of beef more than doubled, while poultry production
tripled. Cheaper prices and effective marketing by the beef industry increased
per capita consumption of beef from 63 pounds in 1950 to 116 pounds in 1970.
Consumption of poultry grew from 20 pounds to 49 pounds.

In contrast, domestic fishermen were slow to adopt the modest improvements in technology that research and development for the war effort had yielded
in the 1940s. The marginal finances of many fishermen discouraged investment
in new technology or larger vessels. As a result, domestic fish landings remained
at about 2.2 million metric tons for several decades after World War II. Unable
to compete in price, quality, or convenience, seafood remained a secondary choice
for consumers. Between 1950 and 1970, per capita consumption of fish fluctuated slightly, and never exceeded 11.8 pounds.

For the most part, the fishing industry did little to counter the competition from beef and poultry producers, and increasingly from imports, except approach government for assistance. In the 1950s, the fishing industry and its supporters in Congress and in the Bureau of Commercial Fisheries (BCF) argued that government agricultural assistance programs were responsible for placing the fishing industry at a competitive disadvantage with other protein producers. Rather than arguing against agricultural assistance programs, advocates for the fishing industry argued that they should simply get their fair share of government support.

"We felt that poultry and beef were getting a tremendous amount of help and the whole bureaucracy was geared towards their preservation," says Bob Jones, longtime executive director of the Southeastern Fisheries Association in Tallahassee, Florida. "We felt that there were hundreds if not thousands of people in the Department of Agriculture's various bureaus whose sole purpose was to maintain a viable beef, chicken, [and] pork industry, and that government funds were rightfully being expended for them. We [received] nowhere near the amounts of money that we thought should be spent on our behalf."

Campaigns by the fishing industry and its supporters to get that money met with limited success. In 1954, Congress passed the Saltonstall-Kennedy Act, which directed 30% of gross receipts from customs duties collected on fishery products to a separate fund in the Department of Commerce. In the words of Interior Secretary McKay, the money was meant for marketing and research programs aimed at helping "the ailing commercial fishing industry of this country to expand production and to develop new markets for fishery products."[2] Most of the funds, however, were devoted to general operations of the BCF, or later, the National Marine Fisheries Service (NMFS).

After the Eisenhower administration rejected appeals from the New England groundfish fleet to impose tariffs on imports of groundfish from Canada, Congress attempted to address some of the industry's concerns by passing the Fish and Wildlife Act of 1956. Although opposition by recreational fishermen and wildlife organizations persuaded Congress not to establish a separate agency for commercial fisheries in the Department of the Interior, Congress did give commercial fisheries a separate bureau in the new U.S. Fish and Wildlife Service. The act also consolidated legislative authority for the federal government's traditional programs of education, marketing, exploratory fishing, and development of new seafood products, fishing gear, and processing technology.

After passage of the Fish and Wildlife Act, government promotion of seafood entered its heyday. BCF marketing staff used brochures, supermarket demonstrations, television programs, films, and other devices to boost consumer confidence and interest in seafood. By 1964, the agency had produced 21 educational motion pictures on fish, fisheries, and cooking, many of which won national and international awards. Producing and distributing films were only small parts of the federal government's efforts to promote fish consumption.

"We would plan a promotion for a year on themes like Lent or the Fish and Seafood Parade in the fall," says Paul Paradis, who was chief of marketing at the BCF during the late 1960s.

Whatever the immediate market, home economists in test kitchens at the BCF developed recipes, which then were incorporated into brochures and distributed by the thousands through field offices. Marketing campaigns often also included intensive work with the print and electronic media. The bureau took pride in generating more than 220,000 column inches of newspaper coverage for fish products during the Lenten period in 1961. Working with industry representatives, the bureau often arranged radio and television reports and interviews extolling the healthfulness of seafood and demonstrating the ease with which it could be prepared. "We did a lot of television shows," says Paradis. "In Boston, you would turn on your TV set at two o'clock in the afternoon and you would get Louise Morgan's show with a report on some seafood or other."

Many people in the commercial fishing industry welcomed the help. "We knew we had an advocate," recalled Bob Jones in 1999. "We had programs, we had money, we had research, we had product development, we had gear development, we had an extensive marketing program. We had people in the agency saying, 'We've got to help you guys. We've got to promote Spanish mackerel and king mackerel. We've got to develop shark. We've got to do all this because according to our estimates, we have blankety-blank out there that's available for harvest.'"

"We took a Spanish mackerel, created one of the finest frozen fillet products, and were able to sell that fish to major cafeterias throughout the United States," says Jones. "That wouldn't have happened without the federal government's assistance. We didn't have [people] in Florida [who] were really professionals at how you promote things."

In the late 1960s, the BCF's marketing programs came under attack by budget-cutters and free-market advocates within the Nixon administration. In a 1969 critique of the U.S. Fish and Wildlife Service's request for additional funding for its marine fisheries activities, including market promotion and other industry assistance, James R. Schlesinger, assistant director of the Bureau of the Budget, wrote: "To the extent that [g]overnment expenditures are a necessary cost of supplying fish and shellfish, they should be a cost to the consumers of those products and not to the taxpayer. If the consumer is not willing to pay all of the costs of the product that he consumes then that product should not be produced and the resources thus released should be shifted to those alternative uses whose values are reflected in the costs of producing the product."

Some members of the fishing industry also objected to the federal government's marketing efforts. "Bigger companies—tuna, and salmon people—tended to do their own advertising," says Paul Paradis. "They didn't think the government should be in on it. If others could do something, then it shouldn't be done for them by government." But even philosophical opponents to government marketing sometimes sought the government's assistance. When several consumers died from consuming tainted canned tuna in 1963, demand dropped dramatically. "The tuna industry came to us with hat in hand," says Paradis. "They wanted us to go out and beat the bushes and get out some press releases, to talk to the food service industry, the mass feeders, to explain that the contamination will never happen again."

The Nixon administration's skepticism about government expenditures on behalf of the fishing industry and the transfer of BCF functions to the Department of Commerce's National Oceanic and Atmospheric Administration (NOAA) in 1970 reduced the government's direct involvement in marketing. Between 1968 and 1972, the Nixon administration cut the seafood marketing staff from 52 to 34 positions, mostly in home economics.

Managing Gluts, Managing Fisheries

While many government marketing campaigns aimed at increasing seafood consumption generally, government agencies often concentrated their efforts on relieving "fisheries product supply/demand imbalances"—in other words, gluts. In 1937, the federal government for the first time provided $2 million in price supports for fishery products. Much later, the federal government began purchasing surplus seafood under the Surplus Commodities Program established by the Agricultural Adjustment Act of 1935. The U.S. Department of Agriculture (USDA) then distributed these supplies through the School Lunch Program and through charitable organizations. In 1963, canned tuna became the first seafood to be placed on the USDA's plentiful food list. Pink salmon followed in 1964.

Other campaigns to reduce gluts were promotional and often involved the industry and the USDA. In 1959, the industry and the BCF promoted consumption of shrimp, in order to "alleviate the burdensome shrimp inventory." A "scallop festival" one year later aimed at reducing enormous inventories of sea scallops created by record domestic landings and increased imports.

Sometimes, campaigns to reduce gluts were too successful, as in the case of haddock. "In the early 50s, the total catch of haddock by the U.S. and Canada was extremely high," says Paradis, who was based in Boston during the 1950s. "The processors kept sticking haddock in their freezers. But pretty soon, they noticed haddock wouldn't sell at any price. The industry came to us and asked that haddock be brought under one of the agricultural surplus programs. So, we sat down with them and worked out a program. We sent out press releases and called on the food editors, talked to several contacts in the food service industry, state institutions, restaurants . . . The one thing that we made clear at the beginning was that if the price went up during our efforts, we would immediately stop them." The campaign worked, and haddock consumption rose.

By the late 1960s, the BCF faced a very different challenge in the haddock fishery: The lack of restraint in catches by fleets from the United States, Canada, and distant water fishing nations drove haddock populations down. By 1968, haddock catches were in a free fall. In 1969, U.S. catches were just 20,788 metric tons, a little more than one-third their levels in 1966. Lacking regulatory authority over the fisheries, the BCF turned to marketing as a tool for reducing fishing pressure on haddock.

"We had sharply declining stocks," says Spencer Garrett, who worked at the bureau's headquarters in Washington, D.C., from 1968 to 1971. "So we were using some interesting and subtle programs to try to reduce fishing for certain species and direct it toward other species. For the New England stocks, we helped fishermen target pollock, which also is a groundfish. And we gave them some economic incentives to do so. Pollock at that time was not considered to be as desirable a fish as haddock or cod. We did a very aggressive marketing program with the states and with other organizations, promoting the marketing of pollock, calling it 'Boston bluefish.' We really created a tremendous market for it."

Increased demand led to increased prices and to increased landings. From a 1969 level of 6¢ per pound, the price paid fishermen for pollock increased by 25% in the next year and continued increasing to a peak of 22¢ per pound in 1979. Between 1969 and 1979, landings more than tripled from 4,113 metric tons in 1969 to 15,635 in 1979.

"The program was very successful, and one measure of that was that the imports of Canadian pollock went up dramatically," says Garrett. The success of the pollock promotion program, however, could not redress domestic and foreign overfishing of haddock. Landings of haddock by the New England fleet, which had begun declining in 1967, continued falling to a low of 3,730 metric tons in 1974.

Although the diversion of fishing away from traditional groundfish species in New England was well intentioned, it suffered from the same shortcoming as development in other fisheries: Exploitation outstripped scientific understanding of the fishery. As a result, NMFS scientists could not determine the status of pollock populations off the Atlantic coast as recently as 1998—30 years after the federal government's efforts to help the New England fleet survive the decline of other species by creating demand for pollock.

Product Development

From the early days of the U.S. Fish and Fisheries Commission, government agencies also helped the fishing industry enhance its economic stability through the development of new seafood products and processing technology. For example, because techniques for storing and preserving fish were relatively primitive, fishermen's catch had to be sold quickly. As a result, fishermen commonly faced low prices caused by periodic gluts of local and regional markets. In 1879, the fish commission began studying ways to preserve fish through freezing. Later research by the Bureau of Fisheries led to improvements in refrigeration that allowed distributors to store fish for later sale in an unglutted market. In the 1920s, the Bureau of Fisheries's Harden F. Taylor assisted Clarence Birdseye in perfecting a process for quick-freezing fillets of cod. The new technique dramatically expanded the market for cod and other fish.

Federal efforts to increase demand by developing and publicizing methods of cooking fish, particularly fish that were new to consumers, began in the 1890s.

Later, the Bureau of Fisheries attempted to interest consumers in dogfish sharks (*Squalus acanthias*), a species that government and fishermen considered "worthless and highly predacious." In response to food shortages created by U.S. entry into World War I, the Bureau of Fisheries sponsored 125 cooking demonstrations around the country in 1918 alone, seeking to interest consumers in such unfamiliar entrees as whale steaks.

Bureau of Fisheries's innovations in packaging also made fish more convenient to prepare, thereby expanding demand among Americans, for many of whom fish remained an uncommon food. In the 1920s, the bureau promoted selling fish as fillets or steaks rather than whole in order to make fish more convenient and attractive to home cooks. The new products caught on with consumers.

Government product development programs paralleled research in private industry that aimed at overcoming consumer attitudes and the difficulty of predictably producing high quality seafood. Reaching the goal of expanding seafood markets depended upon developing products that were convenient, inexpensive, and consistent in quality and appearance. No other seafood product better exemplified the standard than frozen, breaded fish sticks, which Birdseye began distributing in 1953. For consumers, these uniformly oblong portions of breaded fish fillet were inexpensive, easy to prepare, and free of objectionable odors. For processors, fish sticks did not present the difficulties of storage and manufacture that traditional seafood products did. Because they could be made from almost any whitefish, fish-stick manufacturers did not depend upon local sources of fish. When Birdseye began distributing fish sticks in 1953, President Eisenhower hailed the product as a means of increasing fish consumption by eliminating odors and increasing uniformity and convenience. Fish-stick production grew quickly, from 3,410 metric tons in 1953 to 28,636 metric tons in 1955.

In the 1960s, the importance of research into seafood products broadened beyond commercial markets. Both the Kennedy and Johnson administrations believed that the United States must use its technological capabilities to fight world hunger. The oceans appeared to offer an enormous source of protein for closing the gap between population growth and food production. In 1961, the United States hosted a United Nations conference on fish in the diet at which delegates spoke of "plowing the seven seas" so that they would produce twice as much protein as was produced on land.

The ocean's potential contribution to ending world hunger was frustrated by the difficulty of storing and transporting fish from where it was caught to where it was needed. Research begun in the early 1950s by Dr. Nevin Scrimshaw, an independent nutritional scientist, appeared to offer a means of overcoming this difficulty. By the time he became an advisor to President Kennedy, Scrimshaw had found some success in converting fish into a powder called fish protein concentrate, or FPC.

In 1962, the BCF began a small-scale research program aimed at developing a low-cost process for producing FPC from abundant, low-priced fish. Besides combating malnutrition, the BCF hoped to restore "the ecological balance of the oceans by utilizing the many species of fish now ignored or unwanted by commercial fishermen."[3] If the BCF were successful in developing a manufacturing process, the domestic fleet would be able to market fish that it was discarding. Also, domestic fish processors would be able to produce a higher-priced product than fish meal from abundant species of fish.

The proposal to develop an FPC manufacturing process enjoyed strong support in the academic establishment. "The National Academy of Sciences, which really had quite a lot of clout, laid the arm on Congress and said this is a thing you should do," says Roland Finch, who headed the FPC program after 1968. In 1966, Congress passed the Magnuson Act, which authorized funding for the design and construction of two experimental plants for producing FPC. While the Johnson administration emphasized the legislation's foreign policy implications, congressional sponsors were primarily interested in benefiting the domestic fishing industry. (Indeed, the plants were to be located in the districts of the legislation's principal sponsors—Senators Bartlett and Magnuson and Congressman Keith.)

In 1966, the FPC initiative's international dimension expanded dramatically when it was selected as a focus for White House attention by the Marine Sciences Council, which Vice President Humphrey chaired. The aim of the initiative was to identify developing countries to which the FPC technology could be transferred. After surveying several developing countries, the Agency for International Development selected Chile for demonstrating how assistance in producing FPC from local fisheries could solve protein deficiency problems.

"We put quite a bit of money and effort into it," says Jim Crutchfield, an economist who served on a National Academy of Sciences panel monitoring the FPC research effort. "We expected it would do a great deal of good in places and among groups where the need was very great. And I thought it was a damn fine thing that it be pushed on that basis."

Proponents predicted that FPC could help balance the diet for one billion people at a cost of a half-cent per person per day. "Unfortunately, as we got more and more into the project, it just wasn't practical to do that," Crutchfield says. The difficulties of developing the technology, together with bureaucratic infighting, proved insurmountable. Fearing that FPC would compete with non-fat milk powder, the dairy industry enlisted the opposition of the Food and Drug Administration, which initially barred FPC from American markets on the grounds that the use of whole fish rendered the product "filthy."

"It's as if these people had never eaten a canned sardine, or an oyster, or a clam," says Crutchfield. "That was a nonsense objection. But it had a lot of weight. It had the effect of restricting the interest in developing FPC."

In 1967, Health, Education, and Welfare Secretary John Gardner relaxed some of the requirements, under pressure from Vice President Humphrey. But the Food and Drug Administration placed other restrictions on FPC. For instance, FPC was to be produced only from hake, not from abundant small pelagic fish such as herring and menhaden. The Food and Drug Administration also required that FPC be sold only in one-pound bags, effectively preventing its use in commercial food products, such as bread and cookies. In responding to a petition from the National Fish and Meal Association, the Food and Drug Administration later replaced some of these restrictions with a restriction on the amount of fluoride that could remain in FPC after processing. The only way of reducing fluoride levels, however, was to debone fish before converting them to FPC—a step that significantly raised manufacturing costs.

The processing plants also experienced restrictive problems. "The demonstration plant at Aberdeen proved a bust," says Finch. "The original estimates were overly optimistic. The designers had made no provision for storing raw fish at the plant. But the way fishing works, you may get a feast or famine. And if you got a feast, you ended up with a lot of smelly fish after two or three days. Then, the plant stands down.

"From the economics point of view, to make fish protein concentrate for a penny a pound was quite impractical unless you could keep that plant running 200 days a year, 24 hours per day, and fully supplied with fish," says Finch. "It just plain didn't work. After the plant had been built, we tried to operate it for a year or two, but everybody became disillusioned. The bureau's director at the time, Skip Crowther, went back to Congress to ask for a reauthorization of the act, and Congress said 'no.' And I must say, I thought that was a proper decision on their part."

In 1973, the NMFS filed a final report on FPC and shut the project down. With that, product research by the federal government returned to meeting the needs of industry for new products and markets.

Promoting Trade

While per capita consumption of seafood in the United States remained at around 12 pounds from 1950 to 1970, the U.S. population grew by a third, and with it the total consumption of seafood. Until the late 1970s, however, domestic catches hovered around 2.2 million metric tons. Increasingly, seafood imported from abroad filled the gap between domestic supply and demand. Between 1957 and 1967, fish product imports grew from one-third to more than two-thirds of the total domestic supply of seafood and industrial fish products. In 1965, for the first time in its history, the United States became a net importer of fish for human consumption.

By meeting increased demand, the ready supply of imported seafood kept wholesale prices lower than they might otherwise have been. This benefited processors and distributors, for whom the source of their supply was a secondary concern to price and quality. On the other hand, foreign sources of fish depressed prices paid to domestic fishermen for their catches.

No other group of U.S. fishermen assailed imports more vigorously or effectively than the offshore New England groundfish fleet. As early as the 1940s, these fishermen found themselves competing with imports of groundfish fillets from Canada that quintupled in the decade before 1948. Claiming that the lower price of Canadian imports was due to unfairly low labor costs and government subsidies, the New England offshore groundfish fleet sought quotas and higher tariffs on imported groundfish. In 1954, a second attempt to secure tariffs succeeded in gaining a recommendation from the Tariffs Commission to impose limits on groundfish imports and higher tariffs.

These proposals, which might have helped the offshore groundfish fleet, alarmed processors who had come to depend upon Canadian imports. This was especially true of producers of fish sticks. With no public fanfare, fish-stick processors convinced the Eisenhower administration to reject the recommendations of the Tariffs Commission. In doing so, President Eisenhower claimed that fish sticks would help the New England fishing industry. As it turned out, however, domestic producers of fish sticks relied less and less upon domestic sources of

fish. Some processors relocated their processing facilities to Canada in order
to take advantage of the cheaper sources of groundfish there.

When he rejected yet another recommendation for higher tariffs in 1956,
President Eisenhower identified the principal ideological obstacle that the fishing industry faced in seeking protection from imports: administration support
of free trade. In dismissing the Tariffs Commission's advice, President Eisenhower argued that the countries that exported fish to the United States were "not
only our close friends, but their economic strength [was] of strategic importance
to us in the continuing struggle against the menace of world Communism."

After passage of the Fish and Wildlife Act in 1956, the BCF devoted itself
increasingly to helping the U.S. fishing industry compete in foreign markets.
Until 1965, the federal government's export marketing activities were scattered
among several agencies and programs, when the BCF established an Office of
International Trade Promotion. The new office's mission was to develop new
markets and expand sales of U.S. fishery products abroad.

"We worked with the Department of Agriculture and the Department of
Commerce in putting on trade fairs in foreign countries," says Bruce Morehead, who began working in NMFS's marketing program in 1970. "We would
work with companies and arrange for them to display product in Germany, say,
or in Tokyo. Agriculture and Commerce welcomed our efforts because we
weren't trying to duplicate what they were doing, but to strengthen it."

Agency staff provided other services useful to exporters. In 1978, for example, staff prepared 189 reports on current fishery export opportunities for the
fishing industry and fielded nearly 700 queries for information. Staff also analyzed trends in world fisheries, including foreign fisheries and subsidies, and prepared reports on economic, marketing, technological, and political trends based
partly on information from more than 240 diplomatic posts around the world.

In 1976, in the aftermath of the Magnuson-Stevens Act, the fishing industry faced a fundamentally different set of export challenges. In displacing foreign factory trawlers from U.S. waters off Alaska, U.S. fishermen inherited one
of the world's largest fisheries—the Alaska pollock fishery. Besides having to
learn how to catch and process pollock, U.S. fishermen and processors needed
access to foreign markets. This was especially true of the market in Japan, where
pollock mince, called surimi, was fashioned into dozens of popular seafood products. The administrations of both Presidents Carter and Reagan pressed to open
Japanese markets through a "fish and chips" policy. Under this policy, the United

States would grant access of foreign vessels to fish in U.S. waters only if foreign nations agreed to several conditions, including access to markets. In 1982, Congress strengthened this policy through amendments to the Magnuson-Stevens Act. Under these amendments, the U.S. State Department was to delay releasing half of any allocation to a foreign nation's fishing fleet until the State Department found that the nation was meeting its "fish and chips" obligations. The strategy contributed greatly to opening Japanese markets and to the full Americanization of the pollock fishery by the end of the decade.

Vessel Assistance

During and after World War II, government reports regularly lamented the condition of domestic commercial fleets and called for their rehabilitation. These laments reflected frustration with the failure of the U.S. fishing industry to keep pace with the growth of fishing by other countries. In its 1969 report *Our Nation and the Sea,* the Stratton Commission complained: "Landings by U.S. vessels have remained almost constant over the last three decades, and during that period the United States has dropped from second to sixth among the world's fishing nations. U.S. vessels harvest less than one-tenth of the total production potential available over the U.S. continental shelf." The failure of the U.S. fishing fleet to modernize and to increase catches frustrated Vice President Hubert Humphrey and the White House Marine Sciences Council as well.

By the mid-1960s, American fishermen in the North Atlantic and North Pacific were regularly encountering enormous factory trawlers from the Soviet Union, Eastern-bloc countries, Europe, and Japan on their traditional fishing grounds. These modern, steel-hulled stern trawlers, were modeled after factory ships used in the commercial whaling industry. "The United States fleet was similar to the fleet of a developing country," says Dave Crestin, who worked for BCF in Boston at the time. "Compared to our European counterparts and even Eastern bloc countries, we were a developing country. There was no way we could compete with them."

The foreign factory trawlers, which could catch 500 tons at a time and process most of that in a day, were far more efficient than U.S. vessels, for which design and technology had changed little over the decades since World War II. Within the BCF, some staff were convinced that returning U.S. fleets to leadership in world fisheries might require fishing on such a large scale. To demonstrate the possibilities, the BCF and the Maritime Administration dedicated the entire budget for vessel construction subsidies in 1968 and 1969 to the construction of two factory trawlers: the *Seafreeze Atlantic* and the *Seafreeze Pacific*. The federal government paid half of the construction cost of $5.3 million charged by Maryland Shipbuilding & Drydock.

The two vessels, which were more than twice as long as any other ships in the U.S. fleet, encountered problems from the beginning. Besides technical problems on the vessels themselves, crew were difficult to find and retain. Fishermen in New England were not used to going to sea for months at a time. Nor did they find wages attractive, believing as they did that they could make more as independent fishermen. In April 1969, when a crewman was killed in an accident, the crew of the *Seafreeze Atlantic* mutinied. In April 1971, after seven trips, the vessel tied up for good in Norfolk, Virginia, and was soon followed by the *Seafreeze Pacific*. In 1974, the vessels' owners sold the ships at a loss of $11 million.

The desire to expand the capacity of the U.S. fishing fleet arose long before the BCF tested the waters with the two factory trawlers. After World War II, Congress authorized several financial assistance programs aimed at expanding and modernizing the U.S. fleet. The Fish and Wildlife Act of 1956 included a Fisheries Loan Fund that provided low-interest loans to fishermen for the construction and reconstruction of fishing vessels. Between 1957 and 1973, $31.3 million in loans were approved.

In 1960, Congress authorized funding to make up the difference between the cost of constructing a fishing vessel in the United States and the cost of doing so abroad. Under the Jones Act of 1936, vessels landing fish in the United States had to be constructed in the United States, where boat construction costs generally were at least 30% higher than abroad. The Fishing Vessel Construction Differential Subsidy Program was meant to eliminate this discrepancy for fishing vessels that would be suitable for use by the armed services, if necessary.

Some segments of the U.S. fishing fleet, especially the San Diego tuna fleet and the Gulf of Mexico shrimp fleet, took advantage of these programs. These two fleets, which fished distant waters off South America and Africa, required larger, more sophisticated vessels than were necessary for fishing U.S. coastal waters. Between 1957 and 1963, nearly one-third of Fisheries Loan Fund loans were dedicated to the conversion of 30 tuna clippers into purse seiners.

Despite these programs, most U.S. fleets remained small scale and outmoded. According to Dewar, whose 1983 study of the New England groundfish fleet is a landmark in such analyses, these programs produced so little change partly because they were based on a misreading of problems in the fishing fleets. For example, supporters of financial assistance to fishing fleets embraced the mistaken idea that there was a shortage of private money for fleet modernization. In this view, private investors, principally banks, overestimated the risk of loans for fishing vessels. Experience showed this not to be the case, at least not for successful fishermen. Nevertheless, given the poor financial performance of many fisheries, bankers had reason to be careful with their depositors' money and not lend to borderline fishing operations. In the end, even government lenders avoided poor risks and simply focused on fostering loans at more favorable rates to vessel owners who were good risks. Furthermore, few successful fishermen modernized, even with considerable encouragement and technical assistance from the government.

Congress generally created financial assistance programs in response to pressure from a particular segment of the fishing industry. In some cases, the origins and intended beneficiaries of the programs were clear. In others, the beneficiaries were unintended. For instance, the vessel construction subsidy program adopted by Congress in 1960 included requirements that more or less restricted the program to the New England groundfish fishery. Even so, the program ended up benefiting New Bedford scallop vessel owners most, who could afford to build new vessels without government assistance but welcomed the chance to reduce their construction costs.

Finally, some members of Congress and BCF staff, chiefly economists, raised concerns in the early 1960s about excessively large fleets in some fisheries. In 1965, Congress restricted future loans from the Fisheries Loan Fund to those fisheries for which a new vessel would not cause economic hardship to other fishermen in the fishery. Later, the NMFS began restricting other loans and loan guarantees in fisheries for which entrance of additional vessels would be unwarranted, including the Atlantic groundfish fleet and the San Diego tuna fleet. One result of these conflicts and complications was that the level of direct federal assistance to the fishing industry never was sufficient for supporting widespread modernization.

In 1976, passage of the Magnuson-Stevens Act, together with favorable tax laws and growing markets, did what 25 years of modest government subsidies and other assistance had not done: convince U.S. fishermen to modernize their vessels or purchase new ones. Although the NMFS continued with modest financial assistance programs after passage of the Magnuson-Stevens Act, it was the climate of opportunity and tax laws that fed the fleet's growth. "The Magnuson Act is one of the biggest development pieces of legislation we had," says Bruce Morehead. "Its objective was to Americanize U.S. fisheries. And I think we did succeed in that. We got rid of foreign fishing and replaced it with domestic effort.

"By government policy, we were saying develop U.S. capacity to harvest and process fish. A White House conference that got a lot of attention promoted development," Morehead recalls. "There were studies that laid out some of the potential for developing, how many boats were needed. We generated a lot of information that suggested there were opportunities for investment.

"The perception is that the government financed all this development, but that is simply not the case," says Morehead. "Most of it was done with private capital." Indeed, private capital for building fishing vessels was relatively easy to find. This was due partly to tax laws aimed at encouraging investment generally or at benefiting segments of the economy other than the fishing industry. Chief among these tax provisions was the investment tax credit, which Congress established in 1962. This provision allowed investors to apply 10% of the cost of capital investments as a credit against their taxes, thereby sheltering income.

The investment tax credit proved very attractive to non-fishermen. "Fishing vessels became tax shelters for lawyers, dentists, and doctors," says Morehead. Tax reforms adopted by Congress in 1986 brought an end to the investment tax credit, driving many people out of fisheries who had invested primarily for tax purposes.

Other tax incentives contributed to the rapid growth of U.S. fleets after passage of the Magnuson-Stevens Act. The Capital Construction Fund, which Congress established in 1970, allowed owners of all types of boats to defer income tax on profits from vessel operations if the money were placed in a special account for later renovation, construction, or purchase of a ship. By allowing vessel owners to acquire ships with before-tax dollars, the government effectively provided interest-free loans. In the first 25 years of its operation, fishing vessel owners opened more than 7,000 accounts and sheltered more than $1.82 billion in income. Of the $1.58 billion in withdrawals, vessel owners used about half to rebuild vessels and the balance to purchase new or used vessels.

Private capital also was attracted to marine fisheries by the Fishing Vessel Obligation Guarantee Program (FOG), established by Congress in 1972. Under the FOG program, the federal government encouraged lending for the construction and reconstruction of fishing vessels by guaranteeing that the government would assume any defaults on loans. In return, private banks offered loans to commercial fishermen at lower rates and with longer payback periods. Between 1976 and 1995, the FOG program guaranteed 1,250 loans for fishing vessels amounting to $728 million. For the most part, these guarantees were granted only to good risks, who would have been able to obtain commercial loans, but under less favorable terms.

While NMFS staff in the industry assistance office encouraged fishermen to take advantage of these programs, some NMFS staff in the fishery management program sought to avoid looming problems from rapidly expanding domestic fleets.

"In 1978, Joe Mueller, who was the regional economist, and I went to Fleet Bank headquarters in Rhode Island and spoke to members of the board," says Dave Crestin, who worked in the NMFS regional office at the time. "We told them there are already too many vessels in the fishery, that the stocks are beginning to go down, and that their investment in fishing vessels, new vessels or reconstructed vessels, will be in jeopardy. Well, that went in one ear and out the other, apparently, because a hell of a lot of new vessels entered the fishery, and a hell of a lot of new vessels went broke," says Crestin.

Staff in the conservation and management wing of the NMFS sometimes sought to end financial assistance programs nationally, but succeeded only in redirecting them if they succeeded at all. "The Capital Construction Fund should have been reoriented to dovetail more with management so we weren't using that program to overcapitalize," says Bill Gordon, who served as regional director in New England before moving to NMFS headquarters in 1979. "But part of it was the program people themselves who had a direct pipeline to the Congress and to some of their cronies in industry, who used those programs, particularly the Capital Construction Fund, to shelter huge profits from income tax."

In the late 1970s and early 1980s, government policy and promotion, tax incentives, and private speculation combined to stoke a spectacular expansion of U.S. fishing capacity. Between 1973 and 1984, U.S. boatyards constructed more than half of the 30,503 fishing vessels built between 1950 and 1997. In some areas, fleets expanded far beyond what fisheries could support. Between 1977 and 1980, 857 new vessels entered the offshore shrimp trawl fleet in the Gulf of Mexico. Four hundred and thirty-three of these were built with loans guaranteed by the federal government under the FOG program. When Mexico and some South American countries closed their waters to foreign shrimp trawlers, many U.S. shrimp trawlers returned to the Gulf of Mexico, crowding fishing grounds and splitting overall catches into even smaller pieces. The economic impact of lower catches was worsened by rising imports of shrimp from abroad that depressed prices paid to fishermen for shrimp.

As the economics of shrimp fishing worsened, vessels began leaving the Gulf shrimp fishery. Between 1984 and 1990, more than 2,000 vessels left the Gulf shrimp fishery. Some sailed to Hawaii. Others entered the Atlantic scallop fishery or the Pacific groundfish fishery, both of which already had too many boats chasing too few fish.

"The whole context for development was that you couldn't create problems with these programs," says Morehead. "You couldn't overcapitalize fisheries. You couldn't overfish them. That was just an underlying assumption in everything we did."

"But we created too much domestic effort," Morehead observes two decades later. "This is twenty-twenty hindsight. We didn't see it very clearly then."

Summary

From the perspective of the federal government, the domestic fishing industry faced two obstacles: a lack of consumer demand and a lack of capacity to catch and process marine wildlife. Unlike beef and poultry producers, U.S. fishermen were unable to increase production or the quality and convenience of their products.

When the Eisenhower administration refused to impose tariffs on cheaper seafood imports, Congress sought to assist the domestic fishing industry through funding programs in marketing, promotion of U.S. seafood products in foreign markets, and product and technology development. In the 1960s, the federal government also tried to assist the domestic fishing industry by tapping the apparent abundance of the oceans to reduce world hunger. These programs, which sometimes contributed to overfishing, reached a peak in the 1960s before the Nixon and later administrations reduced federal support for such activities.

In the 1950s, the federal government's financial assistance to the domestic fishing fleet for construction of fishing vessels also grew. With few exceptions, this assistance had little effect in increasing the competitiveness of the U.S. fleet. Passage of the Magnuson-Stevens Act, however, spurred unprecedented growth in the domestic fishing fleet. In many fisheries, the growth proved excessive.

Notes

1. U.S. Department of the Interior. 1945. *Annual Report of the Secretary of the Interior: Fiscal Year Ended June 30, 1945.* U.S. Government Printing Office, Washington, D.C.
2. U.S. Department of the Interior. 1955. *Annual Report of the Secretary of the Interior: Fiscal Year Ended June 30, 1955.* U.S. Government Printing Office, Washington, D.C.
3. Bureau of Commercial Fisheries. 1964. *Report of the Bureau of Commercial Fisheries for the Calendar Year 1962.* U.S. Government Printing Office, Washington, D.C.

1946–1956   *Rather than retreating into isolation as it had following World War I, the U.S. government actively pursued international cooperation after World War II. The postwar decade produced several international agreements to manage fishing on the high seas beyond 3 miles of the coast, including the International Whaling Commission, the International Commission for the Northwest Atlantic Fisheries, the Inter-American Tropical Tuna Commission, and the International Commission for the High Seas Fisheries of the North Pacific Ocean.*

The federal government also provided technical assistance to foreign countries. For example, a series of missions to Mexico led to a treaty regarding research on tunas. After the war, the Fish and Wildlife Service assisted the Philippines in rebuilding its fisheries. By 1950, the service had trained 125 Phillippine technicians in various aspects of fisheries.

After World War II, the Fish and Wildlife Service began building its fleet of research vessels and research laboratories, including a technological laboratory in Boston, a field station in San Diego, California, for research surveys off California, and a field station in Pascagoula, Mississippi, for fishing and gear research. In 1948, the service added the Albatross III, *a converted New England trawler, to its research fleet.*

Chapter 3 | Manufacturing Fish

Nothing in the last century better illustrates the low value placed on fisheries habitat than the construction of hundreds of dams and diversions in the name of water and power development. By flooding rivers and creating barriers to salmon migrating to spawning gravel as adults or to the Pacific Ocean as juveniles, dams radically changed the riverine habitat of salmon or eliminated it altogether.

Though they were aware that dams had contributed to the demise of Atlantic salmon in New England rivers, federal and state water agencies plunged forward with plans for reengineering river basins in the West. The plans became grander in the fervor of battling the Great Depression and Nazi Germany. By the end of World War II, dam builders successfully argued for even more ambitious water development programs in the name of prosperity and economic growth based on abundant and cheap power, irrigation water, and transportation. Whatever problems dams might impose upon Pacific salmon would be overcome with proper planning and ingenuity.

Concerns about the impact of dams on Pacific salmon also were undermined by the prospect that fish culturists and river engineers could succeed in compensating for any losses caused by dams. If salmon were disappearing from dammed and diverted streams, fish culturists offered to adapt salmon and their habitat to modern conditions by constructing and operating salmon hatcheries. Furthermore, hydraulic engineers and biologists would develop means of enabling salmon to make their way past a growing number of dams.

Although these techniques were not shown to be effective, they enabled political leaders to avoid confronting the damage sure to be done to salmon runs by dams on the Columbia River and other western rivers. In time, federally funded hatcheries became their own engine of local economic activity and developed political support powerful enough to overcome a record of failure stretching back into the mid- to late nineteenth century.

Hatcheries Instead of Habitat

In the 1860s, enthusiasm for captive propagation of fish grew as techniques for hatching and raising several species of fish were perfected. Just as Spencer Fullerton Baird's campaign to create a fish commission gained momentum, a group of anglers and private hatchery operators decided to promote captive propagation by forming the American Fish Culture Association, the precursor to today's American Fisheries Society. The fish culturists saw an opportunity in Baird's proposal for a fish commission, and became active supporters. Rather than relying on field investigations to address the alleged decline in food fishes off New England, as Baird proposed, the fish culturists argued for raising and releasing fish. The fish culturists' arguments were politically attractive since they offered government officials a way around controversies among fishermen who were suffering declining catches and increasing gear conflicts.

Captive propagation soon dominated the U.S. Fish and Fisheries Commission's activities. In 1872, with Baird's assistance, fish culturists succeeded in securing $15,000 in federal funds to launch a captive propagation program under the auspices of the fish commission—three times the amount of money allocated to Baird's collecting expeditions. Baird himself became caught up in the popularity of this unproven technique, and used his skills as a lobbyist and administrator in building the fish commission's Division of Culture. At one point, for example, Baird decorated the hearing rooms of the House and Senate Appropriations Committees with tanks containing young cod raised from eggs by the fish commission. In 1875, Baird proposed to eliminate the need for regulating salmon fishing in the Columbia River by "artificial hatching of these fish."[1] As Jim Lichatowich observed in *Salmon without Rivers,* Baird had no evidence that hatcheries could offset losses from overfishing and habitat destruction. But that did not stop him or his successor (George Brown Goode) from asserting otherwise. Goode put the case for relying on hatcheries to rebuild and enhance fisheries in this way:

> It is better to expend a small amount of public money in making fish so abundant that they can be caught without restriction, and serve as cheap food for the people at large, rather than to expend a much larger amount in preventing the people from catching the few that still remain after generations of improvidence.[2]

With such influential and politically adept advocates as these two respected biologists, hatcheries came to dominate federal fisheries programs, accounting for two-thirds of federal fisheries funding between 1872 and 1941.

The fish commission's Division of Culture did not stop at attempting to enhance fish populations. It also developed a large program of "acclimatizing" fishes and shellfishes in new waters. In 1872, for example, Baird sent fish culturist Livingston Stone to the Pacific coast to establish a small station on the McCloud River in northern California, for collecting fertilized chinook salmon eggs and shipping them to the East Coast. Although none of the salmon transplants succeeded, efforts with other species succeeded spectacularly. By 1887, rainbow trout was doing so well east of the Rockies that the Division of Culture ceased shipping eggs and fingerlings by railroad car from western hatcheries. In 1879, Stone successfully transplanted 150 Atlantic striped bass in California's Sacramento River. Over several decades, additional plantings of striped bass as well as Atlantic shad built populations that supported commercial fisheries on the Pacific coast.

As state fish commissions and their congressional representatives vied for federal hatchery funding in later years, the federal government's captive propagation programs grew rapidly. By 1899, the fish commission's Division of Culture was producing more than 1 billion fish eggs, fry, and fish of 23 species each year. Using specially designed railroad cars, trucks, and boats, the fish commission delivered the eggs, fry, and fish to state fisheries agencies for stocking streams, lakes, and other waters. Each year, government and private vessels stocked offshore New England waters with 5 billion fertilized groundfish eggs. By 1940, federal fish hatcheries had produced 200 billion fish and shellfish that were released in U.S. and international waters. About three-quarters of the production was marine species, principally cod, pollack, haddock, halibut, and flounder.

These extraordinary efforts, however, had no measurable effect on the abundance of groundfish. The annual catch of Atlantic cod fell from about 136,000 metric tons in 1880 to 32,000 in 1941. Similarly, stocking of streams and coastal waters with shad could not overcome overfishing and habitat loss. Atlantic shad landings fell from nearly 20,000 metric tons in 1892 to less than 5,000 in 1941. But lack of success in restoring cod and shad did not deter fish culturists. If anything, the continuing failure of state governments to conserve fish populations from overfishing and habitat loss added weight to the promises of fish culturists. Even the relatively young fisheries of the Pacific coast seemed to be in need of such help. By 1915, the Bureau of Fisheries was spending one-third of its fish-culture budget on raising and releasing salmon from California to Alaska.

Only in Alaska did reliance on fish culture fail to take hold. Concerns about enforcement of fisheries regulations along Alaska's lengthy and distant coast-line had led President Theodore Roosevelt to commission a study of Alaskan fisheries, which was completed in 1904. Among other things, the study group urged restoring overfished salmon runs through captive propagation. By 1909, two governmental and several private hatcheries were raising and releasing salmon in Alaska. But the bloom soon faded from the promise of hatcheries. In 1913, the Bureau of Fisheries, which succeeded the U.S. Fish and Fisheries Commission, openly questioned the wisdom of relying on captive propagation rather than habitat protection:

> It is not improbable that a general undervaluation of natural productivity and a corresponding overestimate of the results to be expected from hatchery work is responsible for the one time widely diffused belief that the presence of a few hatcheries would cure all the ills of an unremitting pursuit of salmon; while, now that the few hatcheries in operation do not seem to accomplish this miracle, the opposite tendency to decry all hatchery work is supplanting the former extreme optimism.

The debate in Alaska continued until federal hatcheries ended their operations in 1932. Then, stream restoration and manipulation of lake primary productivity became the focus for federal salmon conservation efforts in Alaska. For decades, the rejection of captive propagation in Alaska would remain the exception in the federal government's reliance on captive propagation as the management tool of choice.

Damming for Development

The burst of water development projects on the Columbia River and other western rivers in the 1930s generated criticism and concern from state and federal fisheries biologists and fishing interests. In an early effort to balance cheap power and water with fish and wildlife habitat, Congress passed the Fish and Wildlife Coordination Act in 1934, which required federal agencies to consult with the Bureau of Fisheries before constructing any dam. The Bureau of Fisheries, in turn, was to advise whether dams should include fish ladders or other "economically practicable" design features that would aid fish migration. The act also authorized the bureau to use reservoirs for culturing fish.

When these measures proved inadequate for protecting salmon and steelhead populations on the Columbia River, Congress passed the Mitchell Act in 1938. Like previous legislation, the Mitchell Act emphasized mitigation through fishways, hatcheries, and habitat restoration without requiring significant change in the scope of dam building. As the pace of dam construction on the Columbia River quickened toward the end of World War II, Congress amended the Mitchell Act. The new legislation authorized most of the fish and wildlife mitigation activities in the Columbia River basin that would form the basis of the federal government's response to the dams it would build over the next three decades. By then, hatcheries had become such a mainstay of the dam development program that the act authorized the transfer of federal funds to the states for the operation of hatcheries and other activities.

Even with the new legislative requirements for consultation, the Bureau of Fisheries was no match for the accelerating pace of dam construction. In his annual report for 1944, Secretary of the Interior Harold Ickes described the department's postwar plans for promoting economic development: "We have hastened the construction of huge dams and the installation of generators to furnish power for war production plants. We have extended our irrigation facilities to increase the production of food for war. . . . Our job soon will be to turn this vast block of power from war to peace. It is a Herculean job but I think that we can master it by shifting, gradually if possible, from war to its nearest economic equivalent in the field of conservation; namely, regional development."[3] The program of dam building required by such regional economic development was of staggering dimensions. In 1944, the Bureau of Reclamation proposed the construction of 236 irrigation and multipurpose projects.

While federal water agencies promoted, funded, and oversaw water projects in other western river basins, the grandest of all water development programs was in the Columbia River basin. There, the dreams of river basin development seemed most promising. Besides generating cheap electricity for industrial and residential development in the region, dams and diversions of water could turn thousands of square miles of desert into productive agricultural land.

The salmon runs and watershed of the Columbia River also may have seemed too large to suffer permanent damage from water development projects. Before European settlement, 10 to 16 million salmon migrated up the 1,214-mile long Columbia River and its tributaries each year—the largest runs of steelhead trout and chinook and coho salmon in the world. Nearly every river and stream in the Columbia River's 259,000-square mile watershed hosted its own run of one or several species. While logging, small dams and diversions, and other activities had reduced many runs by the 1930s, salmon still returned to the Columbia River in enormous numbers.

In 1942, the completion of the Grand Coulee Dam in eastern Washington marked a turning point for Columbia River salmon. Originally designed as a low dam to provide irrigation water, the Grand Coulee was ultimately constructed as a high dam with turbines for the production of electricity. The Department of the Interior preferred this approach since the sale of electricity would greatly reduce the price of water paid by irrigators. The final design improved the economics of the project but presented enormous problems for salmon runs on the upper river. While biologists and engineers had succeeded in designing fish ladders that allowed salmon to pass over Bonneville Dam on the lower Columbia River, the 550-foot high Grand Coulee Dam was too high for fish ladders. As a result, salmon that had ascended 600 miles of river were blocked by the Grand Coulee Dam from 1,400 miles of prime habitat on the upper Columbia River.

To compensate for the loss of upriver habitat, the Fish and Wildlife Service began trapping and transplanting adult salmon from below Grand Coulee to tributaries in the lower stretches of the Columbia River above Bonneville Dam. These early efforts to establish new runs of salmon showed promise, and by 1947, the Fish and Wildlife Service claimed that recent runs of salmon had "shown conclusively that the Service [had] been successful in its program for transplanting the salmon runs."[4] Like similar claims made over the next several decades, this claim was based more on hope than on hard evidence. Nonetheless, transplantation of salmon from one river to another became a common activity of federal and state wildlife agencies, and reflected a choice by the Fish and Wildlife Service to concede the upper stretches of the Columbia River. "The tributaries in the lower reaches of the Columbia River have particular importance, since this area must assume the burden of maintaining production for the entire river as the construction of additional main-stem dams destroys the upper river runs," the service reported in 1946.[5] In the same year, Fish and Wildlife Service director Ira N. Gabrielson warned: "When a single dam is considered by itself, it is usually possible to devise modifications that will help a migrating fish population like salmon surmount it with no serious losses. When one dam is followed by a succession of others, blocking the upper reaches of a stream where the spawning grounds are located, the conservation problems become acute indeed."[6]

As postwar plans for dam construction grew, biologists within the Fish and Wildlife Service raised objections. "No competent fishery biologist is willing to assert that the salmon runs can be preserved if the full program construction does go through," biologists commented in an internal memorandum.[7] As the biologists's objections made their way through the upper levels of the Interior Department, however, they were bled of their vigor. In its final version, the statement simply read: "It appears that the losses incurred . . . might be serious enough to make continued propagation in the headwater tributaries impracticable."

By 1947, biologists had been thoroughly routed by water and power developers within the Interior Department. In a remarkably frank and uncompromising memorandum of March 6, 1947, Secretary of the Interior Julius Krug set the department's policy on dams and salmon on the Columbia River. "It is, therefore, the conclusion of all concerned," wrote Krug, "that the overall benefits to the Pacific Northwest from a thoroughgoing development of the Snake and Columbia are such that the present salmon run must be sacrificed. This means that the department's efforts should be directed toward ameliorating the impact of this development upon the injured interests and not toward a vain attempt to hold still the hands of the clock."[8]

As the construction of dams continued on the Columbia River in the 1950s, Assistant Secretary of the Interior Ross L. Leffler, state fish and game agencies, and others urged Congress to strengthen the Fish and Wildlife Coordination Act. In 1957, with the support of all 48 governors, Leffler sought amendments that would require enhancement of fish and wildlife values rather than mitigation for damages done. Agreeing that the act had failed to protect fish and wildlife, Congress amended the act to require that wildlife conservation be given "equal consideration" with other features of water development projects. Projects were to include wildlife conservation measures recommended by the Fish and Wildlife Service and state agencies in order "to obtain maximum overall project benefits."

Although the Fish and Wildlife Coordination Act, as well as later legislation, placed fish and wildlife on an equal footing as a matter of theory, fish and wildlife agencies worked at an enormous political disadvantage in getting this standard observed in practice. In effect, these agencies bore the burden of demonstrating a precise threat to fish and wildlife as well as the practicability of remedial measures that would not compromise the primary purposes for water developments.

In many cases, the recommendations of wildlife agencies were adopted. On the American River in California, for example, the Bureau of Reclamation adopted the recommendation of the Fish and Wildlife Service and constructed a hatchery to compensate for the loss of a salmon fishery caused by the construction of the Nimbus Dam. In some cases, the Fish and Wildlife Service was able to delay construction of dams while it prepared plans for trying to mitigate the damage. When their advice was not heeded, both federal and state wildlife agencies sometimes took their arguments to court. In 1951, the Fish and Wildlife Service and state fish and game agencies sued the Federal Power Commission in an effort to improve dam and diversion projects that the agencies opposed.

As small and large dams, water diversions, and other water development projects proliferated, the Fish and Wildlife Service was overwhelmed with assessing water development plans. In 1951, the service's Office of River Basin Studies reviewed 180 water project reports. In 1958, the number of large water projects swelled to 366, and included dams on the Snake and Columbia Rivers and the Trinity River in California. Ten years later, the Portland office of the service alone reviewed 461 water development projects.

The Lessons of History

In his 1958 report to the president, Secretary of the Interior Fred A. Seaton argued that the department's dam-building program would not make the kind of mistakes that brought about the near demise of Atlantic salmon. "The plight of the Atlantic salmon fishery, for instance, is a story of a century of exploitation based on the belief that resources are unending," Seaton wrote.[9] "Despite the fact that perpetuation of the species depends upon successful spawning, dams were constructed without considering this problem. Finally, stream pollution completed the task of reducing this great resource to a pitiful fragment. However, planners of the Columbia River [b]asin development, undertaken primarily for irrigation and power, recognized the importance of fish and wildlife resources. Therefore, extensive and continuing efforts were introduced to retain the fish and game potential which otherwise would be sacrificed."

While river basin planners adopted abundance as their goal for power and irrigation water, they accepted much less for salmon. In the words of Interior Secretary Seaton: "As long as salmon run, there is evidence that not all the spawning beds have been gouged out by logging, silted over by mining, or covered by reservoir developments." Persistence rather than abundance was to be the standard.

Like interior secretaries before and after him, Secretary Seaton based his optimistic rhetoric on claims by managers of programs that stood to benefit from the demand for their services. For every problem that dams created, there was a group of specialists prepared to develop and test technology. These programs of research and development frequently lasted decades and often produced only minor improvements for salmon. For instance, early in the construction of federal dams on the Columbia River, biologists recognized that maintaining salmon runs would require helping juvenile salmon avoid dams and large turbines on their downstream migration to the Pacific Ocean. When the pace of dam building quickened after World War II, the Fish and Wildlife Service as well as the U.S. Army Corps of Engineers and the Bureau of Reclamation tried to find a technological solution for this problem. In the next half century, biologists and hydraulic engineers tested everything from skimmers and electric nets for intercepting young salmon as they approached dams to underwater lights and modified turbine intakes to keep young salmon out of turbines. Fish and Wildlife Service researchers were somewhat successful in developing technology for intercepting and collecting juvenile salmon in their migration to the Pacific Ocean. In the mid-1960s, the service began using this technology to collect salmon smolts above John Day Dam on the lower Columbia River, which then were transported by truck and barge below Bonneville Dam and released. The young salmon survived the trip in large enough numbers that this practice became a regular feature of the federal government's salmon programs in the Columbia River basin.

Collecting and trucking young salmon around dams and turbines was expensive and only partly effective, however, since the practice did not address the problems created by slack water in the reservoirs behind the dams. As the Columbia River became more like a string of artificial lakes and less like a free-flowing river, young salmon lost the cues and momentum that river currents provided. The slack water of reservoirs also increased the exposure of young salmon to predators. In the 1970s, the National Marine Fisheries Service (NMFS) pressed federal agencies operating the dams to increase the flow of water through the reservoirs in order to encourage the passage of smolts downstream.[10] The agency also argued for releasing water through spillways to sweep juvenile salmon over dams. As drought gripped the Pacific Northwest in 1977, the NMFS closely monitored water flows to ensure that releases of water through spillways would be timed to carry the largest possible number of salmon downstream. Together with trucking of smolt downstream, these measures, the agency claimed, had avoided the extinction of some salmon runs and later would produce adult salmon and economic benefits of millions of dollars.

The use of water flows to improve salmon migration had political limits, however, since increasing water flowing down the river reduced the amount of water available for generating power and irrigating arid lands. As a result, pro-

posals to increase flows inevitably sparked opposition from politically powerful interests such as aluminum smelters, large agricultural operations, and other
ratepayers.

In the 1950s, the wave of dam construction on the Columbia River also
spurred efforts to increase the production of salmon by improving the habitat
of tributaries on the lower Columbia River. Reflecting a view shared with flood-
control managers and electrical power producers, the Fish and Wildlife Service
assumed that the less debris in a stream, the better. In its annual report for 1958,
the service proudly reported that logjams and other obstructions and debris had
been removed from 1,000 miles of streams in the watershed of the lower Columbia River. In the next eight years, the agency oversaw the clearing of another 700 miles of streams. The removal of large logjams did enable salmon
and steelhead to use previously inaccessible habitat, but the removal of debris
also destroyed pools and overhangs that salmon and steelhead require for shelter and forage.

The diversion of water into agricultural fields presented other problems for
Pacific salmon. Each year, as they migrated downstream toward the Pacific Ocean,
millions of salmon smolts were diverted with irrigation water into ditches that
led them into farm fields where they rotted in the desert sun. What had been
an isolated problem spread dramatically during the Great Depression as the federal government irrigated millions of acres of arid lands in Idaho, Washington, and Oregon with Columbia River water. It was left to the service to argue
for placing screens on irrigation diversions as water development in the Columbia River basin expanded. Like other activities in the Columbia River program, however, new water diversions were constructed far more quickly than
were fish screens. In 1970, when the NMFS took over the management of the
Columbia River program, the federal government had installed 720 screens on
irrigation diversions. By the 1990s, less than 1,000 of the 55,000 water diversions in Oregon had been screened.

Nothing Like Hatcheries

During the development of the Columbia River, no other type of mitigation
persisted longer or received more funding and political support than hatcheries.
Political support for captive propagation repeatedly overcame criticism by biologists. In 1940, for instance, fisheries commissioner Charles E. Jackson cham-
pioned hatcheries, saying: "Exhaustive investigation by bureau biologists, and
the report of an independent board of consultants, has indicated that enlarged

hatchery operations will constitute one of the most important elements in a plan for maintaining the runs of salmon in the Columbia River."[11] Jackson's confidence in hatcheries ignored a recent evaluation of existing hatcheries on the Columbia River by one of the bureau's brightest biologists, Willis Rich. In reporting on his 1936 evaluation, Rich concluded "that there is no evidence obtainable from a study of the statistics of the pack [of canned salmon] and hatchery output that artificial propagation has been an effective agent in conserving the supply of salmon."

In the early 1950s, the construction of McNary Dam just below the confluence of the Snake and Columbia Rivers, as well as congressional authorization of additional dams, added urgency to the Fish and Wildlife Service's advocacy for hatcheries. Although hatchery construction lagged behind dam construction, the service oversaw the construction or renovation of 20 hatcheries by 1959 that were collecting and hatching eggs, rearing fingerlings, and releasing smolts by the millions. In the early 1960s, the service began experimental transfers of salmon eggs from one river or hatchery into a different river or hatchery in order to create runs of salmon and steelhead where there were none. Soon, the bureau expanded the experimental program.

In the late 1950s, however, concerns about the effectiveness of hatcheries arose again, when a team of experts recommended that further hatchery construction be deferred until the effectiveness of existing hatcheries had been determined. Over the next decade, the fins of millions of hatchery-reared salmon were clipped so that biologists could record their return to the hatcheries or their capture in commercial or recreational fisheries. By the late 1960s, Fish and Wildlife Service fish culturists were reporting that hatchery-reared salmon had become the backbone of commercial and recreational fisheries, for which catches of salmon fetched three dollars for every one dollar spent at hatcheries. These calculations, which obscured the tremendous damage done by dams and diversions to the habitat of wild salmon, made hatcheries seem like a good investment for political leaders who were being asked to spend taxpayers' money on fish. Return on investment rather than the status of wild salmon runs soon became the standard for assessing the value of hatcheries in the Columbia River basin.

Like other dam mitigation projects, salmon hatcheries enjoyed the powerful advantage of helping politicians "bring home the bacon" to their districts. Not only did the construction of hatcheries, fish ladders, and other such hardware give a temporary boost to rural economies, the operation of hatcheries provided significant amounts of funding to state fish and game agencies. Attempts to trim federal funding for hatchery construction and operations met with stiff opposition from the congressional delegations of Washington, Oregon, Montana, and Idaho. Fishermen whose catches depended increasingly on hatchery-reared salmon also became strong advocates for hatcheries. Over the years, hatchery construction and operation consumed a larger and larger share of the budget for the Columbia River program—79% of the total in 1986.

The persistent reliance of fisheries managers, fishermen, and political leaders on hatcheries also owed something to the ability of hatchery operators to find and report some good news nearly every year. In 1952, for instance, the Fish and Wildlife Service reported that 101,000 sockeye salmon ascended the fish ladders at Rock Island Dam on the middle Columbia River, the largest run since counting at the dam began in 1933. Later annual reports, however, failed to report on the status of this run. In 1965, the bureau reported record runs of coho at Bonneville Dam, most of which entered hatcheries. During the 1960s, hatchery production of coho salmon boosted commercial catches from less than 250,000 pounds in 1959 to 4.2 million pounds in 1966. In 1973, the NMFS took pride in 10 million pounds of coho landings by Oregon trollers and a recreational catch of more than 300,000 coho, most of which, the agency noted, were from hatcheries.

By focusing on changes over a few years, rather than over several decades, status reports also gave a misleading impression of increasing abundance. For example, in 1969, the bureau reported that 1967 landings of salmon in Washington, Oregon, and California had increased by 27 million pounds over the ten-year average. Yet, even these comparatively high catches, which were composed mostly of hatchery-raised salmon, were 80% below catches of several decades before. Catches of wild salmon were a tiny fraction of what they were just a few decades before.

The dependence of commercial and recreational fishermen upon hatchery-reared salmon also had disastrous consequences for remaining runs of wild salmon. While hatchery-reared salmon could withstand high rates of capture, depleted runs of wild salmon could not. Since wild and hatchery-reared salmon mixed, wild salmon were caught at the same high rate as hatchery-reared salmon. Thus, the apparent abundance of hatchery-reared salmon masked the scarcity of wild salmon.

Salmon Decline

The late 1970s brought clear signs that hatcheries, fish ladders, and other mitigation measures were falling short in countering the destruction of salmon and their habitats by dams and diversions. Fifty-five major dams had eliminated nearly half of the 12,000 miles of stream habitat available to salmon and steelhead in the Columbia River basin. Between 1953, when McNary Dam was completed, and 1977, the number of coho salmon returning to the Columbia River fell from 872,000 to 87,000 fish. With astonishing suddenness, hatchery runs of coastal coho salmon in Oregon collapsed from 3.9 million fish in 1976 to 1 million in 1977. A year later, the NMFS reported a record low run of 1,600 chinook salmon on the Snake River.

These declines spurred the U.S. Fish and Wildlife Service and the NMFS to review the status of fall chinook and steelhead for possible listing under the Endangered Species Act (ESA). In response, the Pacific Northwest's congressional delegation pressed for a legislative alternative. In 1980, Congress passed the Pacific Northwest Electric Power Planning and Conservation Act; this act established the Northwest Power Planning Council, which was composed of two representatives each from the states of Washington, Oregon, Idaho, and Montana. Acknowledging that the balancing of purposes in the Fish and Wildlife Coordination Act and the Federal Power Act had failed to protect fish and wildlife from the "cumulative impact of the hydroelectric dams of the Columbia," the act mandated a "remedial program to cover the entire [b]asin."[12] The NMFS suspended its status review.

As part of a program of salmon restoration, the power council developed a water budget to increase the flow of water during the spring migration of juvenile salmon. It was hoped that the increased flow would "flush" young fish down the river, as spring freshets once had. These and other measures, as well as boatloads of plans and discussion papers, failed to stem the decline in salmon runs. Claims of economic hardship by entrenched interests effectively blocked significant reform of the Columbia River system. In seeking consensus among conflicting interests, the council itself settled for "the lowest common denominator acceptable to power interests" and industry, in the words of one federal judge.[13]

Salmon runs continued to decline. In the three decades after the completion of McNary Dam in 1953, Columbia River spring run chinook declined by 66%, summer chinook by 79%, fall chinook by 26%, sockeye and coho by 72%, and summer steelhead by 69%. In 1990, petitions to list several runs of Columbia River salmon under the ESA provoked yet another high-level salmon summit, which produced little meaningful change in the balance of interests between cheap water and power on one hand and depleted salmon runs and flooded salmon habitat on the other. The November 1991 listing of Snake River sockeye salmon as endangered was followed by others. By 1999, 12 stocks of Columbia River basin salmon and steelhead had been listed under the ESA. These listings provided the NMFS with tremendous legal leverage in arguing for changes in the operation of dams and for other measures; however, reflecting the policy of the Clinton administration, the agency sought to build consensus where consensus had escaped others in the past.

In November 1999, the NMFS released its analysis of options for restoring salmon in the Columbia River basin. One option was the removal of several dams—a proposal similar to one that the agency had made in 1976. According to the 1999 analysis, the removal or breaching of several dams on the lower Snake River was the "most risk averse" of the options for preventing the extinction of Columbia River salmon, but the option was hampered by great uncertainties. The agency insisted that the level of precaution to be taken was a political decision that it was not going to make. In describing the agency's role, regional administrator Will Stelle argued: "Our job is to get the science right and to help foster regional debate on choices."[14]

There was room for skepticism that such an approach would lead to the hard choices that restoration of salmon runs on the Columbia River required. The powerful political interests that had benefited from ignoring risks to salmon for so long seemed unprepared to change their successful approach to protecting their own interests. At a Senate hearing in June 1999, a representative of wheat and barley growers in Washington State argued that dam removal was receiving far too much attention. "There are thousands of reasons for the decline of salmon," Lynn Ausman argued in calling for transporting smolts around dams and improving hatcheries.

At the end of the century, the economy of the Pacific Northwest was booming even as the runs of salmon in which the region took such public pride were at record lows. Runs of salmon and steelhead that once numbered 10 to 16 million fish had been reduced to about 1 million fish. Commercial landings of salmon and steelhead, which were as high as 2.1 million fish in 1941, had fallen to just 68,000 fish in 1995. Wild salmon made up less than 10% of the Columbia River's runs and dozens of races of salmon had been wiped out.

While overfishing, logging, and pollution played a role in the demise of some of the world's richest salmon runs, the chief cause for these declines and the greatest challenge to the recovery of salmon and steelhead was the transformation of the Columbia River watershed into an engine for producing cheap water and power.[15]

Wetlands Conversion

For much of the twentieth century, dam construction was the most visible and dramatic form of fisheries habitat destruction. In the latter half of the century, however, other, more gradual and widespread forms of habitat destruction grew in importance. In the 1950s and 1960s, the booming American economy and population growth fueled the conversion of many kinds of wildlife and fisheries habitat to other uses, such as refineries, harbors, farms and feedlots, waste dumps, residential communities, and tourist resorts. This was especially true along the coasts, where more than half the U.S. population soon lived. In the 1960s, a period of exceptional growth, the population of coastal counties grew by 15 to 110 million, a rate of growth much higher than other areas of the country. For the most part, this growth concentrated around major urban areas. After 1940, the population surrounding Puget Sound, Washington, grew by 400,000 people each decade. Areas such as San Francisco Bay and southern Florida experienced equally rapid growth.

Wetlands were particularly vulnerable to development. Unlike other types of land, wetlands were cheap, largely because real estate prices failed to incorporate the value of wetlands, for example, as wildlife habitat or as storm protection. Now and again, federal fish and wildlife agencies attempted to counter this market failure by supporting studies estimating the value of fisheries produced by wetlands. By providing nursery habitat and shelter and by producing food for wildlife, coastal wetlands played an important role in the productivity of coastal fisheries. The coastal wetlands of the southeastern United States, from North Carolina to Texas, were particularly extensive and important since seven of the ten commercially most valuable species in regional fisheries were dependent on wetland and estuarine habitats at some critical stage in their lives. But like many studies since then, the findings about the value of wetlands remained too general and too far outside the more familiar calculations of the marketplace to have much of an effect on decision making.

Until the 1950s, little systematic attention was paid to the loss of habitats, such as wetlands, caused by such growth. In 1950, however, the Fish and Wildlife Service established an office to work with state agencies in delineating and classifying wetlands and their use by wildlife. A national inventory of wetlands was completed in 1954 in the hopes of identifying high priority areas for wildlife where drainage should be controlled or prohibited. That inventory and later ones documented massive losses of fresh- and saltwater wetlands, which Interior Secretary Walter Hickel characterized as "legalized larceny of resources."[16]

In the late 1960s, federal law and practice regarding the conversion of coastal habitats began changing dramatically. On March 14, 1967, Colonel R. P. Tabb, district engineer of the U.S. Army Corps of Engineers in Jacksonville, Florida, issued the first-ever denial of a permit application to dredge and fill in coastal waters, based on concerns about fish and wildlife.[17] (In a dredge and fill project, soil submerged beneath water is dug up and deposited on low-lying land, often to create or improve a navigation channel and to create land for development.) In rejecting the permit application, Colonel Tabb cited BCF research suggesting that the project would cause damage to fish and wildlife in Boca Ciega Bay and would be inconsistent with the Fish and Wildlife Coordination Act.

In 1968, the Fish and Wildlife Service gained additional leverage in stemming the loss of nearshore habitats when the U.S. Army Corps of Engineers expanded the review of dredge-and-fill permit applications by state and federal fish and wildlife agencies. Previously, the corps had restricted reviews under the Rivers and Harbors Act of 1899 to projects that affected navigation. The new policy included projects that affected fish and wildlife habitat. Passage of the National Environmental Policy Act in 1970 created another tool for scrutinizing the impacts of projects on coastal resources by requiring environmental assessments. Finally, the Clean Water Act of 1972 prohibited the discharge of dredge or fill material into U.S. waters without a permit from the U.S. Army Corps of Engineers. Initially, the corps excluded many wetland areas from the protection of the Clean Water Act's Section 404, but expanded its definition in 1975 after losing a lawsuit brought by the Natural Resources Defense Council and the National Wildlife Federation. Quite suddenly, the habitat conservation staff of the NMFS found themselves reviewing thousands of permit applications forwarded by the corps under the Fish and Wildlife Coordination Act.

No region was more beset by projects to alter coastal wetlands and other habitats than the Southeast Region that stretches from North Carolina to Texas. From 1981 to 1985 alone, the NMFS regional office commented upon 23,292 proposals to alter a total of 184,187 acres of coastal wetlands. A little more than 5,000 of these permits received detailed review. On average, the corps accepted the service's recommendations half of the time, and fully rejected them one-quarter of the time. In a study of 584 permits, the NMFS found that its recommendations for mitigation were observed 80% of the time.

"When I first came in, in every corps district, the regulatory functions chief, who handled the permits, was a civil engineer," says Andy Mager, assistant regional director for habitat in the NMFS regional office in St. Petersburg, Florida. "You tried to talk fish and wildlife and they didn't care. They were pro-development anyway, and some of them even had money in some of the developments they were regulating. It got to that point."

Summary

In the 1930s, the burst of dam construction in the Pacific Northwest posed a threat to salmon runs that federal fisheries agencies proposed to overcome largely by producing and releasing salmon from hatcheries. This choice reflected a trust in captive propagation that stretched back to the founding years of the U.S. Fish and Fisheries Commission. Captive propagation of fish had dominated the funding and programs of federal fisheries agencies from the beginning. Despite a lack of success, federal agencies propagated and released fish by the hundreds of billions each year.

Federal fisheries agencies tried to counteract other problems created by dams through constructing fish ladders, transporting young salmon around dams, screening diversions of water into agricultural fields, transplanting salmon from flooded streams to still-flowing streams, and by managing water flows through dams. These efforts were always too little, too late.

As the pace of dam construction quickened in the 1950s and 1960s, Congress increased legal protections for salmon insignificantly, even as it continued investing in hatcheries that enjoyed local political support.

In the 1970s, the signs of decline in salmon populations became unmistakable. During the next two decades, however, the federal government resisted confronting the declines, until Indian tribes filed petitions to list several runs of salmon under the Endangered Species Act (ESA). By the end of the century, many runs of Columbia River salmon remained at historic lows.

The economic boom of the 1950s threatened marine habitats in other, less obvious ways. Chief among these was the degradation and destruction of wetlands. What these habitat losses lacked in scale, they made up for in number, as thousands of acres of coastal habitats were converted to private home, industrial, or commercial use. Federal fisheries agencies enjoyed no more leverage in protecting coastal habitats from small-scale destruction than they did in preventing the loss of salmon runs.

Notes

1. Quoted in Lichatowich, Jim. 1999. *Salmon Without Rivers: A History of the Pacific Salmon Crisis.* Island Press, Washington, D.C.
2. Quoted in Cart, T.W. 1968. The Federal Fisheries Service, 1871–1940. A thesis submitted to the faculty of the University of North Carolina at Chapel Hill in partial fulfillment of the requirements for the degree of Master of Arts in the Department of History. 87 pages.
3. U.S. Department of the Interior. 1944. *Annual Report of the Secretary of the Interior: Fiscal Year Ended June 30, 1944.* U.S. Government Printing Office, Washington, D.C.
4. U.S. Department of the Interior. 1946. *Annual Report of the Secretary of the Interior: Fiscal Year Ended June 30, 1947.* U.S. Government Printing Office, Washington, D.C.
5. U.S. Department of the Interior. 1946. *Annual Report of the Secretary of the Interior: Fiscal Year Ended June 30, 1946.* U.S. Government Printing Office, Washington, D.C.
6. U.S. Department of the Interior. 1945. *Annual Report of the Secretary of the Interior: Fiscal Year Ended June 30, 1945.* U.S. Government Printing Office, Washington, D.C.
7. Quoted in Lichatowich, Jim. 1999. *Salmon Without Rivers: A History of the Pacific Salmon Crisis.* Island Press, Washington, D.C.
8. Lichatowich, Jim. 1999. *Salmon Without Rivers: A History of the Pacific Salmon Crisis.* Island Press, Washington, D.C.
9. U.S. Department of the Interior. 1958. *Annual Report of the Secretary of the Interior: Fiscal Year Ended June 30, 1958.* U.S. Government Printing Office, Washington, D.C.
10. Federal dams in the Columbia River are operated by several different agencies, including the U.S. Army Corps of Engineers and the Department of the Interior's Bureau of Reclamation. Other dams are operated by public utilities, such as Pacific Power and Light.
11. U.S. Department of the Interior. 1940. *Annual Report of the Department of the Interior, 1940.* U.S. Government Printing Office, Washington, D.C.
12. H.R. Rep. No. 96-976, pt. I, 96th Cong. 2nd Sess. Cited in Bean, Michael J., and Melanie J. Rowland. 1997. *The Evolution of National Wildlife Law,* Third Edition. Praeger, Westport, Connecticut; Northwest Resource Information Center, Inc. v. Northwest Power Planning Council, 35 F.3d 1371, 1378 (9th Cir. 1994), also cited in Bean and Rowland (1997).
13. Quoted in Bean, Michael J., and Melanie J. Rowland. 1997. *The Evolution of National Wildlife Law,* Third Edition. Praeger, Westport, Connecticut.

14. National Oceanic and Atmospheric Administration. November 16, 1999. Press release: Federal Agencies Release Four-H "Working Paper" on Salmon Recovery in Pacific Northwest.
15. Anadromous fish in California suffered similar declines. Dams, diversions, mining, logging, and other activities reduced runs of spring chinook in the Sacramento and San Joaquin Rivers from 500,000 to less than 1,000 wild fish. Coho salmon were extirpated in many streams. Alteration of the Sacramento River delta for agricultural and transportation purposes destroyed spawning and rearing habitat for pink and chum salmon.
16. U.S. Department of the Interior. 1972. River of Life, Water: The Environmental Challenge. U.S. Government Printing Office, Washington, D.C.
17. Under Section 10 of the River and Harbors Act of 1899, alterations of navigable waters of the United States required a permit issued by the U.S. Army Corps of Engineers. Common types of alteration included dredging to maintain or create navigation channels and to drain coastal wetlands. Often, the dredged material or spoil was deposited in adjacent wetland areas for the purposes of "land reclamation."

The Fish and Wildlife Coordination Act authorized federal and state fish and wildlife agencies to review applications for such permits and make recommendations whether to grant the permit or to place conditions on the permit.

1956–1960 In 1956, President Eisenhower signed the Fish and Wildlife Act, reorganizing federal fish and wildlife activities for the first time since 1940. Under the new arrangement, the Interior Department's U.S. Fish and Wildlife Service included the Bureau of Sport Fisheries and Wildlife and the Bureau of Commercial Fisheries (BCF).

The Bureau of Sport Fisheries and Wildlife was responsible for managing the service's captive propagation programs, which included salmon hatcheries on rivers of the Pacific Northwest. The bureau administered the Dingell-Johnson program of grant-in-aid to the states for fish restoration and organized the service's comments on water development projects.

In 1960, the BCF employed 1,662 staff, of which 205 were seasonal. Within its $22.3 million budget, 31% was allocated to research, 19% to marketing and technology, 14% to Pacific salmon, 13% to the Fisheries Loan Fund, and 3% to management of fisheries in Alaska. The agency operated 24 laboratories, 68 smaller stations and offices, and 23 vessels of 40 feet or longer. In 1960, the BCF added a technological laboratory, two field research stations, and two exploratory and fishing gear research stations.

Chapter 4 | International Affairs

Throughout modern history, the wide-ranging behaviors of many marine wildlife species, together with their commercial value, created the opportunity for international conflict. It is not surprising, then, that from its beginnings, negotiating international agreements on the management of marine fisheries dominated U.S. policy on marine fisheries.

As early as the sixteenth century, groundfish populations on Georges Bank and the Grand Bank provided the raw material for a lucrative trade in salted fish that attracted fishermen from France, Spain, England, and later, the American colonies. For nearly as long, governments found cause for conflict over fish and fishermen working the waters off Newfoundland. At first, the controversies concerned rights to land in order to salt the catch and reprovision. Later, governments contended over the rights of their fishermen to catch the fish.

Access to these fish remained a bone of contention between Great Britain and the young United States well after the Treaty of Paris brought an end to the American War of Independence in 1783. In 1815, Senator John Quincy Adams, who was later appointed secretary of state by President Monroe, argued for free access to the waters off Newfoundland. Reflecting centuries-old views that were not seriously circumscribed until 1945, Senator Adams said: "Neither nature nor art has partitioned the sea into kingdoms, republics, or states. . . . The ocean and its treasures are the common property of all men, and we have a natural right to navigate the ocean and to fish in it, whenever and wherever we wish."[1]

The doctrine of "freedom of the seas," which was first articulated by the Dutch lawyer Hugo Grotius in 1609, relied partly on the belief that the life of the seas was inexhaustible. At the time and for more than two centuries after European settlement, the populations of marine wildlife in the waters off the Atlantic coast of North America seemed to confirm the theory of abundance. The only matter in dispute was who should benefit from the abundance.

While disputes over fisheries in the Gulf of Maine required periodic negotiation over who got what, concerns over the decline of marine wildlife populations also played a role in spurring negotiations in the Pacific. In the 1890s,
the fishery for Pacific halibut (*Hippoglossus stenolepis*) off Washington, Canada,
and Alaska grew rapidly after railroads made it possible to supply Atlantic Coast
markets. In 1915, landings by Canadian and U.S. fishermen peaked at about
27,000 metric tons then fell by one-third the following year. Gasoline-powered
engines enabled fishermen to respond to the decline by fishing farther offshore
and increasing the amount of fishing gear they deployed.

In 1923, after five years of negotiations, the governments of Canada and the
United States agreed to establish a commission to research the causes of the decline in halibut. William F. Thompson, who had begun studying the halibut
fishery in 1915 as a Bureau of Fisheries biologist, was appointed director of
investigations. Several years of research by the commission concluded that overfishing had been the primary cause of decline in the abundance of Pacific halibut. In response, Canada and the United States expanded the powers of the
International Pacific Halibut Commission and agreed to catch limits that led
to a restoration of the halibut population.

Negotiations between Canada and the United States were less successful in
protecting the enormous runs of Pacific salmon that swam through the two
countries' waters. As in the case of Pacific halibut, both concern over the decline of Fraser River salmon populations and equitable access for U.S. and Canadian fishermen drove negotiations between the two countries in the early 1930s.
Fishermen in Alaska, Washington, and Oregon regularly caught large numbers
of Fraser River sockeye. Likewise, Canadian fishermen regularly caught salmon
reared in streams of Oregon, Washington, and Alaska. Failure to collaborate
in limiting the catch of salmon raised the risk of overfishing individual runs of
salmon. Each country also was concerned about equity in sharing the costs of
conservation. Because salmon reared in the streams of one country could be
caught by fishermen of the other, a nation might not enjoy the benefits of investing in conservation measures such as quotas and habitat protection.

In 1937, the two countries established the International Pacific Salmon Fisheries Commission to regulate coastal fisheries and to restore runs of sockeye
salmon (*Oncorhynchus nerka*). The commission enjoyed initial success in rebuilding Fraser River salmon; however, controversy and international conflict
returned throughout the commission's history.

As the end of World War II approached, the U.S. government foresaw growing competition over fisheries as nations sought to rebuild from the war and

feed growing human populations. In the Fish and Wildlife Service's annual report for 1944, director Ira N. Gabrielson warned: "Post-war competition among nations for the food resources of the high seas and even of coastal and the larger inland waters will be greatly intensified."[2] Buoyed by the success of the Allies in the war and aware of the United States's newly gained leadership, the U.S. government sought to preempt conflicts over shared fisheries through regional organizations. By 1950, a burst of U.S. diplomatic initiatives had created several international organizations, including the International Whaling Commission (IWC), the Inter-American Tropical Tuna Commission, and the International North Pacific Fisheries Commission.

As fishing fleets grew, the effectiveness of these and other treaty organizations was challenged by several persistent problems: the difficulty of achieving agreement on meaningful conservation measures among nations with different views, conflicting goals of development and conservation, risk-prone decision making, fishing by nonmembers, resistance to effective enforcement, the failure to support or act on scientific analysis, inadequate funding, and the lack of effective monitoring programs.

The most important limitations on the effectiveness of international organizations arose from the sovereignty of nations. Simply put, the decisions of a treaty organization were binding only on those countries that agreed to be bound by them. In some cases, large numbers of countries did not belong to regional treaty organizations although their fishermen may have been harming marine wildlife that the treaty organization was supposed to be conserving. Some treaties, such as the International Convention for the Regulation of Whaling, allowed member countries to exempt themselves from conservation measures by formally objecting to a decision by a treaty organization.

In the 1960s, the United States began playing an unusual and growing role in counteracting these shortcomings.

Sanctions

In 1945, President Harry S. Truman set the stage for the United States's eventual role as champion of international standards of marine wildlife conservation. As World War II came to a close and concerns about increasing conflict over fisheries took hold, President Truman issued a proclamation that the United States had a right to regulate fishing beyond its territorial sea by declaring special conservation zones in adjacent high seas areas.[3] If negotia-

tions failed with distant water fishing nations over exploitation of fish populations off U.S. shores, the United States would unilaterally adopt conservation
measures for the special conservation zone. The proclamation aimed at protecting domestic fishermen from direct competition with foreign fishermen.

While the proclamation may have been intended to encourage other countries to negotiate with the United States before fishing off its shores, South American countries interpreted the proclamation as a territorial grab, with cause. By
the late 1940s, the U.S. distant water tuna fleet had expanded into waters as far
south as Ecuador, attracting the displeasure of the governments of Peru, Ecuador,
and Chile. Reacting to the Truman Proclamation, Chile and Peru moved their
jurisdictional limits from 3 miles to 200 miles offshore, encompassing the fishing grounds of the U.S. distant water tuna fleet. In 1952, Ecuador also claimed
a 200-mile zone and began seizing U.S. tuna boats.

Rather than negotiate with South American coastal nations over access to
tuna within their declared fishing zones, the tuna industry pressed the Eisenhower administration and Congress to reject the claims of the South American
countries. In 1954, after the governments of Ecuador and Peru repeatedly seized
U.S. tuna vessels off their shores, Congress passed the Fishermen's Protective
Act authorizing the secretary of state to secure the release of seized vessels and
crew, even if that meant reimbursing American fishermen for fines paid to these
governments. When seizures continued in the disputed waters, Congress strengthened the act in 1968 to allow the secretary of state to withhold foreign aid from
offending countries.

In 1971, Congress adopted the Pelly Amendment and greatly expanded the
scope of the Fishermen's Protection Act from matters of fisheries jurisdiction
to implementation of international conservation measures. The impetus for the
amendment introduced by Washington Congressman Thomas Pelly was the refusal of Denmark, Germany, and Norway to observe salmon conservation measures adopted by the International Convention for the Northwest Atlantic Fisheries (ICNAF). The negotiations that concluded in 1949 with a treaty establishing
the ICNAF were driven by growing concerns over the fisheries of the Northwest Atlantic. Concern among European countries arose from increasing competition among their fleets for groundfish on the Grand Banks. In the United
States, voluntary efforts to reduce the bycatch and discard of young haddock
had failed, largely because some fishermen were unwilling to forego a loss in
marketable catch caused by the use of gear designed to avoid bycatch. In both
cases, the benefits of conservation actions taken by one group would be undermined by the failure of another group to take similar action.

Under the ICNAF, member countries could exempt themselves from conservation measures by formally objecting, as the three countries did. The Pelly Amendment aimed at encouraging the countries to reverse their exemptions. It did so by authorizing the president to ban imports of fish products from countries that the secretary of commerce certified as "diminishing the effectiveness" of an international fisheries conservation program to which the United States belonged.

The Pelly Amendment saw little use until the late 1970s, when conservationists relied on it in their campaign for a moratorium on commercial whaling. Then, conservationists in the United States regularly pressed for certification of Japan, the Soviet Union, and other countries that did not abide by decisions of the IWC. The IWC had been established by a treaty negotiated soon after the end of World War II by countries sponsoring commercial whaling fleets. The treaty authorized the commission to set restrictions on commercial whaling that each member country had to observe, unless it formally objected. Although administrations sometimes certified violating countries, they rarely imposed sanctions. Generally, administrations claimed that other considerations, such as national security or trade relationships, outweighed immediate concerns about the conservation of marine wildlife. For example, after the secretary of commerce certified Japan and the Soviet Union in 1975 for violating quotas adopted by the IWC, President Gerald Ford declined to impose sanctions. The president argued that the two countries would abide by IWC quotas in the future and that sanctions would cause economic problems in the United States.

In 1979, conservationists capitalized on passage of the Magnuson-Stevens Act to generate greater pressure on offending countries. Under the Packwood-Magnuson Amendment, the secretary of state was required to reduce by half any allocation of fishing rights in U.S. waters proposed for a country that had been certified under the Pelly Amendment. For countries such as Japan and the Soviet Union, which had fishing fleets that depended upon access to U.S. waters, the amendment presented a real threat, if it were applied. By the mid-1980s, however, when an IWC moratorium on commercial whaling took effect, foreign fishing had been virtually eliminated from U.S. waters and the Packwood-Magnuson Amendment lost its force. Nonetheless, the threat of embargoes on imports authorized by the Pelly Amendment remained serious enough that the U.S. government used this tool, generally at the urging of conservationists and their allies in Congress, to compel compliance with conservation measures regarding whaling, restrictions on the use of high seas drift nets, and the incidental drowning of marine mammals in tuna nets.

Enclosing the Global Commons

In 1961, the arrival of 61 Russian trawlers on Nantucket Shoals off Massachusetts sent shockwaves through New England's struggling fishing communities. The enormous modern factory trawlers that enabled the Soviet Union to fish any ocean at any time dwarfed the small boats of New England fishermen, most of them built before World War II. Cold war tensions between the United States and the Soviet Union added an ominous dimension to the appearance of the Soviet flotilla off Massachusetts.

Two years later, climate and currents combined to create unusually favorable conditions for hatching and survival of the spawn of haddock (*Melanogrammus aeglefinus*) in the western North Atlantic. In 1965, as young haddock swarmed in enormous numbers over Georges Bank, American fishermen watched helplessly as the Soviet fleet of factory trawlers swept through waters that once had been an American reserve. Soviet catches of haddock increased tenfold to 128,800 metric tons between 1964 and 1965, doubling total catches to nearly 249,000 metric tons. Predictably, catches began falling soon afterwards and reached a historic low of 23,240 metric tons in 1974. American fishermen felt the effects. Catches by U.S. fishermen, which had averaged 62,000 metric tons between 1950 and 1966, plummeted to 3,731 metric tons by 1974.

For federal fisheries biologists and managers, the arrival of the more efficient foreign fleets spelled trouble for New England's groundfish populations. After the decimation of rebounding haddock population by the Soviet fleet, the Bureau of Commercial Fisheries (BCF) scientists at Woods Hole, Massachusetts, predicted a "haddock crisis." "The very large catch of haddock by the Soviet fleet off our New England coast left a feeling of shock and dismay, anger, and resentment in the U.S. fishing industry," says Henry Beasley, who began his career in international fisheries affairs at the BCF in 1966.

While New England fishermen were stunned by the power of the Soviet fleet, they were enraged that the ICNAF had failed to protect them from foreign fishing fleets. By pressing the ICNAF to adopt restrictions that seemed to hurt U.S. fishermen most, the BCF lost credibility as well. Until the explosive growth of foreign fishing in the late 1950s and 1960s, the ICNAF had performed relatively well. In 1951, the United States used BCF research in fashioning a proposal to require larger mesh in the cod-ends of trawls to allow young groundfish to escape. The measure, which was quickly adopted and implemented by U.S. and Canadian fishermen, became a much heralded success. At the time, it appeared as if the ICNAF were going to stop the cycle of depletion that had marked the recent history of North Atlantic fisheries.

As competition for fish grew in the northwestern Atlantic, however, the ICNAF encountered many of the same kinds of problems that plague other international fisheries organizations. The first difficulty had to do with getting the 14 member countries of the ICNAF, many of whom were vying for a share in the fish, to agree upon strong conservation measures. For quite some time, fisheries scientists and managers had known of the need to restrict catches of haddock—among the world's best understood populations of fish at the time. In 1962, the Canadian delegation proposed to limit fishing effort and catches of haddock, but the proposal foundered on the complexity of dividing overall quotas among the member countries that wanted them. Concerns over the economic impacts of the proposed restrictions led to additional analyses and time-consuming discussions.

There was another, equally important limitation. Even if the ICNAF adopted restrictions on haddock catches earlier, the Soviet Union did not have to observe them, since it did not become a member of the ICNAF until 1969. Federal fisheries staff and State Department negotiators had tried to manage around this difficulty by concluding bilateral agreements with the Soviet Union and other countries that were not members of the ICNAF. But these agreements and stronger measures by international treaty organizations such as the ICNAF did not dissipate the tension. Rather, frustration with the lack of relief from foreign overfishing continued to fuel a simmering political crisis.

Reacting to the ICNAF's inability to control foreign fishing off U.S. shores, fishermen began advocating that the United States expand its jurisdiction beyond the 3-mile limit. In 1966, commercial and recreational fishing interests as well as conservation groups overcame opposition from the Johnson administration and convinced Congress to pass a law extending U.S. fisheries management jurisdiction in a so-called contiguous zone between the territorial sea and 12 miles offshore. This extension of U.S. authority did not satisfy demands by New England fishermen to eliminate competition from a growing number of foreign fishing vessels off U.S. shores. As populations of haddock and other species were depleted off New England, Soviet and Eastern bloc fleets of factory trawlers moved south off southern New England and targeted enormous schools of Atlantic mackerel (*Scomber scombrus*) and Atlantic herring (*Clupea harengus*).

Together with fishermen from the Pacific coast and Alaska, where foreign fishing vessels were making huge hauls of fish and shellfish, New England fishermen began pressing for extension of U.S. jurisdiction to 200 miles offshore. At the same time, United Nations negotiations on a new law of the sea were getting underway in New York City. Delegations from many developing countries that saw a threat to their future in the expansion of distant water fishing fleets from Japan, the Soviet Union, and eastern and western Europe, abandoned the international standard of a 12-mile limit and instead began pressing for a 200-mile limit.

Even as an international consensus grew for adopting the new standard within a new law of the sea, the U.S. government resisted. The U.S. position was based largely on concerns of the U.S. military that a 200-mile fisheries zone would jeopardize freedom of navigation. Nor did the BCF initially endorse the extension of jurisdiction. In 1970, the agency argued: "Adoption of a doctrine which puts the waters within 200 miles of the coast—in most parts of the world these are all the waters above the Continental Shelf—under the jurisdiction of individual states does not lead in the direction of maximum utilization of marine resources, principally because the majority of coastal states which would thus acquire jurisdiction are incapable now of exploiting them and will be incapable for some time to come."[4]

Advocates for the 200-mile zone, both within the BCF and in the commercial fishing industry, were also stymied in their efforts by the Interior Department's own priorities, which focused on offshore oil and gas deposits. In 1970, with the creation of the National Oceanic and Atmospheric Administration (NOAA) in the Department of Commerce, fisheries concerns moved from behind the shadow of the oil and gas industry. The fishing industry successfully pressed for two representatives on the U.S. delegation to the Law of the Sea Conference.

Fishing industry representatives also formed a working group that overcame internal disagreements, and proposed a "three species approach" to fisheries jurisdiction. Under this approach, coastal fish populations, anadromous fish, and highly migratory species such as tunas would be managed under different rules. Coastal nations would have preferential rights to coastal and anadromous fish populations beyond an exclusive fisheries zone that would extend 12 miles offshore. To the extent that a coastal state did not have the capacity to catch fish populations that straddled the boundary between national jurisdiction and the high seas, other countries might do so. This principle reflected the belief and desire of the domestic fishing industry and the government itself that the fishing industry's future lay partly in expanding U.S. fishing for species that foreign fleets were then catching off U.S. shores. Tunas and billfishes were to be managed not by coastal nations but by regional organizations, on the grounds that these species migrate through the waters of several countries.

At the United Nations, opposition to expanding jurisdiction to 200 miles offshore soon crumbled. By 1974, the United States was openly supporting provisions that would allow coastal states to declare jurisdiction over marine resources within an exclusive economic zone (or EEZ) that could extend up to 200 miles off their shores. Soon, consensus developed among negotiators at the United Nations that coastal states could claim sovereign rights over fisheries within 200 miles of their shores. The agreement, however, had little practical or legal effect since negotiators were unable to resolve a plethora of other difficult problems, such as jurisdiction over seabed minerals. (A final agreement on the Law of the Sea was not reached until 1982.)

As negotiations dragged on and foreign fleets continued fishing heavily off U.S. shores, advocates for a 200-mile limit and their supporters in Congress became disillusioned with assurances by the State Department that the law of the sea negotiations would soon protect domestic fishermen. Instead, support built in Congress for unilaterally declaring U.S. jurisdiction to 200 miles offshore. By no means was support unanimous. Fishermen in America's own distant water fishing fleets for shrimp and tuna off South America believed that extending U.S. jurisdiction would jeopardize their own interests.[5]

"We fought it," says Bob Jones of the Southeastern Fisheries Association. "I was fighting it long before 1976 in Don McKernan's Ocean Advisory Committee. Dykstra and a few others would bring it up every time back in the late '60s. The only people against it were the shrimp people and the distant water snapper–grouper folks, people fishing Bahamian waters for lobsters, and the tuna people."

The tuna and shrimp fleets were formidable opponents to extended jurisdiction, partly because they were among the few bright spots in U.S. fisheries. Unlike other U.S. fleets, the tuna fleet had modernized by adopting innovative purse-seine technology.[6] Together with the shrimp fleet, the tuna fleet accounted for one-third of the value of the U.S. catch in 1970. The distant water fleets' opposition to a unilateral declaration of 200-mile limit also enjoyed general support from other quarters. The Department of Defense argued that unilateral extension of U.S. jurisdiction would encourage other countries to do the same, thereby impeding naval navigation. The Department of Justice warned that unilateral declaration of a 200-mile limit would violate international law.

Atlantic Bluefin Tuna

Until the 1970s, catches of large and small Atlantic bluefin tuna (*Thunus thynnus*) fetched U.S. fishermen no more than 5 cents per pound and were processed into cat and dog food. Giant bluefin, which could reach 10 feet in length and 1,400 pounds in weight, were a target mostly for recreational fishermen and inspired dozens of tournaments along the Atlantic coast, until the big fish began disappearing in the late 1960s. Beginning in 1963, the U.S. government participated in a working party sponsored by the United Nations, which had the goal to produce a treaty governing fisheries for tunas in the Atlantic Ocean. In March 1969, the negotiations' product, the International Convention for the Conservation of Atlantic Tunas, took effect.

The goal of the treaty was to manage tunas and tuna-like species so as to maintain "their population at levels that will permit maximum sustainable catch." The commission, which was composed of representatives from the member countries, could recommend conservation measures, which took effect within six months for all member countries that did not file a formal objection.

As the International Commission for the Conservation of Atlantic Tunas (ICCAT) was organizing itself, the fishery for Atlantic bluefin tuna was undergoing a dramatic change. In August 1971, an innovative fisherman by the name of Frank Cyganowski entered Cape Cod Bay with a Japanese freezer/long-liner alongside, to which Cyganowski transferred his purse seiner's load of bluefin tuna. The fish were expertly frozen and shipped to Tokyo's Tsukijii market where they were sold (at a premium price) for consumption at hundreds of sushi restaurants. Soon after Cyganowski's maiden sale, prices rose from 15 cents per pound in 1970 to $1.21 by the end of the decade. Cyganowski was soon joined by other fishermen hoping to cash in on the new market. With rising affluence and declining numbers of the large, fatty Atlantic bluefin tunas most prized on the Japanese market, prices rose rapidly.

Supplying the Japanese market for sushi-grade Atlantic bluefin tuna set off a race for the fish unlike any other in U.S. waters. Although five purse seiners took most of the catch, hundreds of enterprising fishermen on small boats swarmed over the tuna's summer feeding grounds off New England. Although the U.S. commercial fishery for Atlantic bluefin tuna never produced more than $23 million in landings, catching a couple of giant bluefin tunas could make a fisherman's entire season. So great was the demand for sashimi-grade bluefin tuna in Japan that a giant bluefin that met Japanese standards would fetch a fisherman at least $8 to $10 per pound, and perhaps much more.

Unlike other U.S. fleets in which large- and small-scale commercial fishermen were bitter rivals, harpooners, hook-and-line fishermen, and the large purse seiners had long united against a common adversary: recreational fishermen, whose numbers, catch, and political influence had grown rapidly. While hundreds of recreational fishermen pursued smaller bluefin tuna from Maine to North Carolina, many recreational fishermen also purchased commercial fishing permits, enabling them to sell any giant bluefins they might catch. Over the years, the conflict between commercial and recreational fishermen over the allocation of the U.S. bluefin tuna quota settled into a ritualistic exchange of insults and accusations that kept the pressure on the government for maintaining quotas. Through the 1980s, maintaining political peace between commercial and recreational fishermen became a major factor in the development of U.S. positions for ICCAT meetings, as did concerns about relations with Japan and the European Union. In this environment, the advice of NMFS scientists, who were among the best in the world, often received scant attention in the formulation of U.S. positions.

Scientific understanding of Atlantic bluefin tuna populations was limited enough that nearly any statement about their status suffered from uncertainty. Unlike the Inter-American Tropical Tuna Commission, the ICCAT did not have its own scientific staff, but relied entirely on the deliberations of a scientific committee composed of representatives from member countries. As at the IWC, scientists from major fishing countries such as Spain and Japan generally presented the argument for maintaining or increasing catches in the face of uncertainty, while government scientists from the United States presented a more conservative view. Whatever advice the scientific committee did arrive at then had to survive the political bargaining among member countries that set the ICCAT policy.

Until the mid-1990s, the ICCAT and its members confined their recommendations regarding bluefin tuna in the western Atlantic to modest restrictions on catches. Although the restrictions halted the decline of Atlantic bluefin in the West, the adult population had been reduced by 80 to 90% of 1975 levels and showed no signs of recovery.

The Magnuson-Stevens Act

With the congressional delegations of New England, the Pacific Northwest, and Alaska in the lead, Congress acceded to the clamor over foreign fishing and the campaign to expand federal authority over fisheries. Reversing decades of U.S.

policy, Congress passed the Fishery Conservation and Management Act of 1976. In this act, which later was named the Magnuson-Stevens Fishery Conservation and Management Act, Congress declared that the United States held exclusive rights to fish and shellfish within 200 nautical miles of its shores. Within the 200-mile zone, most fisheries were to be managed by the NMFS, based upon fishery management plans developed by regional fishery management councils.

The tuna industry convinced Congress that tunas should be managed differently than other species. Under the Magnuson-Stevens Act, the United States did not claim jurisdiction over highly migratory tunas, but left their management to international organizations.[7] In contrast, the distant water shrimp fleet, which possessed neither the political influence of the tuna industry nor a plausible biological rationale, was not so successful. Although the shrimp fishery was more valuable economically, generating 20% of the value of U.S. fisheries, the tuna fishery's smaller wealth was spread among far fewer fishermen, enabling them to organize and wield greater political influence. In past legislative campaigns, the tuna industry also had built a cadre of allies in Congress and the executive branch that enabled them to maintain U.S. policy on freedom of access to tunas wherever they roam. As a result, Congress did not provide protection to the U.S. distant water shrimp fleet when Mexico and some South American countries later declared their jurisdiction over shrimp and other species off their shores. In Congress's effort to protect both New England domestic fleets and West Coast distant water tuna fleets, the domestic shrimp fleet ended up as odd man out.

With passage of the Magnuson-Stevens Act, fishermen in New England and elsewhere were overjoyed that they had successfully disarmed the foreign fleets they blamed for the decline of regional fisheries and for the marginal economic vitality of U.S. domestic fleets. Although the NMFS supported extension of jurisdiction, the agency also warned that without a system for rational management, foreign overfishing would simply be replaced by domestic overfishing. "The prospect of extended jurisdiction offers hope of exclusive access to new resources," read an agency report developed during congressional deliberations that led to the Magnuson-Stevens Act.[8] "[B]ut extended jurisdiction will bring its own problems of management without solving, in itself, the problems of traditional concern." It remained to be seen if the Magnuson-Stevens Act created a system for rational management.

Summary

Because many species of marine wildlife do not remain within the narrow boundaries of the territorial sea, the United States and other countries regularly negotiate agreements on access, use, and conservation of shared marine wildlife populations.

With few exceptions, these agreements are compromised by persistent problems, such as fishing by countries that are not members of an agreement. Particularly since the early 1970s, the United States has attempted to strengthen the implementation of international agreements by imposing economic sanctions on countries that compromised the effectiveness of treaties such as the International Convention for the Regulation of Whaling.

In the late 1960s, the failure of the International Commission on Northwest Atlantic Fisheries to control fishing by foreign trawlers off New England contributed to a drive by U.S. fishermen to expand U.S. jurisdiction over waters to 200 miles offshore. Initially, the federal government resisted supporting this proposal in the negotiation of a new law of the sea through the United Nations.

As negotiations dragged on at the United Nations, U.S. fishermen successfully pressed for action by Congress. With passage of the Magnuson-Stevens Act in 1976, Congress extended U.S. jurisdiction over marine fisheries 200 miles offshore, over the objections of some domestic fishing fleets.

Notes

1. Quoted in Hobart, W.L. December 1995. *Baird's Legacy: The History and Accomplishments of NOAA's National Marine Fisheries Service, 1871–1996.* NOAA Tech. Memo NMFS-F/SPO-18. Seattle, Washington.
2. U.S. Department of the Interior. 1944. *Annual Report of the Secretary of the Interior: Fiscal Year Ended June 30, 1944.* U.S. Government Printing Office, Washington, D.C.
3. The doctrine articulated in the Truman Proclamation later was incorporated into international law when the First United Nations Law of the Sea Conference adopted the Convention on Fishing and Conservation of Living Resources of the High Seas in 1958. (Bean and Rowland 1997). The first United Nations Conference on the Law of the Sea, which began in 1958, was followed by a second

conference in 1960. Treaties fashioned at these conferences emphasized freedom of passage—a key tenet of U.S. foreign policy.

4. Bureau of Commercial Fisheries. 1970. Background for International Fisheries Affairs. Office of the Assistant Director for International Affairs. Mimeographed document. Washington, D.C.

5. In the Pacific Northwest and Alaska, Soviet fleets hit North Pacific hake (*Merluccius productus*) and Pacific ocean perch (*Sebastes alutus*) especially hard in the mid- to late 1960s. Soviet catches of Pacific ocean perch grew from 16,200 metrics tons in 1960 to 383,900 in 1965 and generally remained above 100,000 metric tons until 1980. Only now are Pacific ocean perch showing signs of recovery.

   Japanese fleets annually had caught around 200,000 metric tons of fish and shellfish in the eastern North Pacific Ocean from 1950 to 1964. After that, their landings built quickly, reaching a peak of 1.4 million metric tons in 1970; 80% of the landings were Alaska pollock (*Theragra chalcogramma*). Japanese fishermen also were major players in the fishery for king crabs (*Paralithodes* spp.) and snow crabs (*Chionoectes* spp.). Japanese landings of crab from the northeastern Pacific Ocean built steadily in the 1960s to a peak of 28,800 metric tons in 1968 then fell steadily.

6. A purse seine is a long panel of netting with weights along the bottomline and floats along the topline, which allow suspending the net from the surface. In purse seining, a skiff pulls the net from the stern of a purse seiner.

   The purse seiner and skiff then move in an arc around a school of fish, eventually meeting again. The purse seiner then draws in the bottomline, closing or pursing the bottom of the net and entrapping the school of fish. Purse seines are used to catch species of fish other than tunas, such as menhaden, squid, and anchovies.

7. Under the Fishery Conservation and Management Act of 1976, highly migratory tunas included albacore tuna (*Thunnus alalunga*), bigeye tuna (*Thunnus obesus*), bluefin tuna (*Thunnus thynnus*), skipjack tuna (*Katsuwonus pelamis*), and yellowfin tuna (*Thunnus albacares*). In contrast to these tunas, the act asserted U.S. jurisdiction over other highly migratory species, such as billfishes, swordfish, and oceanic sharks.

   As finally adopted in 1982, the Convention on the Law of the Sea included (as highly migratory species) a much larger group of species, including some mackerel, pomfrets, sauries, and dolphin. Article 64 of the convention called for bilateral or multilateral cooperation in the conservation and promotion of optimum utilization of these species within exclusive economic zones and on the high seas.

The rationale for excluding tunas from domestic management due to their highly migratory behavior was effectively dismissed by Congress in 1990. In amending the Fishery Conservation and Management Act in that year, Congress reversed U.S. policy and included highly migratory tunas under U.S. management jurisdiction, thereby treating them like other highly migratory species, including billfish, swordfish, and oceanic sharks. In the Atlantic, the secretary of commerce was to exercise management authority, while Pacific tunas were to fall under the management umbrella of the regional fishery management councils there. Beginning in 1992, the United States was to recognize the rights of other coastal nations in managing tuna fishing within their own exclusive economic zones.

8. U.S. Department of Commerce. 1976. *A Marine Fisheries Program for the Nation*. Government Printing Office, Washington, D.C.

1965   *In 1965, the Bureau of Commercial Fisheries carried out research in 25 large laboratories and 75 small stations and offices and on 30 research vessels. One naval vessel was converted to conduct marine research. The research vessel* David Starr Jordan *was commissioned. The bureau established an office of international trade.*

    The bureau had an average of 2,216 employees and a budget of $42 million. Besides appropriations and revenues from duties on imported seafood, the bureau received funding from the Great Lakes Commission for sea lamprey control and money from the fishing industry for inspection and grading of fishery products. Under contract with private fur-processing firms, the bureau sold 38,067 fur seal skins for $3,178,385.

    The bureau published more than 2,600 documents. Of these, 48% were statistical, 15% were for commercial audiences, 30% were contributions to scientific knowledge, and 7% were for popular consumption. Seafood marketing staff obtained nearly 40,000 column inches of editorial space in 273 different newspapers. Marketing staff also arranged or participated in 113 radio and television shows promoting seafood. Fifty-eight federal inspectors examined about 225 million pounds of fishery products.

Chapter 5 | A Revolution in Management

In 1867, when Secretary of State William E. Seward arranged for the purchase of the Alaska Territory from Russia for $7.2 million, the United States acquired some of the richest fisheries in the world. Holding exclusive jurisdiction over wildlife in the territories, the federal government was able to apply the results of its research to the management of fisheries. Elsewhere, Congress had restricted its role to advising state governments and treaty organizations. As a result, it was in the territories especially that the Bureau of Fisheries and its successors gained the fishery management experience that shaped their perspectives and practices in later years.

As early as World War II, federal fisheries officials argued for scientific, rational management by biologists rather than legislatures driven by political expediency and hamstrung by inflexibility. In the view of federal fisheries officials, state management of fisheries regularly led to conflicting regulations that hampered the ability of the domestic fishing industry to compete with foreign fleets and growing seafood imports. Yet, every attempt at federalizing fisheries management met overwhelming opposition in Congress.

In the late 1960s, increased fishing by foreign fleets off U.S. shores prompted a flurry of plans and proposed legislation by state and federal fisheries officials and different segments of the fishing industry. While many fishermen and their supporters in the National Marine Fisheries Service (NMFS) and in Congress promoted development of the domestic fishing industry through exclusion of foreign fleets from a broader zone off the United States, other officials in the NMFS urged the creation of a system for "rational management" of fisheries. In the end, Congress tried to combine the two themes in the Magnuson-Stevens Act. In implementation, however, development of the domestic fishing industry prevailed over the relatively weak conservation standards of the act. Continued financial assistance, tax incentives, and the weak restraints on fishing imposed under the Magnuson-Stevens Act encouraged investment and the entry of thousands of people into fishing as a business. Domestic fishing fleets and processing capacity grew at unprecedented rates, as did catches and revenues to fishermen. In this way, the Magnuson-Stevens Act accomplished in a decade what several decades of financial and technical assistance had not: In a matter of years, it enabled many U.S. fishing fleets to become as capable of overfishing as the foreign fleets that were gone from U.S. waters.

The Alaska Experience

Though ridiculed by some people as "Seward's Icebox," the acquisition of the Alaska Territory proved a profitable investment. In 1897, the salmon fisheries alone fetched processors $3 million. The abundance of salmon that generated such wealth also attracted abuse that triggered a remarkably swift congressional response. In 1889, a year after the Alaska Commercial Company landed 1.2 million sockeye salmon by entirely blocking the Karluk River, Congress banned dams and barricades in Alaska salmon rivers. Congress also directed that the fish commission's research vessel the *Albatross* investigate reported declines in salmon runs along the Pacific coast and in Alaska. In 1892, the fish commission reported on its investigations and made several recommendations. Livingston Stone, whom Baird had sent to the Pacific coast in 1872, argued for establishment of a reserve for salmon in Alaskan waters:

> I will say from my personal knowledge that not only is every contrivance employed that human ingenuity can devise to destroy the salmon of our westcoast rivers, but more surely destructive, more fatal than all is the slow but inexorable march of those destroying agencies of human progress, before which the salmon must surely disappear as did the buffalos of the plains and the Indians of California.[1]

High-level investigations in 1904 and 1923 led to even more dramatic changes in federal management of salmon fisheries in Alaska. In 1906, Congress relinquished some of its role in fisheries management by allowing the secretary of commerce and labor, who oversaw the Bureau of Fisheries, to alter management of the salmon fisheries administratively. In 1924, Congress strengthened restrictions on obstructing rivers and on the use of nets and traps.

After the reorganization of federal fish and wildlife programs in 1939 and 1940, the director of the Fish and Wildlife Service spent several weeks each year in the Alaska Territory and in Seattle, Washington, attending public hearings regarding the coming season's fishing regulations. Based on research by the service's biologists and on public comments, the agency adopted regulations that included quotas, area and seasonal closures, gear restrictions, and other traditional management measures.

With the end of World War II, the Fish and Wildlife Service's presence in Alaska grew as commercial fishing expanded. By 1952, the agency's commercial fisheries management program relied on 22 management biologists and enforcement agents, as well as 98 seasonal stream guards, patrollers, and fisheries aides. Biologists monitored salmon runs at 2 dozen weirs on 14 major streams to ensure that 50% of salmon escaped capture and were able to ascend streams to spawn, as required by federal law. Staff patrolled Alaska's waters with 7 patrol vessels, 20 speedboats, and 19 airplanes, which logged 2,013 flight hours. In all, enforcement agents logged 155 cases of violations, which led to the conviction of 248 individuals and 5 companies paying $73,000 in penalties.

While the Fish and Wildlife Service devoted considerable effort to restoring herring and halibut fisheries in the 1940s and 1950s, most of the agency's attention focused on salmon, Alaska's largest and most valuable fishery. In 1940, sockeye (*Oncorhynchus herka*) and pink salmon (*O. gorbuscha*) accounted for 81% of the 147,000 metric tons of fish landed by fishermen in Alaska, and 91% of the $36 million received by fishermen for the catch. For the agency, management of these fisheries was a showcase of modern management that reflected extensive basic and applied research, monitoring, and enforcement. Annually, the agency adjusted quotas based on the estimated number of salmon returning to their natal streams. Leaders in the Fish and Wildlife Service believed that they had discovered the secret of sustainable use of living marine resources—scientific management. In 1942, the Department of the Interior contrasted fisheries management by the states with its use of biological research in Alaska "where the advantages of the flexible modern method as opposed to the traditional system of regulation by specific rigid legislation has been demonstrated."[2]

Despite the measures applied by the Fish and Wildlife Service, western Alaska's runs of sockeye salmon began showing signs of decline soon after World War II. At the same time, fishermen and fishing vessels were pouring into Alaska's fisheries, creating even more concern among government biologists. In its report for 1951, the Interior Department urged that "exploitation must be curbed rather than expanded, and it is in the still almost untapped groundfish fisheries of Alaska that further expansion must be looked for." But these urgings went unheeded, and the salmon fleet continued growing. In 1953, the Interior Department reported that "[n]ever in the history of the Territory has exploitation of the fisheries been so intense, and never has the need been so great for vigorously enforced, sound regulatory controls."

As populations of Alaska salmon continued declining, the Fish and Wildlife Service announced in 1956 that it was dramatically increasing research and reducing fishing effort. Concluding that some pink salmon runs were depleted, the Fish and Wildlife Service closed Prince William Sound fishery for pink salmon and cut catches by half in southeast Alaska in 1956. The agency also required that all fishing gear be registered, and banned trolling for salmon on the high seas. In 1957, Congress repealed the fixed levels of "spawning escapement" it had imposed years before, giving the Fish and Wildlife Service some flexibility in managing the fisheries on individual rivers.

It was too little, too late. The increasingly unpopular restrictions and the apparent failure of federal management of Alaska's salmon fisheries fed the drive toward statehood that had reignited in 1955. In 1958, when President Eisenhower signed the Alaska statehood bill, fishermen in western Alaska landed only 8,700 metric tons of sockeye salmon, less than 12% of the 1938 record catch.

Until passage of the Magnuson-Stevens Act, the fisheries in Alaska remained the principal source of experience in marine fisheries management for federal agencies. Otherwise, the role of federal fisheries agencies in fisheries management remained advisory. There was little federal agencies could do except provide advice and hope that the states followed it. The states sometimes did take this advice. In 1941, for instance, New England states adopted a recommendation by the Bureau of Fisheries to reduce the capture and sale of young haddock. The bureau argued that allowing the young fish to grow would avoid depletion of haddock populations, increase catches by more than 45,000 metric tons, and net fishermen an additional $4 million in revenue. The next year, the Department of the Interior reported that commercial fishermen had reduced the capture and sale of baby haddock by 87%. The states, however, did not adopt the bureau's recommendation to increase the size of mesh in trawl nets in order to allow young haddock to escape. According to the agency's estimates in 1948, trawlers caught and discarded 17 million haddock that would have generated $3 million in sales for the fleet had they been allowed to reach a larger size. The bureau's recommendation was eventually adopted in 1954, but by the International Commission for North Atlantic Fisheries (ICNAF) rather than by the states.

Frustrated Managers

As the standing of the United States among leading fishing nations fell in the 1950s and 1960s, federal fisheries managers expressed increasing frustration with the lack of growth in domestic landings. During the first two decades after World War II, U.S. commercial landings remained at about 2 million metric tons—leading the Department of the Interior to warn in 1964 that "commercial fishing is currently engaged in a struggle for survival."[3] This stood in sharp contrast to the performance of other countries, some of them cold war adversaries. Between 1957 and 1967, world catches increased 92%. The catch of the top five countries, including the Soviet Union, grew 146%, while the landings of the United States, which ranked sixth, fell 13%. The United States relied increasingly upon imports to meet the demand for seafood. By the mid-1960s, imports accounted for more than half of the U.S. supply of seafood, making the United States the largest importer of seafood in the world. In contrast, imports had made up just 25% of the U.S. supply in 1950.

"The United States should be the leading fishing nation of the world because it has all the qualifications for this position,"[4] the Bureau of Commercial Fisheries (BCF) reported in 1968. "It has adequate resources on the broad continental shelves of its long coastlines to support a modern high-seas fishery. It also has markets for fish and fishery products and highly skilled fishermen, scientists, and engineers."

The principal obstacles to increasing catches appeared to be the number and sophistication of fishing vessels and the welter of conflicting state laws that reflected politically expedient decision making, in the view of the Fish and Wildlife Service. Modest government programs to increase the size and sophistication of the fishing fleet had some success in the 1950s and 1960s, although the U.S. fleet remained small and inefficient in comparison with the modernized fleets of Japan, the Soviet Union, and western European countries.

The federal government's efforts to overcome problems caused by ineffective and conflicting state laws had little more success. The slowness and inflexibility of state fisheries management frustrated administrators and scientists in the Interior Department, whose experience managing fisheries in Alaska seemed to confirm their belief in the wisdom of scientific management. In its 1969 report, the Stratton Commission argued that the root of the problem of state management lay with a fundamental political difficulty: "In part, the difficulty reflects the pressures on the States to find some way to limit the take from over-exploited fisheries without excluding any of the participants."[5] In the federal government's view, state fisheries agencies often solved this political dilemma, which any fisheries management agency must face, with management measures that gave the appearance of doing something but actually did little.

Individual states aggravated this shortcoming by failing to coordinate their measures with other states having jurisdiction over the same fisheries. Congress attempted to remedy this problem by establishing regional commissions, beginning with the Atlantic States Marine Fisheries Commission in 1942.[6] Not wishing to challenge traditional states rights, Congress gave the regional commissions no power to promulgate regulations. Instead, Congress limited the roles of the regional fisheries commissions to recommending, coordinating, and cajoling. The commissions sometimes successfully convinced the states to coordinate their management. In 1951, for example, the Pacific commission succeeded in harmonizing regulations in the troll fishery for salmon among Alaska, Washington, Oregon, and California.[7]

By the end of the 1960s, the regional commissions had accomplished so little, however, that the Stratton Commission concluded they were a failure. Rather than strengthen the commissions, the Stratton Commission recommended that the National Oceanic and Atmospheric Agency (NOAA), which the commission was proposing, be given the authority to regulate fisheries in state waters that had been significantly reduced or endangered. Congress did not act on the recommendation.

In the late 1960s, federal fisheries officials led by the dynamic and strong-willed BCF director Donald McKernan renewed efforts to end the traditional management of fisheries by individual state legislatures, at least beyond state waters. A bill developed by the BCF in 1969 would have authorized the agency to regulate fisheries between the outer boundary of state waters at 3 miles offshore and the boundary of the high seas at 12 miles offshore. A state could assume management of fisheries in this zone if it submitted a satisfactory management plan. This initiative, however, generated opposition from the states, which claimed it was an encroachment on states rights. The agency then amended the proposed new management regime to allow state management beyond 3 miles if a state submitted a management plan that met certain national standards; however, while the new language appeased state interests, it attracted opposition from within the federal government. Provisions aimed at limiting entry to fisheries generated opposition from commercial fishermen.

Efforts to improve state management of fisheries gained momentum after the reorganization of federal marine fisheries activities and the creation of the NMFS. In its first annual report, the NOAA's National Marine Fisheries Service committed itself to removing politics from the management of fisheries: "High priority must be placed on more rational systems for managing fisheries resources. Simply stated, there is a need for management systems based on rational plans rather than as a matter of expediency." A year later, the agency reorganized its operations and launched a state–federal fisheries management program that used grants and technical assistance to promote the development and adoption of management plans for fish over their entire range of distribution. In 1972, an effort to develop a management plan for American lobster in New England led to the adoption of a ten-point plan that was implemented for the most part by the individual states. Similar efforts at coordination succeeded in convincing states to adopt uniform opening dates for several fisheries along the Pacific coast and in the Gulf of Mexico. Working with the Council of State Governments, the NMFS also developed a model code for fishery management that it began distributing in 1975.

As foreign fishing off U.S. shores reached a peak in the early 1970s, frustration with the limitations of existing management grew. In 1972, an advisory committee to the NOAA, called the National Advisory Committee on Oceans and Atmosphere (NACOA), summarized its view in words that remained valid for decades to come: "What NACOA finds lacking is pace, more than direction. Some of the right things are being done, but only some and not quickly enough. Coastal matters are being worked out, but only at a snail's pace. International matters are being worked out, but as if avoidance of conflict were itself a victory. Meanwhile the fish stocks slip, the young men go into other work, and as a [n]ation we import most of the fish we eat. What we do have to find out is whether we will or will not do something about it."[8] The advisory committee warned of the dangers posed by increasing competition, the threat of fishing to extinction, deteriorating habitats, and chronically depressed segments of the commercial fishing industry.

Growing conflicts between commercial and recreational fishermen added to the frustration. Although the Interior Department's Bureau of Sport Fisheries and Wildlife (and later the NMFS) had slowly been gathering information on recreational fishing, supporting research on species sought by recreational fishermen and promoting recreational fishing as a pastime through research and grants, the federal government had more or less ignored management of these fisheries. This was partly because roughly 90% of the recreational catch was taken within state waters, and much of the catch was of species that commercial fishermen did not seek. As recreational anglers grew in numbers and new technology enabled them to fish farther from shore, however, conflicts with commercial fishermen over some species developed.[9]

The NACOA report together with renewed United Nations negotiations over a new law of the sea treaty spurred the NMFS to develop a national plan for fisheries that would cover everything from management within a broader fisheries zone to the promotion of marine recreational fishing and aquaculture. While the NMFS staff was preparing the national plan, a consortium of the regional fisheries commissions was conducting its own survey of commercial and recreational fishermen under a congressional mandate.[10] The purpose of the survey was to develop a plan that would "save our commercial fishing industry and serve the sportfishing industry."[11]

"There was quite a bit of rivalry between the fishery commissions and ourselves," says Roland Finch, who oversaw the development of the NMFS plan. "They thought we were sitting on a golden throne and didn't really know what was what. And to some extent, they were right. But we were asking people who did know to tell us."

The regional commissions used the NMFS draft national plan as well as a survey of federal fisheries as background for meetings with fishermen and government officials. The final report of the so-called Eastland Survey contained dozens of recommendations. "The recommendations of the Eastland Survey were much the same as ours," says Finch, "but they wanted to keep the regulations much looser generally." The Eastland Survey expressed far less concern about the status of fish populations off U.S. shores than did the report issued by the NMFS and the Department of Commerce. The preface of that report included these worried words from Commerce Secretary Eliot L. Richardson: "Thirty years ago, our fisheries seemed inexhaustible. Today we know they are not. The fault lies in large measure with man. Man is a voracious consumer, and modern technology has made it possible for fishing vessels to harvest the living resources of the seas in prodigious amounts. . . . Over the past decade, there has been a serious depletion of a vital source of food and a weakening of the American fishing industry, and we must now set to work to restore both our fisheries and our industry."[12] The NMFS report listed 21 fish populations it regarded as depleted in August 1975, including haddock (*Melanogrammus aeglefinus*), Atlantic sea scallops (*Placopeten magellanicus*), Pacific salmons, rockfish, and yellowtail flounder (*Limanda ferruginea*).

The report raised other concerns that would appear repeatedly during the next two decades. The report noted that bycatch in the Alaska pollock fishery was contributing to a decline in Pacific halibut, while bycatch in the New England trawl fisheries for cod and hake was preventing recovery of haddock from the burst of Soviet fishing in the mid-1960s. Reflecting a precautionary approach that remained dormant and largely unarticulated until the 1990s, the agency urged that when fishing on unexploited populations of fish, "proceed with caution" until safe catch levels could be determined. The report urged that even when there was enough information to allow scientists to estimate maximum sustainable yield, catch levels should be set well below that estimate in order to avoid ecological damage.

While the national plan for fisheries was progressing, other NMFS staff began exploring the implications of extending jurisdiction over fisheries out to 200 miles. The agency's interest in extended jurisdiction was generated by the failure of the ICNAF to rein in foreign fishing off New England. "ICNAF was the seed for the Magnuson Act," says Bill Gordon, who served on the U.S. ICNAF delegation in the early 1970s. "We saw ICNAF was not providing the growth potential for coastal fishermen, although we had obtained some relief through negotiations, but we could not phase out foreign fishing because we had no control over it. So, over two years before they began thinking about it in the Congress, a number of us got together and fomented the rudiments of the Magnuson Act, including greater control for a coastal nation out to 200 miles. At that time, we believed that would encompass most of the coastal stocks that were of principal interest to the United States."

Nationally, in the view of these officials, the federal government had to abandon its role as advisor and become a manager of fisheries beyond state waters. Only by assuming this role could the agency ensure the kind of rational fisheries management in federal waters that it had been pursuing in state waters for more than a decade, with little success. Although fishermen in New England and elsewhere strongly opposed giving the federal government management authority, fishermen elsewhere supported the idea.

"Some fishermen, notably those on the West Coast, wanted to see rational management," says Gordon. "They were intelligent enough to understand what would happen in the Bering Sea and in the Gulf of Alaska if there wasn't a management regime in place: Foreign investment would drive heavy capitalization and potentially, overfishing."

As Soviet and Japanese fishing off the shores of Alaska and the Pacific Northwest grew, so did political support for declaring a 200-mile limit. When United

Nations negotiations over a new law of the sea faltered in 1974, Senator Warren Magnuson of Washington State began pressing forward with legislation to expand U.S. control over fisheries off its shores. Within a year, the Senate had passed legislation establishing a 200-mile fisheries conservation zone.

In 1975, both the House and Senate took up legislation to establish a 200-mile zone. In January, Congressman Gerry Studds of Massachusetts and 24 other members of the House of Representatives introduced H.R. 200, the "Interim Fisheries Zone Extension and Management Act." The bill's proposed declaration of a 200-mile fisheries conservation zone provoked determined opposition from the Departments of State, Defense, and Justice, and from the U.S. tuna and shrimp fleets, which fished within the 200-mile zones of several South American countries. When Warren Magnuson succeeded in recruiting Alaska Senator Ted Stevens to the cause of extended jurisdiction, however, the debate turned to how to manage fisheries within the new fisheries conservation zone, or FCZ.

During 1975, the House bill underwent significant changes as representatives from different parts of the industry, different areas of the country, different agencies, and different interest groups converged on the House Merchant Marine and Fisheries Committee. As passed in October, the House bill did establish an FCZ from 3 to 200 miles offshore in which the United States claimed exclusive fishing rights. Foreign nations wishing to fish within the FCZ could do so only under a permit from the secretary of commerce. The United States also claimed jurisdiction over anadromous fish throughout their range, except in the territorial waters of another country.

The bill established an unusual management system that gave the fishing industry and the states a significant role in the management of fisheries in federal waters. Under the bill, eight regional councils, which were composed of industry representatives and state officials, would prepare fishery management plans that would be approved and implemented by the secretary of commerce provided they met certain standards. Rather than directly managing fisheries in federal waters, the NMFS would largely advise the councils on how to prepare management plans that would meet with approval by the secretary of commerce.

Instead of the traditional standard of maximum sustainable yield, the goal of fishery management plans under the Studds bill was to achieve optimum sustainable yield, which the bill defined as "a yield which provides the greatest benefit to the United States as determined on the basis of the maximum sustainable yield . . . as modified by relevant ecological, economic, and social factors." The new goal not only did not cure the acknowledged problems of maximum sustainable yield, but aggravated them by allowing quotas to be adjusted above

sustainable levels for economic or social reasons. In commenting on the definition in the Studds bill, the NMFS sounded a cautionary note, saying that
allowable catch levels above maximum sustainable yield should be unusual. Ultimately, Congress adopted the definition in the Studds bill.[13]

"Everybody was for conservation," says Lee Alverson. "Whether or not they
were going to implement it was another thing. Optimum yield was largely being
promoted at the law of the sea negotiations by some of the developing countries that didn't want to get into the position where they couldn't take economic
and social interests into account. So you could see people squirming to get wig-
gle room on conservation by adopting optimum yield." Use of the new goal
also reflected continuing confidence that sustainable management required mostly
the scientific collection and analysis of information about populations and their
environments, which interacted in stable, predictable ways.

On March 24, 1976, a final bill was approved by both houses of Congress
and sent to the White House. The Fishery Conservation and Management Act
became law on April 13, 1976, and took effect in January 1977.[14]

Passage of the Magnuson-Stevens Act, as it came to be known, revolutionized the management of commercial and recreational fisheries off the United
States. While much of the language in the act had to do with the management
of fisheries, the immediate aim of many supporters in Congress, the NMFS, and
the industry was to expand U.S. fishing. Unlike previous efforts to build U.S.
fisheries, such as passage of the Fish and Wildlife Act in 1956, the Magnuson-
Stevens Act loosed an unprecedented expansion of fleets, landings, and exports.

With passage of the Magnuson-Stevens Act, the federal government became
deeply involved in the management of domestic fisheries that had been largely
unmanaged. Suddenly, the NMFS was transformed from an agency concerned
principally with science and industry assistance to one consumed with sharing
the management of dozens of commercial and recreational fisheries together
with regional fishery management councils dominated by commercial fishermen and state fisheries managers.

Early Implementation

For industry supporters in the NMFS and Congress, as for fishermen in New
England, the Pacific Northwest, and Alaska particularly, opportunities for domestic fishermen depended greatly upon eliminating competition from foreign
fleets. Reflecting an international consensus in the law of the sea negotiations,

the Magnuson-Stevens Act did not immediately exclude foreign fleets from the U.S Exclusive Economic Zone (EEZ), but adopted a more gradual approach. At its simplest, this approach required a coastal country to provide access to fisheries within its EEZ if its own fishermen could not catch all the fish that it determined to be available. Under the Magnuson-Stevens Act, any part of the optimum yield identified by a council that could not be caught or processed by the domestic fleet was to be available to foreign fishing fleets. The vessels of a country that had concluded a governing international fishing agreement with the United States could apply some or all of the foreign allocation. In return for access, foreign countries paid permit fees, a poundage fee for fish caught, and a fee for maintaining U.S. observers aboard their vessels while in the U.S. zone.

By March 1977, the U.S. government had entered into governing international fisheries agreements with Poland, Romania, Spain, Bulgaria, the Republic of Korea, the German Democratic Republic, the Republic of China, the Soviet Union, and the European Economic Community. In all, 699 catching vessels and 21 processing vessels received permits. Foreign fishermen paid $10 million in permit and poundage fees, of which $3 million was returned when foreign fishermen were unable to catch their entire allocation. Allocations to foreign fishermen in 1977 amounted to 2.1 million metric tons, most of which was caught by foreign trawlers off Alaska.

In the 1980s, foreign fishing allocations fell gradually but at an accelerating rate. By 1987, the foreign allocations in all U.S. fisheries combined amounted to 363,426 metric tons, of which foreign fleets claimed 228,461. The decline in foreign allocations reflected not only the imposition of restrictions on fisheries that had been unrestricted but also the growth of the U.S. fishing fleet.

By sanctioning the exclusion of foreign fishermen within 200 miles of U.S. shores, the Magnuson-Stevens Act created a vacuum into which fishermen and fisheries developers rushed. U.S. fleets grew and modernized at breakneck speed. Private bankers, investors attracted by tax shelters, the NMFS, and other federal and state agencies provided financing for the largest buildup of U.S. fishing vessels in the country's history. In the first decade after passage of the Magnuson-Stevens Act, 13,340 documented fishing vessels were constructed—44% of all fishing vessels built between 1950 and 1997. Between 1976 and 1996, the number of large vessels increased by more than 70% to 28,870, while the number of small boats declined by 40%. The expansion of the domestic fleet and processing capacity boosted landings, which grew by two-thirds from 2.6 million metric tons in 1976, near the average after World War II, to 4.3 million metric tons. Growth in revenues to fishermen was even more spectacular; in 1996, domestic fishermen received $3.5 billion for their catch, 2.5 times their income two decades before.

In New England, where the fervor for development was particularly strong, staff within the agency responsible for carrying out the conservation and management requirements of the Magnuson-Stevens Act rushed to provide some room for recovery of groundfish populations that had been hurt badly by foreign fishing during the previous decade. In its waning days in the early 1970s, the ICNAF had adopted restrictions aimed at finally protecting North Atlantic groundfish (somewhat) from the onslaught of larger and larger fishing vessels. The measures appeared to have helped. In 1975, haddock reproduction was the best it had been in many years, due to a combination of lower levels of fishing and favorable oceanographic conditions.

By the time the Magnuson-Stevens Act came into effect in 1977, these young haddock were showing up in large numbers as juveniles. At the urging of NMFS regional director Bill Gordon, the newly formed New England Fishery Management Council adopted a fishery management plan for cod, haddock, and yellowtail flounder in 1977 that included many of the measures that the ICNAF had adopted the year before. The new federal measures enjoyed no more support among New England fishermen than did the ICNAF measures. Quotas for haddock and yellowtail flounder in some areas were so low that they could be taken entirely through bycatch in other fisheries. As fishermen raced to catch as much as they could as quickly as possible, quotas were reached in some areas months before the end of the season. Fishing for groundfish was shut down in area after area, creating a political firestorm. At the end of 1977, the NMFS closed the New England groundfish fishery entirely, which had been temporarily reopened in response to intense political pressure.

Largely because it could not agree on alternatives that would affect fishermen less, the New England council continued with quarterly quotas in 1978. The value of the quotas, however, was undermined as new fishing vessels continued entering the fishery at the rate of one every four days. The limited ability of the NMFS and U.S. Coast Guard to enforce quotas encouraged widespread misreporting and poaching, further undermining confidence in the new management system.

Although fishermen did not report large amounts of groundfish catch, quarterly quotas were soon met in 1978 and fishing was halted. New England fishermen, who had viewed the Magnuson-Stevens Act principally as a means of getting foreign fishermen off their traditional fishing grounds, were outraged.

They reported seeing more haddock than they had seen in decades, and demanded that the quotas be lifted.

"The fishermen were absolutely correct," says Bill Gordon. "The '75 year-class fully recruited to the fisheries by '77 and '78. Most of the fishermen were very young, and didn't remember the days when their fathers and grandfathers were fishing and there would be four or five year-classes in the population. From heavy overfishing on haddock by the Soviets in the early '70s, we had the one big year-class to rebuild the spawning population from. We argued strongly: "Take it easy guys, this is your future.'"

The stand by the NMFS lay bare fundamental tensions in managing fisheries under the new regime of the Magnuson-Stevens Act. With shocking suddenness, implementation of the Magnuson-Stevens Act enmeshed fishermen in a bewildering maze of hearings and scientific and legal analyses, in which the federal government appeared to be the master. Without foreign fishermen or treaty organizations to blame, fishermen and members of fishery management councils found themselves confronting federal fisheries managers and federal regulatory procedures that frustrated rather than facilitated the growth of their fisheries.

Staff in the NMFS were overwhelmed and frustrated as well. "When the Magnuson Act came, it just put a blanket of requirements on the agency that had never existed before," says David Crestin, who worked in the agency's regional office in New England during the 1970s and 1980s. "Under the Magnuson Act, all of a sudden we became a management agency. So we had to take our scientific results and apply them to management, with one big problem: We had no direct implementation authority. Everything was worked through the council system. So we weren't really managers. We became reviewers and scholars of management techniques and whether the Magnuson Act was being adhered to."

Confusion over the NMFS's relationship to the regional fishery management councils further complicated implementation. Trumpeted as a major innovation in natural resource management, the regional fishery management council system created by the Magnuson-Stevens Act divided responsibility for fisheries management among each of eight regional councils and the secretary of commerce, acting through the NMFS. Voting members of the councils included industry representatives nominated by governors and approved by the secretary of commerce, as well as state fish and game directors, and the regional director of the NMFS. Each council was responsible for developing fishery management plans in its region that the secretary of commerce was then to review, approve, and implement, if they met the Magnuson-Stevens Act's national standards. As the agency recognized from the beginning and as later reviews concluded, however, ambiguities about lines of authority bred confusion and adversarial relationships.

"There was quite a political job nominating members of the fishery management councils," says Roland Finch, who oversaw the review of fishery management plans at the NMFS during the early implementation of the Magnuson-Stevens Act. "And that was our responsibility under the act, as well [as] instructing them on what our concept of the act was, with which they wouldn't always agree."

The Magnuson-Stevens Act did not simply give the regional fishery management councils carte blanche in managing fisheries but required that fishery management plans meet a set of national standards. Fashioning the standards had been the vehicle by which the different players sought to protect their interests.

"The original standards were put together on a piece of a large manila envelope," says Lee Alverson about a meeting of an advisory group for the U.S. delegation to the United Nations Law of the Sea negotiations in 1975. "The national standards were seen as protecting the users. People were sitting around debating issues like conservation. They were worried that politics might dominate, and so the concept of using the best available science came up. We were worried that the state of Alaska would exclude fishermen from Washington, so we developed a standard to address that. The various things that would concern people would be discussed and then we would formulate a standard around it."

The national standards required that fishery management plans:

1. prevent overfishing and ensure an optimum yield from each fishery;
2. be based on the best scientific information available;
3. treat individual fish stocks as management units;
4. not discriminate among residents of different states;
5. promote efficiency;
6. allow for contingencies; and
7. minimize costs and avoid duplication.

As with national standards for other programs such as coastal zone management, those that were adopted by Congress for fisheries had to be interpreted—not just by the NMFS, but by members of the regional fishery management councils. "The national standards were intentionally made pretty vague," says Richard Roe, who was one of several agency staff involved in discussions with congressional staff about the language of the Magnuson-Stevens Act. "I could see all kinds of loopholes in them that the councils could move within, depending [on] whether they really wanted to manage or not manage. And that was not real good. It was a pretty loose game. Then, lay on top of that the fact that the councils are made up of people from industry, that is the governors' political appointees, and many of them don't want to manage. Or maybe they want to manage, but if they do, they're going to be drummed off the docks when they go home."

Soon after the Magnuson-Stevens Act was passed, it appeared that the Commerce Department would take a conservative approach to interpreting the national standards. In official statements, the agency seemed to regard conservation as the first order of business. In its national plan for fisheries, for example, the agency provided its view of the act's principal mission: "The underlying purpose of the [a]ct is to provide a basis in law for a strong national program for the conservation and management of our fishing resources—to prevent depletion of our fish stocks through overfishing, to rebuild stocks that have been overfished, and to conserve and manage our fisheries so that the [n]ation may develop their full potential. And with such a program, we can expand the American fishing industry and provide new opportunities for recreational fishermen."

There were incentives, however, to relax the interpretation of the national standards. Besides a common desire to expand domestic fisheries, imposing unpopular conservation restrictions on domestic fishermen ran against the widely held view, especially in New England, that the major problem in U.S. fisheries was the presence of foreign fishing fleets within U.S. waters. "They just wanted to get the foreigners out, that's what it came down to," says Finch. "Everything would be all right once they got the foreigners out."

Strong political support for letting the new council system work discouraged a strong interpretation of the national standard for conservation. "There were those within the agency who believed that we couldn't be rejecting and sending back every proposal that came up from the New England council, or any other council for that matter," says Eldon Greenberg, who served as general counsel in the NOAA during early implementation of the Fisheries Conservation and Management Act. "That was reflected early on in the national standard guidelines, which were pretty loose, as far as I'm concerned."

Compounding the difficulty of applying the national standards was the feeling within the NMFS that the council system itself slighted NMFS's expertise in fisheries management. Staff believed that their plans for avoiding the mistakes of the past had been complicated. "They wouldn't allow the professionals to work within their expertise, except through the council process," says Crestin.

Nor could regional staff of the agency count on the support of senior managers at headquarters of the NMFS in Washington, D.C. The director of the service during the first few years of the Magnuson Act, Robert Schoning, made it clear to staff that fishermen should be given their way and management should be left to the states. Both regional and headquarters staff also had to answer to the leadership of the parent agency, the NOAA. NOAA administrator Richard Frank relied heavily on the advice of a battery of attorneys that required convincing before they approved any action proposed by the NMFS.

The layers of decision making added delays that irritated the councils and fishermen. Rather than simply providing advice and good science, the NMFS seemed to be second-guessing the decisions of some councils. "The fishery management councils managed the fisheries," says Finch. "They said how much could be taken, what the restrictions should be, and they would pass those on to us. We had the rather tedious task of turning them into regulations. Our concern was to make sure that they complied [with] the act. There we were at odds with the fishery management councils. They might think that we hadn't correctly interpreted what they'd said. And we'd say, 'But we interpreted what you said. If you didn't say what you meant, we couldn't do anything about it.'"

In the late 1970s, NMFS insistence on continuing the ICNAF's fishing restrictions in the fisheries management plan for groundfish especially angered New England fishermen. Fishery council members bridled at the agency's advocacy and searched for management measures that would avoid harsh cuts in catches. As often happened in the past and would happen many times in the future, frustrated fishermen and council members appealed to their representatives in Congress.

"We wanted to restrict the New England cod fisheries considerably more than the New England Fishery Management Council would agree to," says Finch. "When we tried to be restrictive, the council members would rush off to their congressmen, and then they would come around and want to know what we were up to."

One of the first casualties of the struggles over management of fisheries in New England and in other regions was confidence in the scientific advice that federal biologists provided the councils. The Magnuson-Stevens Act emphasized basing decisions on the best scientific information available. Often, however, the best scientific information available was not very good. Even in the Alaska and New England regions, where the federal government had carried on fisheries research to support international management organizations for decades, critical information often was lacking. Research and information on the socioeconomic dimensions of fisheries lagged even further behind.

The Magnuson Act also required each council to establish a scientific and statistical committee composed of scientists from inside and outside the NMFS.

In some regions, such as Alaska and the Pacific Northwest, the regional councils relied heavily on their scientific committees. In New England, the council did not even meet with its scientific committee.

The cultures and languages of fishermen and of scientists often did not mix well, further inhibiting agreement over the status of fish populations. For fishermen, who could always find fish if they looked long and hard enough, the extrapolations of scientists were completely unfamiliar and easy targets for criticism. "In ICNAF, the scientists were god, because we were getting our way," says Bill Gordon. "Once we came under the Magnuson Act, the same scientists were considered idiots, so we shouldn't pay any attention to them. Even the executive director of the New England Council said he would hire scientists and recalculate all the stock assessment information because NMFS science wasn't any good."

In 1978, the New England Council sought to defer restrictions in the groundfish fishery and to placate fishermen by "the ultimate gimmickry," in the words of Margaret Dewar, who conducted a thorough review of the fishery in the early 1980s. The council's proposal to the secretary of commerce was quite simple: move the starting date of the new fishing season up from January 1979 to October 1978, thereby giving fishermen a new set of quotas two months early. In September 1978, the secretary of commerce acquiesced to the council's request, preventing a closure of the fishery in the fall of 1978.

In 1980, when heavy fishing, much of it illegal, dumped large volumes of groundfish on the market and drove prices down, fishermen who were confronting higher fuel prices and other expenses began going out of business. Congress responded by passing legislation in December 1980 that offered fishermen low-interest loans if they were in danger of defaulting on boat loans or needed to repair or purchase used fishing vessels. Prices for the main species of groundfish soon recovered and resumed a steady climb that had begun in the mid-1970s. Average prices for cod, haddock, yellowtail flounder, and Alantic ocean perch increased three- and fourfold between 1977 and 1987.

The lack of meaningful controls on the fishery, rising prices, and tax incentives for investment had a result that was as predictable as it was ignored. Between 1976 and 1983, the number of large vessels in the fleet grew fivefold, the amount of fishing effort doubled, and the number of days fished by trawlers grew 73%. Catches grew dramatically, which fed the illusion of abundance, and soon obliterated any chance of rebuilding overfished populations of cod, haddock, redfish, and flounder. Attempts to intervene with stronger regulations earned the NMFS stern warnings from the New England congressional delegation, which succeeded in discouraging the agency from enforcing the conservation standards of the Magnuson Act. Nor did the service receive support from political appointees in the Reagan administration, who were more interested in regulatory relief and placating members of Congress than in the conservation of fisheries.

The political confrontation in the New England groundfish fishery made short work of whatever restraint the Magnuson-Stevens Act's definition of optimum yield might have imposed. By allowing optimum yield to be adjusted to take into account socioeconomic considerations, the act invited sacrificing the long-term health of a fishery and whatever benefits it might generate for the country to short-term economic and political gain. In 1982, under pressure from the fishing fleet, the New England council removed any meaningful controls over the groundfish fishery when it adopted an interim fishery management plan. The interim plan used Orwellian logic in defining optimum yield for the fishery as being whatever amount of fish was actually caught. Intent on imposing as little regulation as possible, the council eliminated quotas and adopted ineffective restrictions on fishing gear and other indirect controls. The secretary of commerce ruled that the interim plan met the national standards.

"I think the New England groundfish fishery was our big failure," says Greenberg. "I don't think we did a good job of managing New England groundfish then or later, for that matter. I'm not sure they've ever done a good job in managing that fishery. We did not impose the kind of strict management measures, which in retrospect it seems clearly were needed."

Summary

Until passage of the Magnuson-Stevens Act in 1976, direct management of marine fisheries by the federal government was confined to the territories. In Alaska, the Fish and Wildlife Service developed methods of "scientific management" that would ensure maximum sustainable use of salmon fisheries, in the agency's view. In contrast, the service could only advise states on the management of fisheries in the territorial sea. Often, states did not adopt the service's recommendations, resulting in conflicting regulations that prevented the growth of the U.S. fishing industry, according to the agency.

When regional commissions established by Congress in the 1940s and 1950s were unsuccessful in coordinating state fisheries programs, the Fish and Wildlife Service again sought to take over management of fisheries in state waters during the 1960s. With the transfer of responsibility for marine fisheries to the Department of Commerce in 1970, the National Marine Fisheries Service (NMFS) promoted improved state management by providing technical assistance, leading to the adoption of several regional fishery management plans.

The environment for fisheries management changed dramatically with the growth in fishing by foreign vessels off U.S. shores in the mid-1960s. As domestic fishermen became increasingly discontented with the international control of these fisheries, momentum grew in Congress to extend U.S. jurisdiction over fisheries to 200 miles offshore.

In 1976, Congress passed the Magnuson-Stevens Fishery Conservation and Management Act, which established a fishery management system for fisheries occurring in federal waters between 3 and 200 miles offshore. Major U.S. fisheries were to be managed under plans developed by regional fishery management councils. The NMFS was to implement plans that met the act's national standards.

Early implementation of the Magnuson-Stevens Act focused upon excluding foreign fishing vessels from U.S. waters and upon expanding U.S. fishing capacity as rapidly as possible. The U.S. fishing fleet and landings grew at unprecedented rates in the first decade after the act passed.

In some regions, the drive to expand U.S. fishing conflicted with the conservation standards of the act, which enjoyed strong support within the NMFS. A significant lack of understanding about exploited fish populations, the complexity of the regulatory process, unclear roles of the councils and the NMFS, the composition of the councils, and vague national standards created tension among fishermen, the councils, and the NMFS.

In New England, where fishermen had generated much of the political momentum for the Magnuson-Stevens Act, these tensions led to weak management of the region's fisheries. By the late 1980s, the region's most valuable fishery had resumed a precipitous decline that began with foreign fishing in the 1960s.

Notes

1. Quoted in Cart, T. W. 1968. The Federal Fisheries Service, 1871–1940. A thesis submitted to the faculty of the University of North Carolina at Chapel Hill in partial fulfillment of the requirements for the degree of Master of Arts in the Department of History. 87 pages.
2. U.S. Department of the Interior. 1942. *Annual Report of the Department of the Interior, 1942.* U.S. Government Printing Office, Washington, D.C.
3. U.S. Department of the Interior. 1965. *Quest for Quality: U.S. Department of the Interior Conservation Yearbook.* U.S. Government Printing Office, Washington, D.C.

4. Bureau of Commercial Fisheries. 1968. *Report of the Bureau of Commercial Fisheries for the Calendar Year 1966.* U.S. Government Printing Office, Wasington, D.C.
5. Commission on Marine Science, Engineering and Resources. *Our Nation and the Sea.* U.S. Government Printing Office, Washington, D.C., 1969.
6. Congress approved the compact establishing the Pacific States Marine Fisheries Commission in 1947 and the compact establishing the Gulf States Marine Fisheries Commission in 1949. In 1962, the compact establishing the Pacific States Marine Fisheries Commission was amended to allow the participation of Alaska and Hawaii.
7. In trolling, up to six stainless steel lines are run from hydraulic spools to outrigger poles from which they are spread and suspended from the boat. Hooks are attached to the mainlines with monofilament leaders at intervals and baited with herring, anchovy, or artificial lures.
8. Quoted in U.S. Department of Commerce. 1976. *A Marine Fisheries Program for the Nation.* Government Printing Office, Washington, D.C.
9. Partly through financial and other assistance by state and federal governments, the number of recreational anglers was expected to grow from 30 to 45 million between 1970 and 1985. These estimates proved to be extravagant, partly because of the difficulty in monitoring such large numbers of people engaging in such an activity, and partly because of wishful thinking and political posturing. In 1985, the NMFS estimated the total number of marine recreational fishermen at 17 million, who caught an estimated 326,000 metric tons of fish. For 1995, the estimated number of participants in marine recreational fishing was about 14 million.
10. The survey was called the Eastland Survey, after Mississippi Senator James O. Eastland, who had introduced the legislation mandating the development of the plan. The legislation was adopted unanimously by the House and the Senate in December 1973.
11. Anonymous. 1977. *Eastland Fisheries Survey: A Report To the Congress.* Atlantic States, Gulf States, and Pacific Marine Fisheries Commissions. Washington, D.C.
12. U.S. Department of Commerce. 1976. *A Marine Fisheries Program for the Nation.* Government Printing Office, Washington, D.C.
13. In the Magnuson Fishery Conservation and Management Act of 1976, optimum yield was defined at 16 U.S.C. 1802(18): "The term 'optimum', with respect to the yield from a fishery, means the amount of fish—(A) which will provide the greatest overall benefit to the [n]ation, with particular reference to food production and recreational opportunities; and (B) which is prescribed as such on the basis of the maximum sustainable yield from such fishery, as modified by any relevant economic, social, or ecological factor."
14. For a thorough and authoritative review of the Fishery Conservation and Management Act, including the amendments embodied in the Sustainable Fisheries Act of 1996, see Bean and Rowland (1997).

Part II | Scarcity

1969–1970   In 1969, the year before it was moved from the Interior Depart-
ment's U.S. Fish and Wildlife Service to the Commerce Department's National Ma-
rine Fisheries Service (NMFS), the Bureau of Commercial Fisheries (BCF) em-
ployed 2,475 employees.

Within a budget of $64.7 million, 33% was allocated to research, 20% to mar-
keting and technology, 12% to Pacific salmon, 14% to assistance for the fishing in-
dustry, 13% to financial aid for states, and 3% to fisheries management in Alaska. The
agency operated 26 large laboratories and 70 smaller stations and offices.

In 1969, the BCF operated 28 research vessels longer than 40 feet. Congress funded
a burst of research vessel construction. Seven of the ten research vessels in the federal
fisheries research fleet in the year 2000 were constructed during the 1960s.

Under Reorganization Plan Number 4 of October 1970, the Nixon adminis-
tration created the National Oceanic and Atmospheric Administration in the De-
partment of Commerce. Within this agency, the reorganization plan created the
NMFS out of the Interior Department's BCF and the marine gamefish activities of
the Bureau of Sport Fisheries and Wildlife. The total NMFS budget amounted to
roughly $47 million in 1971.

Chapter 6

Precautionary Science
and the ESA

A s the ideology of abundance and scientific management reached its peak of acceptance in the early 1970s, a more complex, less optimistic view emerged from within the scientific community. This new view, which centered on an ecosystem perspective and a precautionary approach, gained political influence from growing public concerns about the ethics of killing some kinds of marine wildlife. In the late 1960s, publicity about commercial whaling, seal hunts, and the incidental drowning of dolphins in tuna nets generated widespread public outrage. While many people were horrified by the fate of individual animals and objected to the killing of animals with such complex social behaviors and seemingly peaceful lifestyles, some scientists were concerned principally with the fate of entire populations of marine mammals. Especially in the decline of great whale populations, these scientists saw a fundamental flaw in prevailing policy on the exploitation of marine wildlife.

"Rather early, I was on the scientific advisory committee of the whaling commission because I wanted to find out how in the world these people could do what they were doing," says Dr. Lee Talbot in an interview. Talbot managed a program in international affairs and conservation at the Smithsonian Institution in the late 1960s. "I found that their science was just absolutely awful. Virtually all the scientists were biostatisticians but not biologists."

"They were trying to treat whales as fishes," says Talbot. "They were also using MSY [maximum sustainable yield] and using very simplistic models trying to determine what the maximum sustainable yield would be. What they were doing was pretty primitive and certainly inaccurate from the standpoint of finfishes. But from the standpoint of whales, the obvious result was that they were simply driving them down every year—knocking out one species after another commercially, and some of them biologically."

For Talbot and others, the use of MSY by the International Whaling Commission (IWC) reflected global problems in the exploitation of living marine resources. "I ran into marine problems that paralleled terrestrial conservation problems as far back as the early '50s," says Talbot. "It became evident that our management of marine living resources was very poor indeed globally. In fact, it was characterized by no management, really, in an enlightened sense. Therefore, it seemed to me increasingly important to do something about that.

"I found early that you couldn't get people very much worked up over cod or something like that. They have trouble relating to a cod, so I thought, well, people can relate to a whale."

As campaigns by conservation and animal rights organizations built momentum for an end to killing whales or other marine mammals in the United States and abroad, Congress began considering the Ocean Mammal Protection Act, which led to the Marine Mammal Protection Act of 1972. Broad support for a complete moratorium on the intentional and unintentional killing of marine mammals in the United States provoked opposition from the scientific community, even as it created an opportunity for scientists to promote alternatives to traditional management.

"My view was that the overriding policy of the law should be to maintain the health and relative stability of the ecosystem," says Talbot. "And then, only consistent with this could you manage the target species for harvest or for whatever other reason."

This emphasis upon an ecosystem perspective stood in stark contrast to the prevailing emphasis upon management of single species for MSY. Although Talbot and others did not support the proposed moratorium on taking marine mammals, they expressed little confidence that the continued use of MSY as a standard would lead to anything but overexploitation. "Maximum sustainable yield was an elegant formulation, a generalization of the idealized way that species behave. It was great for training, but was never intended for managing wildlife," says Talbot.

To Talbot and other wildlife scientists at the time, the traditional emphasis upon single-species management for MSY required ignoring ecological factors in the abundance of a species. These factors included competition among animals and species at the same trophic level, relationships between organisms at different trophic levels (such as between predator and prey), and changes in the capacity of an ecosystem to support a species due to changes in climate, pollution, or habitat. Some scientists also questioned the emphasis of MSY upon economic yield to the exclusion of other values, including the health of the ecosystem and aesthetic enjoyment.

Other scientists, outside the government, shared Talbot's desire to expand beyond traditional focuses of fisheries management upon maximum yield from single species. In the 1960s, a small group of marine mammalogists had proposed an ambitious research program to the National Science Foundation that would explore the interactions of marine mammals and their environment, but the proposal was turned down, largely because it cut across scientific disciplines.

"Science can be just as obstinate and reactionary as any other field," says Carleton Ray, who worked closely with the staff of the House Merchant Marine and Fisheries Committee in developing the legislation. "And the traditionalists in science were the population dynamacists, who were very conservation-oriented, but felt that the key was better use of MSY. In fact, when MSY first came around, everyone thought that it was a breakthrough in conservation, and it turned out to be one of the problems. Now, it's been shown, more or less, that we were right: In management, you can't separate out animals from their environment."

The Great Whales

For many marine conservationists, the haul of great whales by commercial whalers serves as the classic case of overexploitation of marine wildlife. Besides ethical questions about killing and causing pain to such highly evolved creatures, critics raised questions about the adequacy of traditional management theory and science. Indeed, management of "the whale fisheries" had generated criticism among scientists long before concerns were raised in the late 1960s about the ethics and humaneness of commercial whaling methods. As early as the 1860s, scientists were raising alarms about the depletion of great whale populations, but the alarms went unheeded. The disappearance of whales from an area after heavy hunting was rationalized simply as a withdrawal into refugia that had yet to be discovered. As whalers expanded their range with diesel-powered vessels that could remain offshore for long periods of time in distant waters, more whales were found and the theory of refugia seemed to be confirmed.

By the 1920s, the decline of many populations of great whales could no longer be ignored. In 1930, when nearly 20,000 blue whales were killed off Antarctica, the League of Nations called upon a panel of whale scientists to prepare an international agreement to manage the whale fishery. The Convention on the Regulation of Whaling prepared by the expert group included provisions protecting right whales, immature animals, and whales with calves. The treaty did not become effective until 1935, a year in which more than 16,000 blue whales were killed off the Antarctic continent and the population had begun a steep decline. Because some whaling nations did not join the treaty and some member nations did not strictly observe it, the 1931 agreement proved ineffective.

Later in the 1930s, the whaling industry itself tried to regulate the catch in order to avoid fluctuations in the markets for whale oil. As public pressure continued to build, the whaling industry organized a conference in 1937 at which a temporary agreement was reached. The agreement included closed seasons, size limits for some species, protection of whales on calving grounds, gray whales, and right whales. The dominant whaling countries, including the United States, signed the agreement.

The outbreak of World War II began the first effective respite for great whales since World War I. Worldwide catches of blue, humpback, fin, sei, and sperm whales fell from 36,643 animals in 1940 to 7,707 in 1942. Soon after the end of World War II, commercial whaling resumed in Antarctic waters, where enormous factory ships were supplied by squads of catcher boats. In the 1946–1947 season, Norway, Britain, South Africa, the Netherlands, and the Soviet Union sent 13 factory ships to hunt the waters of Antarctica for great whales. With the assistance of the United States, Japan sent 2 factory ships to the Southern Ocean in order to meet pressing needs for protein.

The depletion of blue whales and other great whales in the Antarctic before the war prompted U.S. efforts to expand upon past treaties regulating the whale fishery after World War II. In 1946, the U.S. government convened a meeting of whaling nations in Washington, D.C., that led to the adoption of the International Convention for the Regulation of Whaling. The principal purpose of the agreement was "to provide for the proper conservation of whale stocks and thus make possible the orderly development of the whaling industry . . ." As described in chapter 4, the treaty established the IWC, which was composed of representatives from member countries.

Like similar treaty organizations, the IWC suffered from several major flaws.[1] Charged with both conserving whales and promoting the development of the whaling industry, the commission commonly erred on the side of exploitation, often contrary to the recommendations made by its own scientific committee. When the commission moved toward restraining whale catches, whaling countries threatened to withdraw from the commission and sometimes did. Under the treaty establishing the commission, member countries could exempt themselves from a commission decision by filing a formal objection within 90 days.

In the late 1950s, the scientific committee became increasingly frustrated with the rejection of its recommendations by the commission. In 1960, as whale catches continued declining, members of the scientific committee expressed doubts about their ability to determine the exact size or sustainable yield of any species. At the suggestion of the scientific committee, the commission established a committee of three independent scientists to review the previous 30 years of landings statistics for the Antarctic whale fishery. In 1963, the committee submitted its analyses and recommendations. The scientists reported that catch statistics alone showed some whale populations nearing extinction. In Antarctic waters, the catch of blue whales, which had been the mainstay of the fishery in the 1930s, had fallen from 9,192 whales in the 1946–1947 season to 102 in the 1963–1964 season. The special committee called for a 50-year moratorium on catching blue and humpback whales, sowing the seeds of a general moratorium on commercial whaling that the commission approved—two decades later. In 1963, however, the commission rejected the special committee's recommendation, despite its previous commitment to accept whatever recommendations the independent committee made.

The commission also rejected the special committee's recommendation to abandon the blue whale unit in setting quotas. No other feature in the management of commercial whaling more eloquently captured the prevailing view of whales as a commodity. One blue whale unit, which was equal to 1 blue whale, 2 fin whales, 2.5 humpback whales, or 6 sei whales, was based on the average amount of oil that individual species would yield. By ignoring differences among species and reducing whales to a commodity, the blue whale unit enabled the commission to avoid a glut of whale oil on the market, which would threaten the industry's economic viability. After all, the ultimate goal of the commission's charter was "the orderly development of the whaling industry." Although the committee's view did not prevail, it was at the forefront of a movement within the scientific community that would have profound implications.

U.S. Whaling Policy and Practice

Unlike other whaling countries, the United States hunted whales only sporadically, although intensely. In the seventeenth century, New England colonists ventured from shore in small boats propelled by oars and sails to hunt slow-moving humpback and right whales with handheld harpoons as they migrated along the coast. The U.S. whale fishery started to expand in 1712, when U.S. whalers began hunting sperm whales in the open ocean.

American whalers soon dominated this fishery as it spread southward in the Atlantic and into the Pacific by 1789. At one time, hundreds of American whaling ships used Hawaii as their base.

By the 1860s, U.S. catches of sperm whales peaked then rapidly declined. Some whalers moved to other areas of the North Pacific in order to hunt right whales and later, bowhead whales. Other whalers began exploiting newly discovered coastal species along the Pacific coast. American whaling continued sporadically along the Pacific coast until the late 1940s, when it ceased. In 1956, after a hiatus of more than a decade, commercial whaling resumed in the waters off California and entered its final phase. In that year, two catcher boats caught 145 whales, most near the Farallon Islands, and delivered them to a processing plant at Point San Pablo in San Francisco Bay. The 133 humpback, 9 sperm, and 3 fin whales yielded oil and more than 5 million pounds of meat and meal that fetched the Del Monte Fish Company $366,000 (or roughly $2.2 million in 1999 value). As in later years, most of the meat was sold as food for mink; some meat was canned for pets. Whale oil found uses in cosmetics, soaps, paint, and other products.

The renewed whale fishery grew rapidly. In 1960, a second whaling station opened in Richmond in San Francisco Bay, and in 1961, a third station opened in Warrenton, Oregon, at the mouth of the Columbia River. In the next year, one plant added equipment that reduced the time required to flense a whale. In the words of a Bureau of Commercial Fisheries (BCF) report, this avoided "the placing of limits on catcher boats, when whales were numerous, because plants were unable to handle the catch."[2]

In 1961, U.S. commercial whaling reached its postwar peak when 343 whales were landed. The high total catch obscured signs of trouble: U.S. catcher boats were able to find only 64 humpbacks compared to the 199 humpbacks they landed in 1957. The BCF already had concluded that the humpback whales upon which U.S. whalers depended were depleted. Declining catches of humpback whales did not deter the whaling companies. Instead, catcher boats targeted other species as the catch of humpbacks declined. For several years, the catch of fin whales increased, until it too fell dramatically in the late 1960s. In some years, sperm and sei whales made up a large part of the catches.

At the same time, concerns about Pacific whale populations grew among BCF biologists. In 1962, the BCF annual report raised the specter of extinction of a marine species, perhaps for the first time since the Steller's sea cow in the eighteenth century. "The stocks of the five commercially important whales—blue, fin, humpback, sei, and sperm whales—could be almost completely destroyed unless several restrictions were placed upon these species," according to the BCF. Because it had no independent authority to restrict domestic catches of whales, the BCF pursued restrictions through the IWC.

By the mid-1960s, international pressure was building to halt the unregulated slaughter of the great whales. Grudgingly, the commissioners responded with reductions in quotas and even outright bans. In 1965, for example, the IWC banned killing humpback and blue whales in the North Pacific. That year, U.S. catcher boats made their last landing of four humpback whales. In 1966, growing restrictions and declining catches closed the Oregon whaling station operated by Bioproducts, Inc. The next year the Golden Gate Fishing Company on San Francisco Bay ended its whaling operations. The last of U.S. whaling businesses, the Del Monte Fish Company, persisted. In 1967, the company rejected a request by the BCF to abide by voluntary limits on sei whale catches recommended by the IWC. In a pattern of serial depletion of species that commercial whaling followed from its beginnings centuries earlier, the Del Monte Company shifted to less and less desirable species, including sperm and gray whales.

The end of commercial whaling in the United States came swiftly. In 1970, Curtis Bohlen had just been appointed deputy assistant secretary in the Department of the Interior under Secretary Hickel when a student by the name of Bob Brownell approached him about the decline of whale populations caused by commercial whaling. Like most other Americans at the time, Bohlen was little aware of whales, much less their decline. Brownell's account caused Bohlen enough concern to investigate. "The more I talked to people in the scientific community," says Bohlen, "the more I realized that there was a problem that needed addressing."

Several months later, when Bohlen suggested listing eight species of great whales as endangered under the Endangered Species Conservation Act of 1969, Interior Secretary Hickel seized upon the idea. Hickel's enthusiasm was at least partly political and personal. Just months before, Hickel had suffered through a bitter battle over his confirmation as interior secretary, largely because of his background as a developer in Alaska. To counter this criticism, President Nixon had appointed noted conservationist Russell Train to the position of under secretary in the Interior Department in 1969.[3]

"[Hickel] always resented that, because he always wanted to prove that he was a better conservationist than anybody else," says Bohlen, who served as deputy assistant secretary for Fish, Wildlife, and Parks from 1971 to 1977. Listing whales under the Endangered Species Conservation Act of 1969 was just the kind of bold action that could establish Hickel's credentials as a conservationist.

As Bohlen circulated the proposal within the administration, fierce opposition arose, principally because the proposal called for an end to whaling and to the use of whale products in the United States. The Navy claimed that a ban on imports of sperm oil would threaten national defense since the substance was used for lubricating instruments and machines on naval vessels. Commerce Secretary Maurice Stans charged that a ban on whale oil imports would incapacitate "large segments of our economy."[4]

The opposition did not deter Hickel or Bohlen. Just before Thanksgiving, Hickel signed the Federal Register notice announcing the decision to list the great whales as endangered. Bohlen left for Thanksgiving dinner with his family in Boston. But on Thanksgiving Day, Bohlen was suddenly called back to Washington as word spread that President Nixon had fired his interior secretary.[5]

Opponents of listing the great whales seized the opportunity. "We began to get all kinds of calls from the Navy and from Commerce to retrieve the notice from the Federal Register," says Bohlen. "Finally, some office of the White House called and gave me instructions to withdraw it. But somehow, I just couldn't work it out over the weekend. Monday it was printed and the eight species were on."

In 1971, when a domestic ban on commercial whaling took effect, Del Monte received a license to catch 165 whales, but succeeded in landing only 53. Within a year, the Del Monte Fish Company ceased whaling after landing 4 fin whales, 2 sei whales, and 47 sperm whales. Other U.S. businesses continued exporting whale products until 1977, when 710,000 gallons of whale oil were sold for $1.7 million. Several firms including Archer–Daniels–Midland and the Werner G. Smith Company claimed economic hardship and were granted permits to continue imports of whale oil for several years after the listing of the great whales.

A Global Moratorium on Commercial Whaling

Dissatisfied with the 1970 listing of the great whales under the Endangered Species Conservation Act of 1969, conservationists inside and outside the federal government launched a campaign for a global moratorium on commercial whaling. In June 1971, the Senate approved a resolution introduced by

Senator Hugh Scott (R–PA), the Senate's minority leader, calling upon the Department of State to negotiate a ten-year global moratorium on commercial whaling. When the House of Representatives took up the proposal, opposition surfaced from federal agencies and the scientific community. The Department of the Interior, the U.S. commissioner to the IWC, and the Department of State all opposed the resolution. Scientists who had been pressing for adding an ecological dimension to fisheries management opposed the proposed moratorium, and rejected the argument made by supporters that the intelligence and complex social life of whales did not merit special consideration.

As marine mammologist Ken Norris later wrote, an untidy debate over whales ensued. "A prevalent view was not 'Let us change the take of whales so their populations can prosper,' but 'We must take no whales at all, because they are incredible creatures whose lives we hardly understand at all.' The whale became a symbol of man's mindless destruction of nature."

Animal protection activists countered the opposition. Lewis Regenstein, who was operating a one-person office for the Fund for Animals in Washington, D.C., at the time, exploited his contacts at major newspapers. Soon, both the *Washington Post* and the *New York Times* ran editorials supporting the moratorium resolution. While animal protection activists were pursuing the moratorium through Congress and the media, others were pursuing support within the Nixon administration. In 1971, preparations were under way for a United Nations Conference on the Human Environment, which was to be held in Stockholm, Sweden, in May and June 1972. From his position as senior scientist on the President's Council on Environmental Quality, Talbot urged that the United States introduce a resolution supporting a commercial whaling moratorium. Blocked by the State Department, Talbot approached the organizer of the UN conference, Maurice Strong, whom Talbot had met while working for the International Union for the Conservation of Nature (IUCN) and Natural Resources in the 1950s and 1960s. Strong placed the moratorium resolution on the agenda and with that, Talbot was able to begin developing a U.S. position.

Within the scientific community, opponents viewed a moratorium as a hysterical reaction to bad management that should be dealt with through improved management techniques. Both the State Department and the NMFS renewed their opposition, arguing that sperm oil was essential for the military and that ending whaling would cost jobs. Eventually, the controversy reached the White House, where a final meeting was attended by representatives of the State Department, the NMFS, and the Joint Chiefs of Staff. Using contacts developed by conservation activists, Talbot invited representatives of several chemical companies to the meeting. Talbot asked the three representatives from the chemical industry if they could make a synthetic oil with all the characteristics of sperm oil. All said that they could do so within six weeks, if it were economically advantageous.

As the Stockholm Conference approached, Talbot and others began preparing the U.S. delegation to become active advocates for the moratorium resolution. Talbot approached friends in other countries that he had made while working for IUCN, and arranged for a dozen other delegations, including Iran, Kenya, Mexico, and India, to make statements in support of the moratorium when formal discussions began. When the conference's deliberations turned to the resolution on a whaling moratorium, the United States expressed its strong support, and was followed by a dozen other delegations. Of the whaling countries represented at the conference, only the Japanese delegation raised objections. The resolution was approved by a vote of 53 to 0, with Brazil, Japan, and South Africa abstaining.

A week later, Talbot accompanied Train, the newly appointed U.S. commissioner, to a meeting of the IWC. Despite the endorsement by the United Nations Conference on the Human Environment, the U.S. proposal for a moratorium on commercial whaling was rejected by the commission.

A New Endangered Species Act

"The Endangered Species Act of 1973 stems from the listing of the great whales," says Bohlen. "The 1969 act required a species to be threatened throughout its range. Our own solicitors office in Interior said we couldn't list the whales because you couldn't prove they were threatened throughout their range. [These difficulties] led to the realization that [the Endangered Species Conservation Act of 1969] was a very inflexible instrument, and the desire to amend it."

The Endangered Species Conservation Act of 1969, which Secretary Hickel used to end commercial whaling in the United States, was based on the Endangered Species Preservation Act of 1966. That act called for federal agencies to protect native forms of wildlife threatened with extinction. The 1966 act, however, provided no enforcement authority. The power to restrict taking of endangered wildlife remained with state fish and game agencies.

The 1969 act expanded the scope of the federal government's endangered species program to species or subspecies of fish and wildlife "threatened with worldwide extinction." With the exception of imports for zoological display, scientific and education activities, and captive breeding, the importation of listed species was prohibited. The 1969 act also urged some federal agencies to avoid adverse impacts by their projects on listed species, but did not require that they do so. Nor did the 1969 act ban killing listed species.

"The more we talked, the more we realized it probably made sense to go to a completely new act, which would accomplish several things," says Bohlen. "One, it would enable you to list a given population rather than proving the species was threatened throughout its range. Two, creating a second category, which became the threatened category, that enabled the secretary to take steps before a species was actually endangered."

There were other concerns. "The problem was that the '69 act was hortatory," says Lee Talbot. "It was full of weasel-words, such as 'insofar as possible or practicable,' or 'consistent with the main mission.'" Growing public support for environmental protection strengthened political interest in increasing endangered species protection. "There was a huge groundswell of public concern and support that expressed itself in editorials in the *New York Times,* the *Washington Post,* and the *Boston Globe,*" says John Grandy, who was on the staff of the National Parks and Conservation Association at the time. "CBS television inaugurated a regular program that would begin with a picture of the Earth and the title, 'Can the Earth Be Saved?' It was great."

Other events contributed to the growing interest in protecting declining wildlife in the United States and abroad. Early in 1973, the State Department hosted final negotiations on the Convention on International Trade in Endangered Species of Wild Fauna and Flora, or CITES, as mandated by the Endangered Species Conservation Act of 1969. The treaty discussions attracted widespread media attention. The discussions also laid the conceptual groundwork for key features of the Endangered Species Act of 1973, such as the listing of species that were not yet in danger of extinction but were declining toward endangerment.

With the support of the White House, Lee Talbot of the President's Council on Environmental Quality, together with Bohlen and Nathaniel Reed of the Department of the Interior, enjoyed a free hand in developing and vetting new endangered species legislation. Advocates overcame the efforts of federal agencies to protect their prerogatives by reducing mandatory wording to hortatory wording of key provisions.

In 1972, staff of the Nixon administration and John Dingell's Merchant Marine and Fisheries Committee worked closely together in developing a strong bill for committee consideration. "I met with Lee several times and with a number of other people," says Frank Potter, Dingell's senior staffer on the committee. "And we came out with what turned out to be pretty damned close to the final version of the Endangered Species Act. That's the first and probably the last time in my awareness of a bill going into the process and emerging very close to the way it started out." This was partly due to the obscurity of the Dingell committee. "The Merchant Marine Committee was sort of a jerky little committee that nobody paid much attention to, other than the shipping industry and the sand-and-gravel people," says Potter. "They didn't much care about endangered species."

The House bill included several key changes to the 1969 act, including the creation of a new category, threatened species. Instead of requiring that all populations of a species be in danger of extinction before receiving protection, the bill authorized the protection of individual populations of a species. H.R. 37 also banned not only the killing, but the harming, of endangered species, and allowed for the regulation of activities that might harm species threatened with extinction.

These were important provisions, but not the core of the legislation. "The interesting part of the bill was Section 7 that said that all agencies will use their authorities in pursuing the purposes of the act, which were very broad," says Potter. "Not that they will do it at their discretion, or that they will use their best efforts, but that they will just do it."[6]

Section 7 required not only the protection of endangered species but efforts by federal agencies to increase their populations. Federal agencies were to consult with the Interior Department's Fish and Wildlife Service or the Commerce Department's National Marine Fisheries Service (NMFS) to ensure that activities they conducted, funded, or permitted did not harm listed species or their habitat.

"I don't think there were more than four or five of us, including Lee and Frank, who really understood the import of Section 7," says Bohlen. "None of us could have envisaged how Section 7 turned out, although we knew its potential." The objections of a small group of private interests were overwhelmed by the strong support for doing something dramatic for endangered species.

While the Senate considered a weaker bill, Congressman Dingell pushed forward with a strong bill, which cleared the full Merchant Marine and Fisheries Committee in July 1973. On September 18, after limited debate, the

House of Representatives approved H.R. 37, the Endangered Species Act (ESA) of 1973, by a vote of 390 to 12. Negotiations with the Senate resolved the concerns of the states about preemption of their management authority, while retaining the strength of the House bill. On December 28, 1973, President Nixon signed the ESA of 1973 into law.

Summary

In the 1960s, there arose an alternative approach to wildlife management that emphasized an ecosystem perspective and precaution in exploiting wildlife. A growing number of scientists questioned the traditional model of single-species management of wildlife populations for maximum sustainable yield. At the same time, advocates for animal rights were building political support for an end to the hunting of wildlife, including commercial whaling. Generally, scientists and government wildlife managers rejected these appeals as emotional and inconsistent with scientific management.

For many conservationists at the time, commercial whaling became a symbol of the reckless overexploitation of wildlife. Over the decades, international treaty organizations had overseen the decimation of many populations of great whales, and continued to reject concerns from scientists that some species were approaching extinction.

Before World War II, the United States had sporadically hunted whales, and resumed small hunts along the Pacific coast in the 1950s. Because commercial whaling was managed under international treaty, the Bureau of Commercial Fisheries was limited in what it could do to limit catches. In 1970, the listing of the great whales under the Endangered Species Conservation Act of 1969 brought a sudden end to commercial whaling by U.S. citizens. Soon afterwards, the U.S. government became the primary sponsor of a resolution to place a ten-year global moratorium on commercial whaling. Although 53 countries attending a United Nations environmental conference in Stockholm, Sweden, approved the resolution, the International Whaling Commission rejected the proposal, and whaling continued.

The difficulties in listing the great whales under the Endangered Species Conservation Act of 1969, as well as the limitations of the act, led a small group of individuals in the Nixon administration and Congress to purse a major reform of endangered species legislation. With unusual swiftness, Congress adopted the Endangered Species Act of 1973. Among other major innovations, the act required that federal agencies not only avoid activities that might jeopardize the survival of a population of wild animals or plants, but also that they promote the recovery of wildlife threatened or in danger of extinction.

Notes

1. The International Convention for the Regulation of Whaling entered into force on November 10, 1948. In 1949, 11 countries attended the first meeting as members: Australia, Canada, France, Iceland, the Netherlands, Norway, South Africa, Sweden, the United Kingdom, the United States, and the Soviet Union. Delegations from Argentina, Brazil, Chile, Denmark, and New Zealand also attended. By 1950, Brazil, Denmark, Mexico, New Zealand, and Panama had joined the commission.

   Membership has fluctuated over the years. As the campaign for a moratorium on commercial whaling escalated in the late 1970s, supporters recruited non-whaling countries in order to gain enough votes to achieve the necessary three-quarters majority. By the 1990s, the commission was no longer a club of whalers and former whalers, but included many countries with no tradition of whaling or access to whales. In 2000, membership had grown to 40 countries as follows: Antigua and Barbuda, Argentina, Australia, Austria, Brazil, Chile, Costa Rica, Denmark, Dominica, Finland, France, Germany, Grenada, India, Ireland, Italy, Japan, Kenya, the Republic of Korea, Mexico, Monaco, the Netherlands, New Zealand, Norway, Oman, the People's Republic of China, Peru, the Russian Federation, Senegal, the Solomon Islands, South Africa, Spain, Sweden, Switzerland, St. Kitts and Nevis, St. Lucia, St. Vincent and the Grenadines, the United Kingdom, the United States, and Venezuela.

2. Power, E.A. and C.H. Lyles. 1964. *Fishery Statistics of the United States, 1962.* U.S. Government Printing Office, Washington, D.C.

3. Train's conservation credentials were well known. In the late 1950s and early 1960s, Train had become heavily involved in the conservation of African wildlife. He served on the board of several organizations, and as chairman of the board of trustees of the African Wildlife Leadership Foundation. In 1965, he was one of the founders of the Conservation Foundation and served as its first president. He also helped launch the World Wildlife Fund.

   Train's work in Africa brought him into contact with Lee Talbot, who later served as Train's assistant when Train led the U.S. delegation to the IWC in 1973, which sought a moratorium on commercial whaling. After leaving the Department of the Interior in 1970, Train was appointed the first chairman of the President's Council on Environmental Quality. Train recruited Talbot to be the council's first senior scientist.

4. Quoted in Regenstein, Lewis G. December 1974. A History of the Endangered Species Act of 1973, and an Analysis of its History; Strengths and Weaknesses; Administration; and Probable Future Effectiveness. Master's Thesis. Emory University, Atlanta, Georgia.
5. According to Bohlen, there was general dissatisfaction within the Nixon administration with Hickel's management of the Interior Department. The secretary's firing, however, was triggered by a letter to the president opposing the war in Vietnam. An aide who opposed the war had prepared the letter for Hickel's signature, then released its contents to the press before the president had seen the letter.
6. Under Section 7(a)2, every federal agency must "insure that any action authorized, funded, or carried out by such agency . . . is not likely to jeopardize or threaten the continued existence of any endangered species or result in the destruction or adverse modifications of habitat of such species . . . "

Amendments to the act triggered by the controversy over the halt in construction of the Tellico Dam in Tennessee to protect the snail darter defined critical habitat and formalized a process for determining whether activities would jeopardize a protected species' continued existence. This process often requires the Fish and Wildlife Service or the NMFS to prepare a biological opinion that describes the anticipated impact of the proposed activity on listed species. If the activity is found to jeopardize the species' continued existence, then the services are to recommend measures for mitigating these impacts, if possible.

1977   In 1977, the National Marine Fisheries Service's (NMFS) activities were organized into offices for international fisheries, fisheries development, scientific and technical services, fisheries management, executive and administrative support, program planning and budget, marine recreational fisheries, and policy development and long-range planning.

In the first year of implementation of the Magnuson-Stevens Act, the NMFS budget was $82 million. Of this, 28% was devoted to assessment, monitoring, and prediction; 21% to conserving marine resources, which included fisheries, marine mammals, and endangered species; 15% to restoring and increasing fishery resources through hatcheries and other methods; 36% to management of fisheries and utilization research; and 1% to financial support services for the fishing industry. In return for gaining access to fish populations within U.S. waters, 13 countries paid $11 million in fishing fees.

Under the Fishing Vessel Obligation Guarantee program, the NMFS approved $26 million in guarantees for loans to build or rebuild vessels in 1977. Under the Fishing Vessel Capital Construction Fund, fishing vessel owners deposited $27 million of operational income in accounts sheltered from taxes for later use in constructing or reconstructing vessels. In 1977, fishermen used such funds to build 160 vessels and rebuild 45.

Chapter 7 | New Values, New Roles

> We have, for too long now, accepted a view of non-human life
> which denies other creatures feelings, imagination, consciousness,
> and awareness. It seems that in our craze to justify our exploitation
> of all non-human life forms, we have stripped from them any at-
> tributes which could stay our hand.

With these words, Joan McIntyre's introduction to *Mind in the Waters,* published in 1974, expressed new values that successfully
challenged traditional views of marine wildlife and led to passage
of two landmark laws. Until the late 1960s, government decision makers, busi-
nesspersons, scientists, wildlife managers, and the general public viewed marine wildlife principally as a commodity. Wildlife managers confidently asserted
that they could make wildlife populations more productive through exploitation. Aesthetic, ethical, and ecological concerns were utterly absent from governmental decision making on wildlife. For the most part, orthodox wildlife
management went unchallenged.

During the mid- to late 1960s, however, new voices arose. Animal rights activists raised ethical questions about the suffering of wildlife at the hands of
human exploiters. The Pacific tuna fishery, in which purse seine nets were drowning hundreds of thousands of dolphins each year, came under attack. The clubbing of baby harp seals, with soulful eyes that captured the hearts of thousands
of people, fed public furor over traditional uses of marine mammals. The har-
pooning of whales and the decline of whale populations provoked criticism on
ethical and scientific grounds.

Even as society's values were changing, many professional wildlife managers
and scientists inside and outside the federal government dug in their heels against
what they viewed as pure emotionalism. As they did so, however, public outrage grew and soon swept over Congress, leading to the passage of two major

pieces of legislation: the Marine Mammal Protection Act (MMPA) of 1972 and the Endangered Species Act (ESA) of 1973.

The impact of these laws went beyond their specific provisions because they introduced new principles into marine wildlife management. Both the MMPA and the ESA created classes of wildlife that received special protection and were not to be managed for sustainable yield. By imposing a moratorium on most activities harmful to marine mammals, the MMPA shifted the burden of proof. Instead of requiring a demonstration that an activity was harmful, the MMPA required a demonstration that it was not. The ESA mandated that federal agencies not conduct or sponsor activities that would jeopardize the continued existence of a species listed as threatened or endangered. Finally, both acts explicitly recognized that individual species are members of broader communities and ecosystems.

While the design of these laws reflected the experience and expertise of key individuals in the Nixon administration and in Congress, growing controversy over the humaneness and scientific basis for whale and seal hunts generated much of the political support that led to the laws' enactment.

Campaigns to protect endangered species and marine mammals reflected broader concerns about the environment that reached a peak in the late 1960s. Then, damage to the environment and people's health from pollution became a common concern of politicians and the public, leading to passage of major legislation in the early 1970s.

Pollution

"It looks more hopeful than ever that pollution will gradually become a less menacing evil as our fight against it progresses," wrote Interior Secretary Ickes in 1945.[1] "Domestic sewage and almost every kind of industrial waste can now be disposed of by practical and commercially profitable means." The secretary's optimism about ending pollution was more a matter of speculation than of experience. As with the effect of dams on Pacific salmon, the Fish and Wildlife Service itself seems not to have shared the secretary's optimism. Director Ira N. Gabrielson's annual report seethed with alarm over the pollution of rivers and bays with sewage and industrial wastes. "The effect on animal resources has been so wastefully destructive," Gabrielson wrote, "that pollution is now one of the most serious and complex of conservation problems occupying the attention of the Fish and Wildlife Service."[2]

State and federal conservation agencies were hard pressed to protect wildlife from possible damage by increasing volumes and types of pollutants. Industrial and municipal wastes were discharged at will into rivers and bays, with little more justification than "out of sight, out of mind." The goal of feeding a growing population, which drove programs to develop the domestic fishing fleet, also encouraged expanded farming and use of agricultural chemicals. Between 1944 and 1964, more than 6,000 agricultural chemicals from 200 compounds were introduced into the market.

The effects of pesticides on marine fish and other wildlife generated serious attention in the late 1950s. In his annual report for 1958, Arnie J. Suomela, commissioner of Fish and Wildlife in the Department of the Interior, warned that "[t]he pesticide problem is becoming acute." Suomela expressed particular concern about the danger to commercial fisheries "where housing developments have been established on 'reclaimed' tidal flats or near them and where the 'mosquito menace' can lead to indiscriminate use of pesticides."[3] In 1958, Congress passed legislation authorizing renewed studies on the effects of pesticides on fish and wildlife. By 1960, Bureau of Commercial Fisheries (BCF) laboratories in the Gulf of Mexico had concluded that several chemical compounds, including DDT, sevin, heptachlor, aldrin, and dieldrin, were toxic to white shrimp.

The Fish and Wildlife Service already was familiar with DDT, a pesticide that had been used to kill disease-carrying insects in the Pacific theater during World War II. After the war, the service became concerned with the growing use of the wonder chemical for such purposes as eradicating agricultural pests and mosquitos near burgeoning suburban developments and in countries suffering from malaria epidemics. Early research by Fish and Wildlife Service biologists had found no harm to wildlife, except at high levels of application. When the service found that some insects had become resistant to DDT, it only recommended caution in increasing dosages; however, studies by BCF biologists late in the 1950s found that such common pesticides as DDT, endrin, and lindane were highly toxic to shrimp and fish. By 1962, BCF biologists were reporting that most tested pesticides were toxic to marine animals at levels far below recommended application rates.

The concerns of government biologists suddenly became public concerns with the publication of *Silent Spring* in 1962. The popular book, written by former BCF biologist and editor Rachel Carson, combined with a critical report by the President's Science Advisory Committee to undermine the image of modern chemicals as benign tools of progress. Soon, careful evaluation of agricultural chemicals and other potential pollutants enjoyed support in the administration and Congress. The Fish and Wildlife Service began screening a far larger number of chemicals for effects on wildlife and established a system to monitor pollutants in mollusks collected from major estuaries in the Gulf of Mexico. Gradually, accumulated evidence led to the banning of several pesticides, such as DDT.

Federal wildlife agencies never enjoyed sufficient funding and staffing to screen even a few of the hundreds of new chemicals introduced each year, or to carry out the kinds of detailed analyses necessary for demonstrating a direct link between the use of a particular chemical and a decline in the health or abundance of marine wildlife. If anything, the complexity of chemicals' effects on marine wildlife became clearer, and with it, the difficulty of identifying specific effects. This analytical difficulty was compounded by the suite of chemicals used or produced in industrial processes that entered rivers and bays.

Through the 1960s, concern over water pollution grew at higher and higher levels of the government. In 1966, Interior Secretary Udall warned that a "[r]eversal of pollution damage to our fisheries resources will require a complete overhaul in traditional thought."[4] In a special message to Congress three years later, President Johnson called for an all-out attack on marine pollution. In 1971, Secretary of the Interior Walter Hickel fulminated: "There has been too little resistance to prevailing and threatened pollution when payrolls are involved. . . . It is contrary to human welfare to contribute in any way, however slight, to the degradation of the sea's capacity to support life."

Of greatest immediate concern to government agencies were health hazards from seafood contaminated with pollutants. In 1971, contamination of seafood by heavy metals made newspaper headlines when the Food and Drug Administration warned consumers of possible health hazards in eating swordfish, which carried high levels of methylmercury. While some industry leaders criticized the warning as alarmist, others were concerned about the pollution. At the 1971 annual meeting of the National Fisheries Institute, the president Lee Weddig warned: "Perhaps the only way the public will ever be awakened to the need to support the programs that will protect the environment is through the shock of sudden realization that pollution has a direct negative effect. It may well be the mercury problem is the bitter medicine that the industry must swallow in order to achieve a cure to a much broader, more devastating illness."[5]

The mercury scare joined a growing list of pollution problems. In 1972, the Interior Department pointed to the discharge of 29 billion gallons of sewage and industrial wastes into coastal waters every year. "This intemperate action is equivalent to filling 1,000 ships the size of the *Torrey Canyon* every 24 hours and letting them empty their holds along the seacoasts of the [E]ast, [W]est, and Gulf," read the department's report *River of Life, Water: The Environmental Challenge.*[6] Among other things, these discharges were slowly reducing the areas in which shellfish such as oysters and mussels could be harvested for human consumption. Interior Secretary Walter Hickel complained that "[t]he right to produce is not the right to pollute." In a remarkable jeremiad against coastal pollution, Hickel charged that "[w]e have become such proficient spoilers that not even the seas are too big for us to ruin."[7] In 1972, President Nixon asked Congress to pass a clean waters act and to authorize $4 billion for waste treatment facilities.

The broad support for taking some action against water pollution swept through Congress, which produced several major pieces of legislation in 1972. Among other things, the Clean Water Act of 1972 required permits for the discharge of industrial and other wastes, created a program of grants to improve sewage treatment, and called upon the states to reduce polluted runoff from land. The act launched a massive program of sewage treatment plant construction in which the federal government invested more than $67 billion between 1972 and 1997.

The treatment of sewage from millions of households before discharge into the ocean led to dramatic improvements in water quality, but also created enormous amounts of sludge that required disposal. By the 1990s, sewage treatment plants were producing about 325 million tons of sludge each year. While the Marine Protection, Research, and Sanctuaries Act (also known as the Ocean Dumping Act) mandated a phaseout of dumping industrial and municipal wastes at sea, several cities on the Atlantic coast continued dumping sludge, creating concern among NMFS biologists, commercial and recreational fishermen, and environmentalists. The NMFS, however, had little leverage in bringing an end to the dumping of sewage sludge or other materials. Title I of the act gave the Environmental Protection Agency responsibility for issuing permits for ocean disposal of wastes other than dredge spoil, for which the Corps of Engineers held the responsibility. Permits could be granted if the dumping would not "unreasonably degrade or endanger human health, welfare or amenities, or marine environments, ecosystems, or economic potentialities." The NMFS's role was restricted to raising its concerns under the Fish and Wildlife Coordination Act and the Ocean Dumping Act. In the 1990s, research by NMFS biologists eventually contributed to a congressionally imposed phaseout of all sewage sludge dumping in coastal waters.

Federal fisheries agencies had even less influence on so-called nonpoint sources of pollution, which increased as uses of coastal lands grew more intense after World War II. For example, the expansion of farming after World War II transformed the landscape in many coastal areas by leveling forests, filling wetlands, and removing buffers of bushes and trees along streams and rivers. These changes in the landscape, together with channelization of rivers for flood control, increased the flow of chemical residues from farmlands into coastal waters. Farmers also applied ever greater amounts of fertilizers to their lands, tripling the amount of active nutrients in fertilizers between 1960 and 1995 to more than 21 million tons. Crowding large numbers of chickens, hogs, as well as beef and dairy cattle into feedlots generated enormous amounts of nutrients that flowed into streams and bays. Taken together, these farming activities increased the amount of nutrients entering streams and bays as much as tenfold in the last century.

By the mid-1960s, algal blooms, fish kills, oil spills, and the closure of shellfish beds due to pollution were becoming widespread. Leaders in the Department of the Interior and in the White House Marine Sciences Council during the Johnson and Nixon administrations believed that coastal pollution and coastal land use were inextricably linked. In a speech in July 1967 at the University of Rhode Island, Vice President Hubert Humphrey called for solving "the related problems of conflicting uses of our shoreline and the pollution of our estuaries and streams."[8] In his 1971 Message to Congress on the Environment, President Richard Nixon called for a national land-use policy that would encourage states and local governments to develop more rational patterns of land development. These calls for action culminated in 1972 with the passage of the Coastal Zone Management Act, under which the federal government provided grants to states for the development of federally approved plans for managing growth in coastal areas. Managed by an office in the National Ocean Service, a sister agency to the National Marine Fisheries Service (NMFS), the program led to the adoption of coastal zone management plans by 32 of 35 coastal states by 1998. Many of these plans were influenced by advice from regional offices of the NMFS.

The efficacy of state coastal zone programs varied greatly around the country. In some states, they curbed the most damaging types of development, while in other states, the restraints were minimal. As land uses further intensified in coastal areas and other sources of pollution were reduced, runoff became the chief source of pollutants in coastal waters. While heavy metals, oil, industrial chemicals, and agricultural chemicals continued to be a problem, nutrients running off the land into rivers and coastal waters were creating even more dramatic problems than the algal blooms of previous decades.

There was little that the NMFS could do to reduce the impact of so massive a problem, except study it and urge other government agencies to consider the downstream impacts of activities many miles upstream.

Humaneness or Management

"I stood about five feet from one seal which was permitted to escape after receiving a glancing blow, and it waddled past me toward the water with blood streaming from the socket where an eye had been knocked loose," reported Alice Herrington to members of the Friends of Animals in 1970.[9] "This same seal had fish net embedded in its coat, which I was told was the reason for not chasing it. The fur is not valuable commercially when it has been mangled with net. The terror of the seals during the long hours of waiting and watching the murder of their friends and relatives was pathetic."

In 1970, most Americans might have mistaken this report for a description of the Canadian hunt of baby harp seals that had so outraged people in the United States and Europe in the late 1960s. They would have been mistaken. Herrington was not reporting on the Canadian hunt of harp seals, but upon the hunt of northern fur seals (*Callorhinus ursinus*) that the U.S. government had sponsored and managed for more than a century. In the early 1960s, the Friends of Animals, the Humane Society of the United States, and other animal protection groups began raising concerns about the humaneness of the fur seal hunt. Like the harp seal hunt, fur seal hunters killed the seals by clubbing. Unlike the harp seal hunt, however, the hunt on the Pribilof Islands did not target week-old seals, but juvenile male seals that scientists had determined were surplus to the population.

To government managers of the hunt, these differences between the two hunts were critical and the mounting criticism misdirected. At one point, the NMFS openly complained: "Through misinformation, much of the attention given to the Canadian harvests was directed to the management program on the Pribilof Islands."[10] The criticism of the Pribilof fur seal hunt was particularly vexing for federal managers of the hunt, since they had long considered it a model of scientific management of a wild marine species. In 1954, Interior Secretary Douglas McKay boasted that "[t]he successful handling of Alaska's fur-seal herd by the [f]ederal [g]overnment has been cited by naturalists as an outstanding example of proper conservation and channeling of an animal population in the natural state."[11] By eliminating the hunt of seals on the high seas and culling the herd, federal managers had rebuilt a depleted population of wild animals. "Since the [g]overnment first assumed direct responsibility for this resource 45 years ago," McKay wrote, "the herd's ranks have swollen from 125,000 to 1,500,000 seals."

The recovery of northern fur seal populations was a remarkable achievement. Soon after the United States purchased Alaska in 1867 and assumed management of the fur seal herds on the Pribilof Islands, the federal government attempted to bring the hunt under control, but with little success. In the early 1890s, researchers on the fish commission's research vessel the *Albatross* investigated the decline in fur seal numbers. They concluded that the cause for the decline was not the hunt on the islands, but the wasteful killing of adult seals on the high seas by sealers on ships flying the flag of Great Britain.[12] Many of the seals killed at sea were not recovered.

Three years later, the United States and Great Britain concluded an agreement to bring pelagic sealing by their citizens under control, but some British and U.S. sealers changed the country under which they registered their vessels to evade the treaty's restrictions. Pelagic sealing became even more profitable as declining supplies of fur seal hides drove prices up.

In December 1908, when the BCF was given responsibility for management of the northern fur seal fishery, the agency characterized it as "little less than a national disgrace."[13] As the fur seal rookeries on the Pribilof Islands declined, the U.S. government pressed for an agreement among the four sealing countries. In 1911, Great Britain, Japan, Russia, and the United States finalized the Treaty for the Preservation and Protection of Fur Seals. The treaty included a ban on pelagic sealing and authorized a supervised hunt on the islands. By requiring that all members of the treaty share in the profits from the island hunt, the fur seal treaty encouraged compliance with the ban on pelagic sealing.

The treaty included no criteria for determining quotas. As a practical matter, quotas were set at levels considered to be maximum sustainable yield (MSY). The United States, which was responsible for overseeing the landside hunt, could ban hunting in a year if it compensated the other parties to the treaty, or if the population of fur seals had fallen below 100,000 animals. As the population returned to its size at the time the United States gained control of the Pribilof Islands in 1867, the federal government restricted the hunt largely to avoid a glut on the market that would have driven prices down.

Economics were a key concern for federal managers of the hunt, partly because the hunt generated revenue beyond its costs. The federal government, and later the state of Alaska, received a share of the profits from the sale of the furs at biennial public auctions. Between 1867, when the United States took possession of the islands, and 1945, the sale of fur seal skins netted the U.S. government $20 million. In 1959, federal proceeds reached a post–World War II peak of $3.3 million out of total sales of $4.9 million. Small revenues were also generated through the sale of other products. The seals' carcasses were converted to meal and oil until 1963, when 85,354 fur seal carcasses yielded 300,000 pounds of meal and 22,000 gallons of oil. After 1965, northern fur seal carcasses were processed into frozen meat, principally for use on mink farms. In the peak year of 1968, nearly two million pounds of frozen fur seal meat were produced.

By the late 1960s, the fur seal hunt and other similar hunts in Canada and other countries came under attack as being brutal and inhumane. At the same time that animal protection groups were increasing their campaign to end the fur seal hunt on humane grounds, the much-vaunted scientific management of the fur seal herd was beginning to show its shortcomings. Fundamental to the BCF's management of the herd was its presumed ability to determine what size population would produce the most surplus fur seals—the population's MSY.

This mathematical exercise was confounded by a number of factors, some of which were of the bureau's own creation. For example, MSY calculations required a number of generous assumptions, such as that the ocean environment of the seals was stable over long periods—which it was not. Furthermore, the BCF did not consider how the population dynamics of fur seals might be influenced by other species and activities other than the hunt, such as a burgeoning fishery for groundfish in Alaskan waters. Indeed, the North Pacific Fur Seal Commission and the federal government appeared more concerned that a large population of northern fur seals might reduce commercially valuable fish populations: The larger the fur seal population, the less the fish that fishermen might catch. The bureau also did not aim at calculating simply the number of surplus fur seals, but rather the number of surplus fur seals "that have the highest quality skins"—males three to four years of age.

Finally, the agency assumed that it could use pup counts on the islands to accurately estimate the size of the entire herd. These counts, however, proved to be an imperfect indicator of overall numbers. In 1949, for example, the BCF estimated that the fur seal population had grown to 3.8 million animals. In contrast, the NMFS concluded in the late 1980s that the population had never exceeded 2.2 million animals—1.6 million animals less than the peak estimated by the agency in 1949.

Combined with years of high pup mortality, these large estimates engendered the belief that there were too many northern fur seals, for the good of the fur seals themselves and other living marine resources. In 1956, the BCF broke with its tradition of killing only juvenile males, for which skins were more easily marketed, and called for killing females to reduce the population of fur seals. By 1962, 151,254 female fur seals had been killed on the Pribilof Islands, and the harvest of females appeared to be having the desired effect. In 1964, the BCF declared its program to reduce the fur seal population successful. The killing of females, however, continued until the early 1970s, partly to supply the market for less desirable female skins that the agency and its contractors had created.

These adjustments in management tactics, which reflected traditional views of marine wildlife as commodities, did nothing to calm the growing controversy over government sponsorship of a seal hunt that relied upon the clubbing of animals. By the late 1960s, animal rights activists had succeeded in raising questions in Congress about whether the fur seal hunt represented the kind of policy the United States should pursue regarding marine mammals. This controversy would combine with others to generate the political support that would later lead to the MMPA.

The Marine Mammal Protection Act

> The lifestyle they describe is about as idyllic as anyone could wish. The dolphin herd seems to be a kind of seagoing commune. The animals spend their days in uninhibited sex play, relatively effortless food gathering, and exuberant games. They have no significant natural enemies. But in the last few years, a predator has arisen like no other in nature. It kills not for food nor [sic] sport. The dolphins die because they are in the way, an inconvenience, a worthless byproduct.[14]

With a bow to the ethos of the aquarian age in the mid-1970s, Dick Cavett thus introduced viewers of the television special *Last Days of the Dolphins?* to the drowning of dolphins in purse seine nets that were set for yellowfin tuna in the eastern tropical Pacific Ocean. In the late 1960s, Ken Norris had learned of dead dolphins in the holds of American tuna purse seine vessels returning to San Diego. Norris assigned a graduate student, Bill Perrin, to investigate. Soon, Perrin had gathered evidence that dolphins were dying by the hundreds of thousands each year in the U.S. tuna fishery. In the Pacific Ocean off South America, U.S. tuna fishermen located schools of tuna by pursuing those of dolphins that swam above. Fishermen would then encircle tuna with purse seine nets, trapping thousands of dolphins at a time. Since fishermen had no interest in marketing dolphin, the animals were routinely discarded, dead or dying.

Once Perrin's observations became known, outrage over the drowning of dolphins mushroomed, as scientists questioned the impacts of the fishery on wildlife populations and many Americans questioned the ethics of drowning animals as intelligent and social as dolphins. Neither the NMFS nor tuna industry representatives ever publicly expressed any serious ethical doubts about incidentally drowning dolphins in tuna nets.

Together with commercial whaling and the fur seal hunt, the drowning of dolphins in tuna nets provided the fuel that drove the controversy over management and preservation of marine mammals to so quick a resolution in Congress. "The result was a fair amount of pressure and passage of legislation earlier than what one might have anticipated," says Frank Potter. "Usually, when you start talking about creating a piece of legislation, the gestation period is two or three Congresses. And the MMPA [took] only two. We had hearings late in one Congress, and passed it the next year."

In March 1971, Senator Fred Harris (D–OK) and Representative David Pryor (D–AR) introduced the Ocean Mammal Protection Act. The bill, which called for a virtual ban on killing marine mammals and on importing marine mammal products, was the latest attempt by animal protection groups to bring an end to the northern fur seal hunt, commercial whaling, and the drowning of dolphins in tuna nets. Political momentum was in their favor. At a time when environmental awareness was growing by leaps and bounds, marine mammals epitomized the abuse of the natural world in many people's minds. Members of Congress reported that they were receiving more mail on marine mammals than on any other issue, with the exception of the war in Vietnam. At a hearing on marine mammal protection in September 1971, Congressman Edward Garmatz (D–MA) said, "During my 24 years as a member of Congress, I have never before experienced the volume of mail I have been receiving on the subject of ocean mammals."[15]

Whatever support marine mammal protection enjoyed among the general public, the Harris-Pryor bill's proposed moratorium on domestic capture of marine mammals hit a raw nerve among wildlife managers and scientists. "That's what raised the alarm signal among a lot of the management community," says Dr. Carleton Ray, who became heavily involved in fashioning what became the MMPA of 1972. "What led to the great divisions of the time was when one person actually testified that she didn't want management, but conservation. 'Let's just stop: no research, no nothing. Let's just don't touch whales.'"

The wildlife management community quickly mobilized to defend values that themselves had once been considered radical: scientific management that aimed at producing a sustained yield of wildlife. Organizations from the National Rifle Association, the Wildlife Management Institute to the National Audubon Society, and the World Wildlife Fund formed a coalition to oppose the Harris–Pryor bill. Leading scientists, who embraced MSY even as they searched for ways of including ecological considerations, attacked the bill as unscientific. Although other scientists argued that marine mammals could not be managed for sustainable yield, traditionalists had the advantage of support in state and federal agencies, including the NMFS and the U.S. Fish and Wildlife Service.

The wildlife management community's supporters in Congress responded with a bill called the Ocean Mammal Management Act. Introduced by Congressman Glenn Anderson (D–CA), the bill called for setting limits on killing marine mammals "to insure that such species . . . can be managed on a sustainable yield basis." Reflecting the interests of the tuna industry in Congressman Anderson's district, the bill exempted the tuna fleet from the bill's restrictions.

With the support of Congressman John Dingell (D–MI), the committee's chairperson, the Anderson bill sailed through the Merchant Marine Fisheries Committee and appeared headed for easy passage on the floor of the House of Representatives in December 1971. The bill's supporters, however, had not considered the ability of animal protection groups to mobilize public opinion. Just days before the floor vote, Lewis Regenstein of the Friends of Animals again engineered editorials in the *Washington Post* and the *New York Times* lambasting the Anderson bill. The bill went down in defeat.

The defeat fractured the coalition that had formed in defense of traditional ideas about scientific management of wildlife. Dingell decided to support some form of moratorium on taking marine mammals, rather than rely on traditional management for sustainable yield. In 1972, Dingell introduced a bill that later became the MMPA of 1972. This bill included features that broke entirely new ground in wildlife management and conservation. Some of these new ideas had been discussed in the previous year, but had not survived the pitched battle between management and preservation.

As the debate over marine mammals resumed in 1972, these new concepts gained support. Some of the principal advocates for these new approaches served in senior positions within the Nixon administration. In joining the staff of the President's Council on Environmental Quality in 1971, Lee Talbot had received approval from Russell Train, the council's first executive director, to pursue putting the management of living marine resources, and other wildlife, on an ecosystem basis.

"Right at that time, John Ehrlichman and John Whittaker in the White House were looking for additional environmental issues which would give the president a political boost," says Talbot. "I had the marine mammal business and I proposed that to them, and they agreed." By working directly with Frank Potter, Talbot was able to promote his ideas without the involvement of the NMFS and the U.S. Fish and Wildlife Service, both of which were strongly opposed to any new legislation that might change their management prerogatives.

The House of Representatives soon passed a new bill that included a five-year moratorium on killing marine mammals. The House bill encountered opposition in the Senate where some senators argued that marine mammals would overpopulate and starve if their populations were not cropped. By the fall, however, both houses of Congress passed the MMPA, in which the mix of management and protection was a disappointment to traditional wildlife managers and animal protectionists.

Like the Endangered Species Act, the MMPA prohibited a range of activities that fell under the general definition of a "taking." The MMPA defined taking as meaning "to harass, hunt, capture, or kill" any marine mammal or attempting to do so. Congress did not define the term harass, which was a new concept in wildlife management. In practice, it came to refer to a wide range of activities that adversely affected marine mammals by triggering changes in their behavior. Animal rights activists objected to the exceptions, while wildlife managers and some scientists objected to the moratorium.

"That was a complete reversal of natural resource policy practice up to that point," says Dr. William W. Fox Jr., who served in several positions at the NMFS, including director. "Traditional practice was to allow fishing to occur unless scientists could prove that it was harming fish populations."

Besides the tension between preservation and management, the framers of the MMPA had to resolve the longstanding conflict between states rights and national standards. On one hand, the federal government had traditionally deferred to the states in the management of wildlife within their borders. Furthermore, state fish and wildlife agencies vigorously protected their prerogatives whenever the federal government appeared about to compromise them. On the other hand, the federal government had a national interest in ensuring the conservation of wildlife. As a matter of fact, few states had meaningful programs for the conservation of marine mammals or other marine wildlife.

"I certainly understood and believed that the marine mammal act was essentially a mechanism to stop the uncontrolled taking, hunting of these species, and set up a system whereby the states would manage them," says Bohlen. "We all assumed that once the state met the conditions laid out in the bill, they would then take over management. We never contemplated that the feds would remain the managers. The feds would just establish standards by which these species would be managed."

In the end, Congress decided to preempt state authority in the management of marine mammals, unless it met certain conditions. Within a year, the state of Alaska applied to the secretary of commerce for return of management authority over northern sea lions (*Eumetopia jabatus*), beluga whales (*Delphinapterus leucas*), harbor seals (*Phoca vitulina*), spotted seals (*P. largha*), ringed seals (*Phoca hispida*), and bearded seals (*Erignathus barbatus*). At the same time, the state

applied to the secretary of the interior to return management authority for walrus (*Mirounga angustirostris*), sea otters (*Enhydra lutris*), and polar bears (*Ursus
maritimus*).

In 1975, the Department of the Interior returned management of walrus to
Alaska, while the state's request to manage the other nine species was being considered. After lengthy hearings, an administrative law judge concluded in June
1977 that the state's proposal to the Department of Commerce met the requirements of the MMPA.

It appeared as if the state of Alaska would soon be managing several of its
major marine mammal populations, thereby vindicating the mechanism that
Congress had fashioned for maintaining state–federal relations; however, litigation by Alaska natives based upon another provision of the MMPA champi-
oned by the Alaska congressional delegation derailed the process. In *People of
Togiak* v. *United States,* Alaska natives successfully argued that in returning management of Pacific walrus to the state, the federal government had approved
state management of subsistence hunting. A federal court agreed that this approval violated the MMPA's exemption for Alaska natives' hunting of marine
mammals for subsistence and handicrafts. The state of Alaska responded by
dropping its request for management of walrus and the other nine species.[16]

In 1981, Congress attempted to resolve the conflicts that had prevented the
return of management authority to Alaska by amending the MMPA. Congress
overturned the court's decision and allowed the state to manage hunts by Alaska
natives if the state otherwise qualified for the return of management authority. Other provisions of the amended MMPA were a mixed bag for Alaska and
other states. For example, once a state successfully demonstrated that its program was consistent with the MMPA, it still would have to make the same difficult determinations as the federal government had to make before allowing
the taking of any marine mammals. Furthermore, the federal government would
continue to regulate incidental taking in fisheries and the use of marine mammals for research and public display.

Although California, Oregon, and Washington each took tentative steps toward requesting return of management authority for marine mammals in the
1980s, no other state actually did so after Alaska's 1975 request. As marine mammal populations expanded under the act's protections, and as conflicts with fishermen, other protected species, and coastal residents grew, the lure of champi-
oning states rights and managing marine mammals faded.

"I think after a point some of the states were happy enough not to have to
deal with these problems," says Bohlen.

Rather than leaving implementation entirely to the agencies, as it did with the

ESA, Congress established a Marine Mammal Commission to serve as a watch-dog over implementation of the MMPA. The commission was composed of three commissioners appointed by the president, a committee of scientific advisors, and a small professional staff. In carrying out their responsibilities, such as granting exceptions to the moratorium on taking, the agencies were to consult with the commission. If the agency did not accept the recommendations of the commission, the agency was to explain its reasons for doing so. Largely because of the stature of the commissioners as well as the professionalism and dedication of its staff, the commission came to play a crucial role in implementation of the MMPA by the agencies. Often, the commission had to prod the agencies to implement the MMPA rather than continue their traditional programs.

For the NMFS, the requirements of the MMPA and the ESA demanded a dramatic change in behavior and orientation toward commercial fisheries in particular. Rather than promoting and assisting in the development of fisheries and the fishing industry, the agency found itself having to manage the impact of fishing on marine mammals and other species of little or no commercial value. Besides having little experience in managing domestic fisheries, the agency chafed at applying the new standards of the MMPA, since these placed the agency at odds with the commercial fishing industry. In this way, the MMPA and the ESA initiated a change in the relationship between the federal government and the commercial fishing industry that passage of the Magnuson-Stevens Act would complete.

"The 1950s and 1960s were the glory days," says Spencer Garrett, who began his career at the BCF in 1965. "Once we became a regulatory agency, we had no friends."

Summary

Early optimism about ending the damage from water pollution was overcome by the introduction of hundreds of new chemicals and the growth of coastal activities in the 1950s. Research by Fish and Wildlife Service biologists in the 1940s and 1950s demonstrated the harmful effects of some chemicals such as DDT, but the agency never had sufficient funding to screen even a small fraction of the chemicals introduced each year.

By the 1960s, government leaders at all levels were calling for a campaign against marine pollution, as coastal water quality declined and concerns about the healthfulness of seafood grew. In 1972, Congress passed several pieces of legislation aimed at attacking the growing pollution problem. These included the Clean Water Act, the Ocean Dumping Act, and the Coastal Zone Man-

agement Act. Although consulted by the agencies responsible for the implementation of these laws, the National Marine Fisheries Service (NMFS) had
little influence on government policy regarding marine pollution.

In the late 1960s, animal rights activists outraged at the killing of marine
mammals introduced new values into debates over the uses of marine wildlife.
For the most part, federal wildlife agencies and the scientific community rejected these new values and promoted scientific management of wildlife populations. Within a remarkably short time, Congress responded to the controversy over marine mammals by passing the Marine Mammal Protection Act
(MMPA). Passage of the MMPA was driven by controversies over several key
issues. In the late 1960s, the commercial hunt of fur seals on the Pribilof Islands provoked criticism from animal rights organizations that the hunt was
inhumane. The federal government and the scientific community largely rejected the criticism and pointed to the management of the fur seal herd as a
model for the management of other wildlife populations. The drowning of dolphins in tuna nets also provoked widespread public outrage.

Initially, the campaign for protection of marine mammals was blunted by
opposition from traditional wildlife managers and the scientific community;
however, after animal rights groups blocked a weaker bill, several key members of Congress and the Nixon administration began supporting alternative
legislation that later became the MMPA.

Among other innovative features, the MMPA imposed a moratorium on the
"taking" of marine mammals that could be lifted only if the taking was shown
not to harm a population of marine mammals. The MMPA also placed the conservation of marine mammals within a broader goal of maintaining the diversity and productivity of entire ecosystems. Congress also placed responsibility
for conservation of marine mammals on the federal government, preempting
state authority over the management of marine mammals. A mechanism for returning management authority to the states was never successfully used.

By investing the NMFS with the responsibility for conserving marine mammals, Congress placed the agency at odds with its traditional partners in the
fishing industry.

Notes

1. U.S. Department of the Interior. 1945. *Annual Report of the Secretary of the Interior:
   Fiscal Year Ended June 30, 1945.* United States Government Printing Office, Washington, D.C.

2. Ibid.
3. U.S. Department of the Interior. 1958. *Annual Report of the Secretary of the Interior: Fiscal Year Ended June 30, 1958.* United States Government Printing Office, Washington, D.C.
4. U.S. Department of the Interior. 1966. "The Population Challenge . . . What It Means to America." *United States Department of the Interior Conservation Yearbook No. 2.* U.S. Government Printing Office, Washington, D.C.
5. Quoted in Anonymous. July 1971. "NFI Weighs Crippling Contamination Crisis." *National Fisherman.* Page 20A.
6. The *Torrey Canyon* was a 118,000-ton oil tanker that struck a reef in the English Channel on March 18, 1967, spilling 860,000 barrels of crude oil. Much of the oil washed onto the beaches of southern England and killed large numbers of shorebirds and other marine wildlife. At the time, the spill was the largest in history.
7. U.S. Department of the Interior. 1972. *River of Life, Water: The Environmental Challenge.* U.S. Government Printing Office, Washington, D.C.
8. Quoted in Wenk, Edward Jr. 1972. *The Politics of the Ocean.* University of Washington Press, Seattle.
9. Quoted in Regenstein, Lewis. 1975. *The Politics of Extinction.* Macmillan Publishing Co., New York, NY.
10. National Marine Fisheries Service. 1973. *Report of the National Marine Fisheries Service for Calendar Years 1970 and 1971.* NMFS, Seattle, WA.
11. U.S. Department of the Interior. 1954. *Annual Report of the Secretary of the Interior: Fiscal Year Ended June 30, 1954.* U.S. Government Printing Office, Washington, D.C.
12. As a rule, all types of vessels must register with a government. When a vessel registers with the government of a country, the vessel is said to "fly the flag" of that country. A vessel may fly the flag of a country other than the country in which its owners and operators reside.
13. Quoted in Cart, T. W. 1968. The Federal Fisheries Service, 1871–1940. A thesis submitted to the faculty of the University of North Carolina at Chapel Hill in partial fulfillment of the requirements for the degree of Master of Arts in the Department of History. 87 pages.
14. From Minasian, Stanley M. (Producer). 1975. "The Last Days of the Dolphins?" Save the Dolphin and Environmental Defense Fund. San Francisco, CA.
15. Quoted in Regenstein, Lewis G. December 1974. A History of the Endangered Species Act of 1973, and an Analysis of its History; Strengths and Weaknesses; Administration; and Probable Future Effectiveness. Master's Thesis. Emory University, Atlanta, GA.
16. The state concluded that its constitution prevented it from adopting management measures based on racial or ethnic concerns.

1982–1988   Beginning in 1981, the administration of President Ronald Reagan requested less than $100 million in appropriations—half the level allocated by Congress in the previous year. Congress rejected the proposed budget cuts. Between 1982 and 1988, the National Marine Fisheries Service (NMFS) budget grew from $149.2 to $165.2 million in nominal dollars, or about 10%. When adjusted for inflation, however, the NMFS budget declined by 21%. Nominal funding for several key NMFS functions decreased: fisheries management from $28.7 to $26.5 million; enforcement and surveillance from $9.6 to $7.1 million; and information analysis and dissemination from $21.4 to $17.7 million. Funding for developing resource information increased, from $40.3 to $72.4 million.

In 1987, the agency had 2,310 full-time staff. Of these, about two-thirds were associated with the research centers, 16% with regional offices, and the balance with headquarters in Washington, D.C. Shares of funding were similar in distribution.

The work of the agency was dominated by the review and implementation of fishery management plans and amendments. Between 1983 and 1988, the number of regulatory actions proposed and adopted by the NMFS grew from 175 to 360.

Chapter 8 | Agency Resistance

The successful campaigns for the Marine Mammal Protection Act (MMPA) and the Endangered Species Act (ESA) did not lead directly to changes in the behavior of the Commerce Department's National Marine Fisheries Service (NMFS). Instead, implementation of these laws' new approach came about largely as the result of lawsuits filed by environmental or animal protection groups, or by amendments to the original legislation. The slow progress was caused partly by inadequate funding, which reflected the low priority that protected-species programs enjoyed in the NMFS, its parent agency the National Oceanic and Atmospheric Administration (NOAA), the Department of Commerce, and Congress.

The language of many key provisions of the laws left considerable room for interpretation and discretion, creating opportunity for disputes over the application of the laws to specific situations. While the lack of precision in language sometimes reflected the difficulty of stating general rules about complex and diverse issues, imprecision in language was also a politically expedient means of shifting the burden of resolving controversial issues to the agency. In implementing the two laws, the NMFS risked creating conflict with its traditional clients, commercial and recreational fishermen, and of provoking intervention by Congress if the agency appeared to be sacrificing the short-term interests of these constituent groups. The citizen suit provisions, which enabled private citizens and organizations to compel implementation through the courts, provided the agency with another incentive not to enforce the two laws vigorously. By implementing the laws only when directed to do so by the courts, the agency avoided a direct confrontation with its traditional constituents and with their congressional supporters.

Commercial and Aboriginal Hunts

Rather than apply the moratorium and other standards of the MMPA to the northern fur seal hunt on the Pribilof Islands, Congress directed the Departments of State and Commerce to review whether the fur seal treaty was consistent with the MMPA. The two departments later issued a superficial three-page report that concluded the treaty and the MMPA were compatible. The hunt continued, as did the campaign to end it.

In the early 1980s, the campaign to end the hunt hit a fever pitch as organizations that had supported the hunt in the past joined animal protection groups in opposition. Many wildlife organizations had maintained their tacit support of the hunt because they did not share the concerns of animal protection groups over the hunt's methods. Also, they had accepted the government's argument that if the treaty were to expire, the Japanese would resume the much messier method of hunting fur seals on the high seas, where far more seals would be killed than would be recovered and kept. Furthermore, the argument went, fur seals would soon overpopulate the islands, leading to disease and starvation.

"In the early part of those years, we supported the Pribilof fur seal hunt because we had listened to the same rhetoric that everyone else listened to," says John Grandy, who was on the staff of the National Parks and Conservation Association in the early 1970s. "It's how Ronald Reagan changed the economy of this country: If you say it long enough, somebody may believe you." By the 1980s, when he was executive director of Defenders of Wildlife, Grandy reversed that organization's past support and came out strongly against the hunt.

As they responded to growing public concerns over the humaneness of the hunt, wildlife conservation organizations also reacted to growing evidence from the NMFS that the northern fur seal population was declining at an annual rate of 4 to 8%. The agency exonerated the continuing hunt on the Pribilofs, as well as the rapidly growing commercial catch of groundfish in the Bering Sea, as being causes for the decline. Instead, the service suggested that the population decrease was due partly to entanglement of fur seals in discarded fishing gear and to the harvests of females during the 1960s.

When Congress evaluated the commercial fur seal hunt in 1983, it so much as acknowledged that the hunt would soon end. In reauthorizing the Fur Seal Act, Congress established a $20 million trust fund to develop economic alternatives for the Aleuts who had been moved to the Pribilofs to conduct the hunt.

In 1984, the International Fund for Animal Welfare sued the Department of Commerce, claiming that allowing the hunt violated the standards of the

MMPA. The court dismissed the case, finding that while the population of fur seals was below levels allowed by the MMPA, the fur seal treaty allowed hunting to occur. In the same year, the Humane Society of the United States petitioned the NMFS to list the northern fur seal as threatened under the ESA. While the agency initially found that there was substantial information in support of the petition, it later rejected the petition.

In practical terms, the federal court's ruling and the agency's decision not to list northern fur seals as a threatened species mattered little. In 1984, opponents of the commercial fur seal hunt succeeded in bringing about its end by blocking Senate ratification of the Fur Seal Treaty's renewal.[1] To the end, the NMFS, the State Department, and other treaty supporters warned that rejection of the treaty would lead to wasteful pelagic sealing as well as disease and death among overpopulating fur seals. Contrary to the warnings, pelagic sealing did not resume. Nor did fur seals proliferate and become a danger to themselves. Indeed, in 1988, the NMFS designated the northern fur seal as depleted under the MMPA, since its population had fallen to less than half its size during the 1950s.

Both the MMPA and ESA also exempted the hunt of bowhead whales (*Balaena mysticetus*) and gray whales (*Eschrichtius robutus*) by Alaska natives. This exemption continued similar allowances under international treaties stretching back to the 1930s. Between the end of commercial whaling for bowheads in 1910 and 1969, Alaska natives landed an average of 12 bowhead whales each year, using traditional methods as well as technology borrowed from commercial whalers. While the U.S. government pursued a global moratorium on commercial whaling in the early 1970s, Alaskan Eskimos began expanding their hunt of bowhead whales. A booming economy, driven by petroleum production on the North Slope, enabled many more Alaska natives to purchase small motorboats for hunting bowheads.

At the request of the International Whaling Commission (IWC), the NMFS began monitoring the hunt and gathering information about bowheads in the early 1970s. Early counts suggested that the population was highly endangered and that the hunt was wasteful. An increase in the number of inexperienced whalers led to the loss of many whales once they were struck by harpoons.

In March 1974, a coalition of animal welfare groups called Project Monitor formally requested that the Department of Commerce protect bowhead whales. The petition argued that the Eskimos' hunt of bowheads violated provisions of the MMPA and ESA that prohibited wasteful taking of depleted species. The NMFS took no action.

During the 1976 hunt, Eskimo whalers lost nearly half of the 91 bowheads they struck with shoulder-held harpoon guns. At the June 1977 meeting of the IWC's scientific committee, NMFS biologists estimated that the bowhead population of the Beaufort Sea numbered about 1,300 animals. Concerns about the low abundance of bowheads deepened as reports reached the commission that Alaska Eskimos had harpooned as many as 108 bowheads in the 1977 hunt, but retrieved only 26. When the scientific committee recommended an end to the hunt, the U.S. delegation followed U.S. policy, which emphasized acceptance of recommendations by the scientific committee. As a result, Bill Aron, who was serving as U.S. commissioner, cast his vote with all other commissioners in support of the zero quota.

"We were surprised by the bowhead whale vote," says Richard Roe, who oversaw the NMFS's marine mammal and endangered species programs at the time. "We had been vociferous at the IWC for a moratorium on whaling. We had prohibited whaling in the United States, except for subsistence hunting in Alaska for bowheads and some gray whales. So we kept pounding the table at the IWC, looking particularly at the Japanese and the Soviets and the Norwegians, who were pounding the hell out of the big whales worldwide, no question about it."

"Out of the blue, at the 1977 meeting, the IWC passed a zero quota on bowhead whales. They said, 'Hey wait, you guys are telling us we need a moratorium on whaling and you're whaling up there on a highly endangered species.' We didn't know much about bowhead whales in those days," says Roe. "The population estimates were pretty pathetic. It looked like there [were] only a handful left."[2]

Reaction to the whaling commission's decision, and to the U.S. delegation's support of the zero quota, was swift. Angry Alaskan Eskimos sent a delegation to Washington, D.C., to secure the support of their congressional delegation. A battle between the Carter administration and the Alaska delegation over the allocation of public lands in Alaska to parks, wilderness, mining, logging, and Alaska natives gave North Slope Eskimos tremendous political leverage. Both the Carter administration and environmental groups such as the Sierra Club depended upon Alaska natives to counter the tendency of the Alaska delegation to support exploitation of the state's natural resources on a massive scale. In this political environment, the use of wildlife by Alaska natives took on added importance.

Within the NOAA, a debate raged whether to formally object to the zero quota and allow Eskimo whalers to continue hunting bowhead whales, or to accept the quota for the time being and to work within the whaling commission to raise it. In the face of protests by Robert Schoning, then director of the NMFS, the new administrator of the NOAA, Richard Frank, opted to accept the zero quota. Among other things, he reasoned, rejecting the commission's decision would undermine U.S. efforts to reduce quotas on other species and to secure an overall moratorium on whaling. Nonetheless, the zero quota could precipitate political disaster in U.S. government relations with the aboriginal peoples on whose stewardship the future of bowheads depended.

At a special meeting in December 1977, the whaling commission revisited its decision on bowheads. The U.S. delegation presented its management and research plan for bowheads and requested a 1978 quota of 15 bowheads landed or 30 struck, whichever occurred first. The commission agreed to a 1978 quota of 12 landed or 18 struck, whichever occurred first. Although Alaska Eskimo representatives stormed out of the meeting, the U.S. delegation believed they had averted a total rupture in relations with the Alaska native community.[3]

Over the next several years, the controversy over the bowhead whale hunt by Alaska natives subsided as the U.S. government and the IWC developed a regime for managing traditional subsistence whaling. At the same time, supporters of a moratorium on commercial whaling transformed the composition of the IWC, making its membership more open to a moratorium. In 1972, when the IWC first rejected the call for a moratorium made at the United Nations Conference on the Environment, 8 of the 14 member countries of the IWC conducted whaling. In 1980, only 10 of the 40 members sponsored whaling. Many of the new members had been recruited by conservation organizations that also worked closely with governments, such as the U.S. government, in generating support for a moratorium.

At the same time, scientists on the IWC's scientific committee found it increasingly difficult to apply the "new management procedure" that the IWC had adopted in 1974 as an alternative to a moratorium on all commercial whaling. Under the new procedure, populations of whales were classified based upon their level of abundance compared to the level that scientists calculated was necessary to produce maximum sustainable yield (MSY). Key information such as natural mortality rates and the pre-exploitation population size was lacking, more often than not. Together with the limitations of population models, the lack of information caused estimates to fluctuate widely from year to year. By the early 1980s, members of the scientific committee could not agree on how to classify most populations of whales, other than those that clearly deserved full protection.

Rather than leading to larger quotas, as might have happened in the past, the uncertainty over the status of many whale populations led the IWC to adopt lower quotas for many populations. The uncertainty also added to the momentum toward an indefinite moratorium on commercial whaling. In the United States, the end of commercial whaling attracted the support of the Reagan administration, for which environmental policies otherwise ran directly counter to those of the previous decade. The moratorium offered the Reagan administration one way of placating critics in Congress and in the conservation community and of claiming a victory that had eluded the previous three administrations.

At the 1982 meeting of the IWC, the necessary three-quarters of the members voted to approve the U.S. proposal for an indefinite moratorium on commercial whaling. Although several member countries continued whaling, catches were far below recent levels. The burden of proof had clearly shifted to those who wished to resume whaling.

Reluctant Implementation of Critical Habitat

Among the provisions of the ESA was that other agencies had to consult with the NMFS to ensure that their activities would not jeopardize the continued existence of listed marine species. This gave the NMFS considerable leverage in influencing a wide range of activities. Indeed, NMFS's early use of this new power led to several precedent-setting cases. For example, the agency's review of a proposed refinery in coastal Maine led to a finding that the risk of an oil spill from tankers servicing the refinery would jeopardize the continued existence of the critically endangered right whale (*Eubalaena glacialis*). A federal court later ruled that the Environmental Protection Agency had violated the ESA when it issued a permit for the refinery, despite NMFS's expert opinion.

For the most part, however, the NMFS only reluctantly implemented the ESA in the decade following its enactment. The agency's reluctance expressed itself partly in delays. For example, after the Interior Department proposed the listing of green (*Chelonia mydas*) and loggerhead (*Caretta caretta*) sea turtles in January 1973, more than five years passed before the NMFS actually listed the species. The agency did not list another species under the ESA until 1985, when it listed the Gulf of California harbor porpoise (*Phocoena sinus*) and the Guadalupe fur seal (*Arctocephalus townsendi*) in response to petitions by conservation organizations. The agency did not begin systematically surveying the status of vulnerable marine species until the 1990s.

Even when evidence was overwhelming, the agency rarely proposed listing species on its own. The decline of Snake River sockeye, for example, was an open secret, as dams were constructed on the lower stretches of the river from 1955 to 1975. In 1955, before the four dams on the lower Snake had been constructed, 4,361 sockeye salmon had been counted at Redfish Lake. After the 1975 completion of Lower Granite Dam, which effectively cut off sockeye salmon from upper reaches of the river, the number of sockeye declined precipitously. By 1981, just 218 sockeyes were counted at Lower Granite Dam, and in 1991, just 8 reached the base of the dam. In November 1991, the NMFS listed Snake River sockeye salmon as endangered—in response to a 1990 petition by the Shoshone and Bannock tribes.

The lackluster implementation of the ESA by the NMFS reflected several factors. First, the agency's mission of sustainable development of marine living resources was at odds with the mission of the Department of Commerce. In the debates over the ESA of 1973, conservationists had urged that endangered species activities remain with the Interior Department rather than being shared with the Commerce Department. "Interior is less likely to succumb to commercial pressures than Commerce," said Stephen Seater, a Defenders of Wildlife staff biologist, at a congressional hearing in 1973.[4]

Whether or not political pressure was exerted from upper levels of the Commerce Department, NMFS staff felt out of place in the department. "We found that the leadership in Commerce didn't have the foggiest idea about fisheries, or marine biology, or the critters, or anything we did," said Richard Roe. "We also found NOAA to be a not very friendly organization, either. The focus of NOAA was then and still is the physical sciences of the oceans and atmosphere, and the biological side of things was given short shrift in the early days," says Roe. "We were a stepchild. It's too bad, because looking back, if we had just worked closer with the oceanographers and the oceanographers with us, we would have found out a lot of things we don't now know. The critters and the environment are inseparable. But we took different pathways. We didn't capitalize on each other's expertise."

After the Magnuson-Stevens Act renewed the NMFS's role in expanding the domestic fishing industry, the agency's role as protector of marine mammals and endangered species was further marginalized. "There were some of us who thought there might be future conflicts with regard to our responsibilities for managing fisheries on the one hand and protecting endangered and threatened species on the other," says Eldon Greenberg, who served as general counsel in the NOAA during the Carter administration.

Without external pressure from the Marine Mammal Commission or conservation organizations, the NMFS generally subordinated the conservation of protected species to the development of commercial fisheries. The delays and half-measures that characterized the agency's approach to the conservation of Hawaiian monk seals is a case in point.

Hawaiian monk seals (*Monachus schauinslandi*) were found on and around the small, sparsely inhabited islands and atolls that stretch 1,200 miles northwest of Kauai. Extraordinarily docile, Hawaiian monk seals were easily hunted by shipwrecked sailors and commercial sealers in the nineteenth century. Although the last one of these animals was thought to have been killed in 1824, it turned out that the remoteness of the northwestern Hawaiian islands had provided refuge for small numbers. Gradually, the population rebuilt itself until it numbered around 3,000 animals in the 1950s when the first systematic surveys were undertaken. By the late 1970s, however, the population had declined again by half.

The decline in the population did not provoke action. "The service essentially described the Hawaiian monk seal as a relict species doomed to extinction and refused to do anything about it," says John Twiss, executive director of the Marine Mammal Commission until 2000. "And the service continued to refuse to do anything about it until I went and got Senator Inouye to earmark and put in their budget $500,000 for the Hawaiian monk seal."

In 1976, the NMFS listed the Hawaiian monk seal as endangered. Bowing to opposition from the state of Hawaii and commercial fishing interests, however, the agency did not designate critical habitat for the species at the same time. Critical habitat is essential to the conservation of a listed species. The designation of critical habitat alerts agencies to the dependence of a listed species on an area and thereby assists them in avoiding activities that could jeopardize the species' continued existence.

In December 1976, the Marine Mammal Commission recommended that the NMFS reconsider designating part of the range of the Hawaiian monk seal as critical habitat. More than a year later, as biologists began reporting dramatic declines in the number of seals on the islands, the agency began preparing an environmental impact statement to evaluate options for critical habitat designation. Soon after the agency issued its draft impact statement, however, it suspended further consideration of critical habitat until a team of experts could develop a recovery plan for the species.

While the agency broadened its review of critical habitat, it pressed ahead with a management plan for a new fishery in the very waters where Hawaiian monk seals feed. Developed in cooperation with the state of Hawaii and Sea Grant, the new fishery aimed at tapping unfished populations of spiny lobster

(*Panulirus marginatus*). In a review of the fishery management plan, protected species staff suggested that Hawaiian monk seals could be harmed by entanglement and depletion of food resources. But rather than adopting measures to address these concerns, the NMFS simply pointed to the new recovery plan for Hawaiian monk seals as sufficient safeguard. Despite mounting criticism by conservationists, the agency approved the fishery management plan in March 1983.

With the completion of the recovery plan in 1983, the NMFS returned to considering critical habitat. Staff biologists in Hawaii, as well as the monk seal recovery team, recommended that critical habitat extend out to 20 fathoms around the islands used by the seals. The recommendation was based partly upon observation of 5,000 dives by male monk seals off one of the islands. In about half of these dives, the seals descended to depths greater than 20 fathoms.

When the biologists' recommendation reached the regional office, however, the regional director, Charles Fullerton, rejected it. Thus, when the NMFS proposed the designation of critical habitat for Hawaiian monk seals, it did not include water deeper than 10 fathoms. Despite the recommendation of its own recovery team and the Marine Mammal Commission, the agency argued that deeper waters were not in need of special management and therefore were not deserving of designation as critical habitat.

When the NMFS failed to finalize the designation within 12 months as required by the ESA, Greenpeace International and the Sierra Club Legal Defense Fund filed suit in federal court. In April 1986, the agency responded and finalized the designation of critical habitat—ten years after it was first recommended by the Marine Mammal Commission. Only continued litigation forced the agency to expand the boundary to 20 fathoms in May 1988. By that time, the population of Hawaiian monk seals at French Frigate Shoals, the species' largest grouping, had begun declining again. The most dramatic decrease was among juvenile monk seals for which rate of survival had plummeted from between 80 and 90% to just 15%. Many young seals appeared starved, and females at French Frigate Shoals were thinner and smaller than females at other rookeries.

Both the NMFS and the Western Pacific Fishery Management Council dismissed a request from the Marine Mammal Commission to close the spiny lobster fishery around French Frigate Shoals. Quite contrary to its public pronouncements in support of precautionary management, the agency claimed that such measures were not justified, since there was no proof, the agency argued, that spiny lobster were important prey for Hawaiian monk seals. The agency also insisted there was no proof that fishing had caused the decline.[5]

The Conflict over the Tuna Fishery

In the late 1960s, the public uproar over the drowning of hundreds of thousands of dolphins in tuna nets sent the industry and the NMFS scrambling for technological solutions that would allow the fishery to continue. Several vessel owners developed gear and fishing practices that held out hope for greatly reducing the dolphin kill without sacrificing tuna catch. In 1972, the service had established "Operation Porpoise Lifeline," a program of research on gear to reduce dolphin deaths. Assured by the NMFS and the industry that a technological solution was imminent, Congress gave the industry a two-year grace period before it had to meet the MMPA's goal of reducing incidental capture to "insignificant levels approaching zero mortality and serious injury rate."[6]

The grace period came and went with little progress in reducing the drowning of dolphins. The NMFS seemed more intent on continuing its role as the industry's friend than in implementing the act. "The Marine Mammal Protection Act of 1972 really put the agency in a box," says Richard Roe. "We were supposed to curtail the dolphin catch in the tuna fishery, [and] yet on the other hand, we were supposed to be helping that fishery catch yellowfin tuna."

"The National Marine Fisheries Service was responding very negatively," says John Twiss. "It was clear that the upper levels of the service viewed the Marine Mammal Protection Act as a gross imposition on them," said Twiss, "and did not see anything good about it. They sought to thwart its implementation at every turn imaginable. Nowhere could it have been more apparent than with the tuna–porpoise issue. The National Marine Fisheries Service was basically covering up the problem. But they couldn't really cover up the problem because it was too obvious to everyone."

As the 1975 fishing season neared, the NMFS issued regulations regarding the capture of dolphins in the tuna fishery. Although the agency had adopted several recommendations from conservation and animal protection organizations, it did not set a limit on the number of dolphins the tuna fishery could capture and drown. On October 4, 1974, the Committee for Humane Legislation filed suit in federal court to block issuance of general permits to the tuna fleet that would allow them to incidentally catch and drown dolphins. The committee claimed that the regulations violated the MMPA.

When federal attorneys responded by challenging the group's standing to sue under the act, the Environmental Defense Fund successfully intervened against the government's claim. Richard E. Gutting Jr., the Environmental Defense Fund's attorney, noted that the court's favorable ruling was "the first judicial recognition of the right of environmental groups to bring lawsuits under the Marine Mammal Protection Act of 1972."[7] The citizen-suit provisions of the MMPA, together with similar provisions in other legislation from the same period, fundamentally changed the implementation of federal wildlife law. Previously, enforcement of federal wildlife law had been entirely in the hands of government agencies. The citizen-suit provisions, on the other hand, empowered private interests to enforce the law, whether they were conservation or industry interests.

In 1975 and 1976, animal protection and environmental groups pursued their campaign of litigation to force declining quotas of dolphin kills on the tuna fleet. On May 11, 1976, Judge Charles R. Richey agreed that the NMFS had violated the MMPA by issuing permits to the tuna fleet, and ordered that dolphin kills be banned beginning at the end of the month. The NMFS appealed and announced that it was setting a quota of 78,000 dolphin kills for the rest of 1976. The service also promised to place observers on tuna vessels to monitor the catches and to begin determining the optimum sustainable population (OSP) levels for the various dolphin populations captured in the fishery. While the Court of Appeals upheld Richey's ruling, it suspended the ban through the rest of the year in order to avoid economic impacts on the tuna fleet.

When the ban went back into effect in January 1977, the Court of Appeals confirmed that the tuna fleet could not capture dolphins until the NMFS had determined the OSP for each dolphin population and issued new regulations and a new permit to the American Tunaboat Association. OSP was an entirely new concept for measuring the health of wildlife populations. Rather than aiming at a specific level that would produce the maximum number of new animals, as embodied in MSY, OSP was a range. The upper bound was the largest number of animals that an ecosystem could support, while the lower limit was the number of animals that produced the greatest annual increase in the population. Any population that fell below the lower limit was to be classified as depleted and subject to additional protection. Using results from an international workshop of experts, the agency prepared estimates of dolphin population levels, and concluded that one population, the eastern spinner dolphin (*Stenella longirostris orientalis*), was depleted. While setting a quota of 62,000 dolphin kills for 1977, the agency prohibited all but truly accidental captures of eastern spinner dolphins.

In December 1977, after administrative hearings and the issuance of environmental impact statements—processes that were foreign to the agency and its industry constituents—the NMFS established declining quotas for the years

1978–1980. Although it had argued during congressional debates in 1972 that it would soon solve the tuna–dolphin problem, the tuna industry pressed for a 1978 quota of 96,000 dolphins, 18,000 more than the previous year's quota. The NMFS proposed a quota of 29,000, and the Environmental Defense Fund, representing a coalition of environmental and animal protection organizations, proposed a quota of 53,000. It was surprising that environmental organizations proposed a higher quota than the NMFS, but these groups were concerned that dramatic quota reductions would produce a backlash against the MMPA in Congress. Under the scheme finally adopted by the agency, no more than 31,150 dolphins were to be captured, much less killed, by the U.S. tuna fishery in the eastern tropical Pacific Ocean during 1980. This level was less than one-tenth the number caught in purse seine nets during 1972.

As a matter of fact, the U.S. tuna fleet caught only half the allowed number of dolphins in 1980. One reason for this dramatic decline in bycatch of dolphins was the presence of observers on some or all U.S. tuna vessels. Among other things, observers were able to monitor the catch and mortality of different species of dolphins, the performance of individual boat captains and crews, and to eliminate the bias normally found in self-reporting. In 1981, however, the U.S. tuna fleet challenged the legality of placing observers on tuna vessels. After enjoying initial success in the courts, the industry's claims were ultimately rejected in appeals that reached the Supreme Court.

Continuing agitation by conservation and animal rights organizations as well as intervention by Congress all but ended the drowning of dolphins in the nets of U.S. tuna fishermen. The use of dolphin-saving fishing techniques contributed to the decline in incidental capture of dolphins by U.S. fishermen. The larger reason for the decline, however, was that the U.S. fleet moved its operations to the western Pacific where tuna fishermen could not exploit the close association between dolphins in tuna found in the eastern Pacific. As the U.S. tuna fleet ceased delivering its catches to the mainland United States, major canneries in San Diego and San Pedro, California, shut down, as canners also shifted their operations to the western Pacific.

The fleets of other countries filled the gap left by the U.S. fleet. In the mid-1980s, the incidental kill of dolphins in the tuna fishery of the eastern Pacific increased dramatically. These high levels declined as foreign tuna fishermen learned the dolphin-saving techniques that had been perfected by U.S. fishermen and as access to the U.S. canned tuna market required catching tuna without catching dolphins.

Chapter 8. Agency Resistance 145

What Are You Fishing For?

The whistles and cheers of 5,000 shrimp fishermen and their families filled the convention center in Thibodaux, Louisiana, as Governor Edwin Edwards approached the microphone on a spotlit stage. Applause gave way to silence. The governor began: "If it comes between shrimpers and sea turtles . . . bye-bye turtles!"[8]

The bleachers shook beneath thousands of feet beating in agreement. The governor paused, then dared the federal government to require shrimp fishermen to install turtle excluder devices (TEDs) in their nets.[9] "The same federal government that has tried to put me in jail is trying to make you pull these turtle exclusion devices." Hoots and guffaws swept through the cavernous hall.

The size and responses of the crowd were a measure of the importance of shrimp fishing in coastal Louisiana and the fear and anger that TED regulations inspired, not to mention the oratorical panache of the governor. Facing a lawsuit by environmental organizations, the NMFS was reluctantly proposing the use of TEDs in order to end the bycatch and drowning of thousands of sea turtles listed as threatened or endangered under the ESA, but many shrimp fishermen from North Carolina to Texas didn't buy the solution because they didn't buy the problem. Shrimp fishermen refused to believe that the infrequent capture of sea turtles by individual fishermen could lead to the drowning of 11,000 sea turtles annually, as federal scientists and conservationists claimed.[10]

The controversy over sea turtle conservation and shrimp fishing had been simmering for many years before the May 1987 convocation in Thibodaux. In 1973, leading scientists concluded that shrimp trawling was the principal threat facing the critically endangered Kemp's ridley sea turtle (*Lepidochelys kempii*). In later years, shrimp trawling was implicated in the decline of other species, most notably loggerhead sea turtles (*Caretta caretta*).

In 1978, the NMFS began a program to design and test devices that would reduce the capture of sea turtles. Within several years, NMFS gear specialists had developed a TED design that, the agency claimed, reduced the capture of sea turtles by 97% without significant loss of shrimp catch; however, all but a few fishermen resisted using TEDs designed by the agency's gear specialists, even when the devices were offered at no cost. Besides objecting to the size of the device, fishermen complained that TEDs would inevitably reduce shrimp catch. Their concern over any loss in shrimp catch reflected the uneconomic status of the overcapitalized shrimp fleet. During the late 1970s and 1980s, both the size of the shrimp fleet and the volume of imported shrimp had grown greatly, reducing catches, prices, and income for most fishermen.

For their part, environmentalists had hoped that TEDs would prove to be an acceptable solution to the conflict between shrimp fishing and the survival of sea turtles. The alternatives were unworkable. Closing areas critical to sea turtles, for example, would have affected very large areas and hundreds, even thousands of shrimp fishermen. On the other hand, the TED developed by the NMFS nearly eliminated the catch of sea turtles without reducing shrimp catches greatly. Environmentalists initially accepted the NMFS view that with some promotion, fishermen would voluntarily use TEDs.

Late in 1985, after concluding that the promotion of voluntary TED use was futile, environmentalists began pressing the NMFS to require the use of TEDs in order to comply with the ESA. The NMFS rejected the request, urging an expanded program of TED promotion instead of regulation. Environmental organizations then turned to the Magnuson Fishery Conservation and Management Act and the Gulf of Mexico Fishery Management Council to achieve their goals. The Gulf of Mexico's fishery management plan for shrimp, adopted in 1981, encouraged the development of fishing gear to reduce the capture of sea turtles.

Representing several other environmental groups, the Center for Environmental Education (later the Center for Marine Conservation and now The Ocean Conservancy) appeared before the Gulf council in March 1986. Arguing that the fishery management plan's requirement for the development of fishing gear had been met, the environmental organization insisted that the council must require the use of TEDs in order to comply with the ESA. The U.S. Fish and Wildlife Service, which held a nonvoting seat on the Gulf of Mexico regional council, also requested that the council require the use of TEDs under its fishery management plan for shrimp.

Although it was the bycatch of sea turtles that had led the Center for Environmental Education to involve itself in the fishery management process, the center took on the bycatch of finfish and other marine life as well. In catching more than 125,000 metric tons of shrimp each year, shrimp fishermen also caught and discarded hundreds of thousands of metric tons of finfish and marine life. The bycatch of some species threatened other fisheries in the Gulf, such as commercial and recreational fisheries for red snapper (*Lutjanus campechanus*). In its fishery management plan for shrimp, the Gulf council acknowledged the problem of finfish bycatch and called for reducing it "when appropriate," expecting that gear research by the NMFS would lead to a technological solution.

At the time, available research indicated that 80–90% of the catch in shrimp trawls was bycatch composed of juvenile finfish, jellyfish, skates, and sea turtles. Most of the bycatch was discarded dead or dying because it was of a species or size that had no market. Although later research found lower levels of bycatch, shrimp remained a minor part of the catch in shrimp trawls. In its request to the council, the center argued that requiring TEDs would address this longstanding problem as well, since the most recent TED designs reduced finfish bycatch by half.

When the NMFS and the Gulf of Mexico Fishery Management Council rejected these requests in the summer of 1986, environmental organizations threatened to compel the use of TEDs through the courts. In a last-ditch effort to avoid open conflict, conservation organizations agreed to enter mediated discussions with the leading shrimp fishing organizations. The talks nearly foundered when representatives of the shrimp fleet and the NMFS refused to address the bycatch of finfish. Environmental representatives agreed to set aside the problem of finfish bycatch for the time being.

After 14 days of negotiations, the groups reached an agreement for phasing in the use of TEDs, which all but one industry representative signed. As the NMFS began developing regulations to implement the agreement under the ESA, however, opposition built among shrimp fishermen, particularly in the Gulf of Mexico. After 17 raucous public hearings in the spring of 1987, the NMFS published final regulations requiring TEDs in some areas at some times. Lawsuits and congressional intervention as well as vacillation by the Bush administration delayed the actual use of TEDs, but by 1994, TEDs were required in all shrimp trawls from North Carolina to Texas.

As ambitious as the TED regulations were, they did not address the bycatch and discard of finfish and other marine life. The agreement negotiated between environmental and industry representatives allowed the use of other devices than TEDs if they were proven to reduce sea turtle captures by 97%. The regulations did not require reductions in finfish bycatch, although some designs later approved by the NMFS did reduce bycatch somewhat.

The failure to address the bycatch of finfish in the shrimp fishery only increased concerns among several environmental organizations for which previous programs had centered on marine mammals and other "charismatic megafauna." Although shrimp trawl bycatch did not threaten the existence of any finfish species, the discard of so much marine life raised questions about fisheries management under the Magnuson-Stevens Act. Roger McManus, who was president of the Center for Marine Conservation during much of the 1980s and 1990s, recalls the organization's early involvement in fisheries. "The origins of our fisheries work was back when we started discussing TEDs. When we were talking about TED policy, our thinking really wasn't just sea turtles. It was this whole problem of bycatch. But at the time, the only tool we had to go after it was the turtles."

Toward Fisheries Reform

Just as the early 1970s brought dramatic change to federal policy and practice regarding marine mammals and endangered species, so too did the early 1990s bring dramatic change in federal management of marine fisheries. As decades before, much of the change in the 1990s was brought about by the activism of organizations and individuals having concerns over marine wildlife that ranged from conservation to animal protection. These concerns were in fundamental conflict with the emphasis of prevailing fisheries management policy upon maximum utilization.

Many of those who were most active in the transformation of federal fisheries management in the 1990s gained their experience and basic views about the management of living marine resources in campaigns for the conservation of marine mammals and endangered species. These individuals brought with them a fundamental lack of confidence in traditional measures such as MSY and single-species management that had led to the serial depletion of great whale populations. They also had gained first-hand experience with the damage that could be done to wildlife populations by the unintended capture of marine life by fishermen. Whether individuals or organizations were concerned most for the animals themselves or for their role in the web of life, conservationists broadened the values of marine life beyond their commercial use.

The newcomers to fisheries also introduced many of the campaign techniques that had been so successful for them earlier. Besides skillful use of the news media, grassroots campaigns, and building coalitions among themselves and with progressive fishermen's organizations, these new actors on the fisheries scene also relied on the stature and skills of scientists in analyzing and articulating the need for conservation. Finally, and most importantly perhaps, charitable foundations began providing significant new funding for fisheries programs at organizations such as The Ocean Conservancy, the Natural Resources Defense Council, the World Wildlife Fund, Environmental Defense, and the National Coalition for Marine Conservation. This funding proved crucial to campaigns for stronger protection of a group of animals that did not inspire wonder, awe, or pity as the great whales and dolphins had done more than two decades before.

Summary

The Marine Mammal Protection Act (MMPA) exempted the fur seal hunt from the moratorium on taking. Humane organizations were joined by some conservation organizations in the 1980s in their campaign to put an end to the hunt. Over the objections of the National Marine Fisheries Service (NMFS) and the State Department, these organizations succeeded in blocking congressional renewal of the fur seal treaty in 1984.

The MMPA and the Endangered Species Act (ESA) also provided an exemption for the hunt of bowhead whales conducted by Alaska natives. In the mid-1970s, rapidly rising losses of bowheads in the hunt attracted the attention of the International Whaling Commission (IWC), which temporarily imposed a zero quota on the hunt in 1977. This action later was reversed and a modest catch allowed after the U.S. government submitted a management plan and rationale for the hunt. As estimates of the bowhead population size increased, the IWC increased quotas.

In 1982, concerns over the humaneness of commercial whaling and the lack of knowledge about whale populations led to the IWC's adoption of a moratorium on commercial whaling. Long a policy goal of the U.S. government, the moratorium reflected a precautionary approach to exploiting marine wildlife when uncertainty about the effects of exploitation was high.

The NMFS only reluctantly implemented the MMPA and the ESA in the first 15 years after their passage. Imprecise language in the laws, conflicts with the agency's traditional client—the fishing industry—and lack of understanding and support at higher political levels discouraged strong implementation. In the 1980s, the agency resisted appeals from conservation organizations and the Marine Mammal Commission to protect endangered Hawaiian monk seals and their habitat, largely because of potential conflicts with growing fisheries. Lawsuits eventually compelled the agency to declare critical habitat for the species. Similarly, lawsuits by conservation organizations forced the agency to require reductions in the incidental capture and drowning of dolphins in tuna purse seine nets. Innovations in fishing gear and techniques and the movement of the U.S. fleet out of dolphin-rich waters led to dramatic reductions in dolphin kills in the fishery.

After voluntary efforts to end the capture of endangered and threatened sea turtles in shrimp trawls failed, conservation organizations appealed to the NMFS and the Gulf of Mexico Fishery Management Council in 1987 to require the use of turtle excluder devices (TEDs) in shrimp nets. After several years of negotiations among fishermen's and conservation organizations, lawsuits, congressional debate, and a National Academy of Sciences study, TEDs became required fishing gear on shrimp trawlers from North Carolina to Texas. The failure of the TED regulations to address the massive bycatch of finfish and other marine wildlife led several conservation organizations to consider direct involvement in the federal management of fisheries.

Notes

1. A small subsistence hunt by Alaska natives continued, although it too was hotly disputed by animal protection groups for several years after the end of the commercial hunt. In 1987, 1,802 northern fur seals were killed in the subsistence hunt. Aleuts on the Pribilof Islands had carried on a smaller-scale subsistence hunt in the late 1970s, taking 350 seals in 1977.
2. By the early 1900s, commercial whaling had depleted the several populations of bowhead whales found in Arctic waters. Like their cousins, the right whales, bowhead whales were extremely vulnerable to hunting due to their very slow swimming speed and their tendency to float rather than sink after death. For centuries, Eskimos and other Arctic peoples had relied on the meat and blubber of bowheads for food.

   Since 1931, international treaties had banned commercial hunting of bowhead whales. Nonetheless, Indians, Aleuts, and Eskimos were allowed to hunt bowheads to meet subsistence needs. The MMPA of 1972 and the ESA of 1973 also prohibited commercial hunting of bowhead whales while allowing Alaska natives to hunt them for subsistence purposes.
3. As additional research revealed more bowheads, the commission raised quotas and controversy over the hunt subsided. By 1987, when biologists estimated there were 4,855 bowheads, the commission had raised the overall quota to 32 strikes for 1987. In 1995, the NMFS estimated there were 7,524 bowhead whales. In 1997, the IWC approved a five-year block quota of 280 bowhead whales.
4. Quoted in Cohn, Jeffrey P. Winter 1997/1998. "How the Endangered Species Act Was Born." *Defenders.* Pages 6–13.
5. In 1997, after persistent badgering by the Marine Mammal Commission, the NMFS began investigating the role of spiny lobster in the diet of Hawaiian monk seals. Late in 1999, preliminary results from this research strongly suggested that spiny lob-

sters were an important part of the diets of most juvenile monk seals and adult female monk seals at French Frigate Shoals.

The uncertainty surrounding the impact of the fishery on a declining population of endangered Hawaiian monk seals did not deter the NMFS from taking additional risks. In 1998, the agency approved a proposal from the regional fishery
management council to direct fishing away from several islands where overfishing
of spiny lobster was occurring to other areas where there had been little or no fishing in recent years, including French Frigate Shoals. In 1999, the NMFS agreed to
make the new fishery management measures permanent—a decision hardly consistent with precautionary management.

6. 16 U.S.C. 1371(a)(2)

7. Gutting later moved to the National Fisheries Institute, in which the membership
is made up mostly of fish processors and distributors. He eventually became the
organization's president. Quoted in Environmental Defense Fund. March 1975.
"EDF Enters Suit to Save Thousands of Porpoises." *EDF Letter.* Vol. VI, No. 2.
http://www.edf.org/pubs/newsletter

8. Author's notes.

9. The turtle excluder device (TED) developed by the NMFS in the late 1970s and
early 1980s was a collapsible, boxlike frame that held a slanting grid of bars. A TED
was placed in the throat of a trawl net in front of the bag or cod-end. As large ob-
jects such as sea turtles entered the net and encountered the bars, they were guided
through a trapdoor in the top or bottom of the net. By 1985, the NMFS had added
features to its design that reduced the bycatch of finfish by half or more.

Sea Grant and individual fishermen developed other designs of TEDs. The
Georgia Jumper was simply a grid of bars sewn into the net at an angle. Other designs used large-mesh netting rather than bars to guide sea turtles through a flap in
the net. None of these designs reduced finfish bycatch as much as NMFS's TED;
however, non-NMFS devices were lighter and more manageable, and—most importantly to fishermen—they were not designed by the NMFS.

10. In its congressionally mandated study, a panel of the National Academy of Sciences
concluded that 5,500–55,000 Kemp's ridley and loggerhead sea turtles drowned
in shrimp trawls each year before the use of TEDs was required in the shrimp fishery.

1995 Support for National Marine Fisheries Service (NMFS) funding grew under the administration of George Bush and reached a peak in the Clinton administration. In 1995, Congress appropriated $269 million to the agency.

Between 1985 and 1995, the budget for protected species management grew from roughly $5 to $25.1 million. Between 1989 and 1995, the budget for enforcement increased from $6.7 to $15.5 million. The NMFS Office of Enforcement was responsible for enforcing 25 federal laws as well as the general criminal statutes of the United States. Under the Magnuson-Stevens Act, NMFS enforcement agents monitored compliance with 33 fishery management plans covering 540 species. Of nearly 2,100 enforcement cases in 1994, 979 had to do with violations of the Magnuson-Stevens Act, 353 concerned the Endangered Species Act, 294 the Northern Pacific Halibut Act, and 143 the Marine Mammal Protection Act.

In 1991, the NMFS reestablished an office of habitat protection. Funding for habitat conservation activities increased from $5.7 million in 1985 to $8.0 million in 1995. In 1994, the Clinton administration also proposed (and Congress approved) significant increases in funding for resource information (from $68.8 to $92.1 million) and fishery industry information (from $14.6 to $19.4 million).

Chapter 9 | Science, Uncertainty,
| and the Politics of Scarcity

U
ntil 1976, when the Magnuson-Stevens Act involved the federal government in the management of most domestic fisheries, the National
Marine Fisheries Service (NMFS) and its predecessors had few opportunities to apply the results of their research and analyses directly to the management of individual fisheries. The agencies prided themselves upon providing
states with the best advice that their scientific and policy experts could offer, but
ultimately, the states decided whether to accept or reject the advice. As a result,
all of the federal government's direct experience came from managing fisheries in
the territories and under the auspices of international agreements, such as the International Commission for the Northwest Atlantic Fisheries (ICNAF). In these
forums, U.S. scientists benefited from peer review of their research and drew upon
the research and experience of scientists and managers in other countries.

Whatever the setting or decision-making body, however, management decisions did not begin and end with scientific advice and analysis. In some organizations, scientific advice was accorded high value, whereas in other organizations it was not. In some settings, scientists were insulated from political agendas,
but in others they were not. In pressing for international controls on growing
foreign fishing off U.S. shores in the 1960s, the federal government relied heavily on scientists. "The United States, Great Britain, and Germany, in particular, strongly pushed for dependence on scientific advice," says Bill Gordon, who
served on U.S. delegations to ICNAF. "There were outstanding scientists in
other countries, but their political leadership didn't necessarily pay much attention to them."

The uncertainty and imprecision of scientific advice, however, provided room
for nations and interest groups to interpret the advice in their favor. Depending upon the internal politics of a state or federal fisheries agency or an international organization, scientific advice was followed more or less faithfully. At
the ICNAF, for example, representatives of nations for which fleets depended
upon easy access to fish populations off North America disputed the science

153

presented by U.S. and other scientists. The criticisms provided a rationale for conducting more research before taking action. Nonetheless, the U.S. government gradually succeeded in convincing a majority of ICNAF commissioners that catches should be reduced.

In the 1970s, efforts to control foreign fishing off U.S. coasts through bilateral and multilateral agreements were overtaken by the passage of the Magnuson-Stevens Act. The act, which emphasized basing decisions on the best scientific information available, greatly increased demand for scientific information and analyses of domestic fisheries, most of which were largely unmanaged. As a result, the role of science at the NMFS changed dramatically, from a focus largely on exploratory fishing and biological studies to providing fishery management councils with estimates of catch levels that would meet the act's goal of optimum yield.

The inadequacy of scientific advice about sustainable levels of fishing, not to mention the political interpretation of that advice, meant that fishery management councils inevitably set allowable catch levels higher or lower than actual sustainable levels. The consequences of the two types of error were very different. If a fishery management council set catch levels lower than populations of fish could sustain, then fishermen would lose whatever short-term economic benefits they might have derived from higher catches. Given the general interest in expanding catches after passage of the Magnuson-Stevens Act, this type of error was relatively rare. If catches were set at levels higher than fish populations could sustain, fishermen would gain short-term economic benefits from higher catches, but fish populations and catches in later years would decline. If catches repeatedly exceeded the productivity of fish populations, populations of fish would decline to dangerously low levels.

At the time, the widespread acceptance of the ideology of abundance gave no cause to reduce expectations of potential catches in order to account for the poor quality of information on many fisheries. Rather than adopting the conservative standards it had adopted in 1972 via the Marine Mammal Protection Act (MMPA), Congress set a standard for conservation in the Magnuson-Stevens Act that it called optimum yield (OY) and based that standard on maximum sustainable yield (MSY). The act further weakened the standard by allowing quotas to be set above MSY to account for social, economic, and ecological factors. This provision effectively allowed fisheries managers to err on the side of exploitation when in doubt about the impact of fishing on fish populations.

Whereas estimates of OY that would allow increased fishing received little scrutiny, estimates that would lead to restrictions often were bitterly attacked. When the NMFS pressed for restrictions in the New England groundfish fishery soon after passage of the Magnuson-Stevens Act in 1976, New England fishermen attacked the agency's scientific analysis. The New England Fishery Management Council soon eased restrictions in the New England groundfish fishery and catches grew for a time; however, they plummeted as heavy fishing prevented recovery of groundfish populations from overfishing by foreign fishing vessels in the 1960s.

By the early 1990s, the biological and economic costs of overfishing were becoming plain as flagship fisheries such as the New England groundfish fishery declined to dangerously low levels. In 1991, director Bill Fox released a strategic plan for the NMFS, which argued that one factor in overfishing was the tendency of fishery managers to make "risk-prone" decisions on quotas when confronted with political pressure to increase quotas and with the imprecision of available stock assessments. Rather than erring on the side of exploitation, Fox argued that the precarious state of many U.S. fisheries required erring on the side of conservation when there was uncertainty about how marine wildlife populations would respond to exploitation. Under this set of values, which reversed decades of practice, the cost of poor or no valid population assessments was lower quotas. An investment by the government in improving assessments offered one of the few ways to increase quotas without violating the precautionary approach that Fox was urging.

Linking increased catches and economic activity to basic fisheries research proved persuasive to Bush administration budget managers. The NMFS budget for research increased, reversing more than a decade of stagnation and decline; however, the modest growth in funding, which often was accompanied by congressional directives on how the funding was to be spent, did not keep pace with the need. As a result, most fisheries still were not regularly surveyed.

Along the Pacific coast, for example, scientists did not have annual trawl surveys and decades of study to draw upon in advising the Pacific Fishery Management Council regarding Pacific groundfish. Instead of attempting a traditional estimate of MSY, scientists had recommended that the council adopt a different measure—a rate of fishing that would reduce egg production to 35% of what it would have been in an unfished population. There was little empirical evidence from research on Pacific groundfish for this rate, which was borrowed from analyses in New England. At the time, however, it seemed to be a conservative standard.

Because populations of most species were largely unexploited, catches initially rose as the fishing fleet grew in the wake of the Magnuson-Stevens Act's passage. By the 1980s, however, populations had been fished down, the Pacific council began imposing restrictions, and some fishermen began seeking opportunities elsewhere. Although conservationists and some scientists raised concerns about the levels of fishing, scientific advisors to the Pacific council continued supporting the target of reducing groundfish populations to the 35% level.

By the middle of the 1990s, however, scientific support for the target evaporated as the result of new research and assessments showing that many species of Pacific rockfish were not nearly as productive as had been assumed. With a suddenness that stunned the Pacific council and fishermen alike, scientists concluded that several of the species they were able to assess actually were severely overfished. Scientists recommended cutting OYs by half for many other groundfish species for which status could not be determined. The Pacific council responded by greatly reducing quotas for many species and nearly eliminating allowable catches for others.

The economic and social stress generated enough of a political firestorm that the fishery was declared a natural disaster and Congress appropriated modest amounts of funds for relief to fishermen and coastal communities. But a much larger task lay ahead: to reduce by half a fleet that had expanded, with government encouragement and assistance, in the hopes of tapping into abundance that would never be.

Shifting the Burden of Proof

"It was very rare that you stopped somebody from fishing," says Suzanne Iudicello, former vice president for programs at the Center for Marine Conservation. "The whole presumption is: Fish until someone makes you stop. The burden on someone trying to stop fishing is pretty darned high."

In 1987, Iudicello and colleagues at Greenpeace and other conservation organizations turned the presumption on its head when they succeeded in blocking the NMFS from granting a permit to the Federation of Japan Salmon Fisheries Cooperative Association. The permit would have allowed Japanese fishermen to capture Steller sea lions (*Eumetopias jubatus*) and northern fur seals (*Callorhinus ursinus*) while fishing for salmon off Alaska. In previous years, the agency had routinely granted the permit, although it was unable to satisfy a requirement of the MMPA that incidental capture in fisheries not drive a population below its optimum level. The agency simply did not know how many sea lions or fur seals were in the North Pacific, how many were captured in Japanese gill nets, or what the impact of those captures were on marine mammal populations.

The agency suffered from similar ignorance regarding nearly all other marine mammal populations, partly because it had conducted little or no research on them. Between 1974 and 1987, the NMFS routinely allowed the incidental capture of marine mammals in dozens of fisheries without determining the status of those populations and without getting even the most basic information from fishermen. The NMFS presumed that these levels of capture had little effect on marine mammal populations, although the minuscule amount of funding allocated for assessing marine mammal populations prevented any real evaluation. Furthermore, the agency had little idea how many captured marine mammals survived, were injured, or died from the ordeal. Although these permits required fishermen to obtain a "letter of inclusion" detailing the numbers of mammals taken, many fishermen reported inaccurately, if they reported at all. In 1985, the Marine Mammal Commission informed the NMFS that the commission would no longer review permit applications because information on marine mammal populations was so poor.

"The prior permits had been granted willy-nilly," says Iudicello. "If you look at them, they say a thousand of these and fifteen hundred of those and five hundred of these, and they just bear no relationship to any kind of deliberative process."

The NMFS's lax application of the MMPA came to a sudden end in 1987 when a federal court ruled in the case *Kokechik Fishermen's Association* v. *Secretary of Commerce.* Together with a lawsuit by the Center for Marine Conservation and Greenpeace, this lawsuit by western Alaskan salmon fishermen took issue with the permit that the NMFS had issued to Japanese salmon fishermen, which allowed them to capture 6,039 Dall's porpoises (*Phocoenoides dalli*). The court agreed with the plaintiffs. When an appeal by the federal government and the Japanese fishermen's association failed, the Japanese drift net fleet was excluded from U.S. waters.

The *Kokechik* decision shocked the agency and the commercial fishing industry, although the ruling simply enforced a standard that had been in the MMPA since 1972. On one level, the ruling was a shock because it represented such a different standard for making decisions than was common in setting quotas for commercial fisheries. There, the burden was upon those who wished to restrict fishing. The absence of information was a license to fish. Under the MMPA, fishermen who were likely to capture marine mammals while fishing bore the burden of proving that these captures would not disadvantage marine mammal populations.

The second cause for shock was more practical.

"When it came time for U.S. fishermen to get permits to take marine mammals in the course of fishing . . . the story was a little different," says Iudicello. "'Oh my god, you can't shut down fishing on the West Coast just because these people are going to kill some sea lions and fur seals!' people said. The political reality brought all parties to the table." In 1988, the Service itself acknowledged the scale of the problem in congressional testimony: "To give you an idea of how large the problem is, incidental taking associated with fisheries in U.S. waters involves over 20 species and 10,000 marine mammals. It is becoming more and more difficult to manage the taking of these marine mammals so as to allow the 3-billion pound American fisheries to continue."

Representatives of fishing interests, primarily from Alaska, and several national environmental organizations convened a series of meetings to work out a solution to their mutual concerns about the lack of information on marine mammal populations, the frequency of conflicts between marine mammals and fisheries, and the level of captures and mortalities in commercial fisheries. The groups were so critical of the NMFS that the agency was not included in the discussions.

In June 1988, the environmental and fishing organizations presented a joint proposal to the Senate Committee on Commerce, Science, and Transportation and to the House Committee on Merchant Marine and Fisheries. "We cut a deal," says Suzanne Iudicello, formerly at the Center for Marine Conservation and a principal in the negotiations. "We said, 'OK, we won't shut you down. We'll go forward with the MMPA reauthorization with a five-year, information-gathering moratorium, a time-out. You can fish, but in order to fish, you have to collect all this information, you have to give it to NMFS, and NMFS has to collect information.' When the deal was presented to Congress, the Merchant Marine Committee on the House side and the Commerce Committee on the Senate side accepted the deal because it had the enviros and fishermen coming to them happily hand in hand."

In November 1988, President Ronald Reagan signed a reauthorization of the MMPA that largely followed the groups' original proposal. "NMFS was not pleased," says Iudicello. "They thought the whole idea was stupid and pretty much balked at it. But they did carry out the program over the five-year period of time." Implementation came in spite of the fundamental difficulty of some tasks and levels of funding and staffing that had been ravaged in the previous eight years of budget cuts under the Reagan administration.

Among other things, the legislation required the agency to do something that no federal agency had ever done: determine how many vessels operated in which fisheries and ensure that they registered for the data-collection program. In 1990, the first year of the program, 18,820 fishing vessels registered, and of these, 13,756 submitted reports on their contacts with marine mammals during fishing operations. In 1991, all fishermen registered in some fisheries, while in other fisheries only 15% registered.

Once registered, fishermen were to submit reports of their fishing activities and contacts with marine mammals. The data recorded by fishermen in logbooks were notoriously unreliable. Concerned about collecting information that would later be used to restrict their activities, fishermen sometimes underreported their capture of marine mammals. For example, in the Gulf of Maine sink gill net fishery for groundfish, observers placed on vessels documented the death of 3,013 marine mammals—12 times the number reported in logbooks. While these and other problems seriously undermined the value of the information that was collected, the program did offer a general idea of the magnitude of marine mammal catch for particular species in particular fisheries.

The 1988 amendments also sketched out a process for developing a new regime regarding incidental captures in fisheries that involved both the Marine Mammal Commission and the NMFS. Based on guidance from the Marine Mammal Commission and its committee of scientific advisors, the NMFS was to prepare a proposal to govern incidental takes in marine fisheries for public discussion. The new director of the NMFS, Dr. William W. Fox Jr., took full advantage of the opportunity. Fox had previously served on the Marine Mammal Commission and was familiar with the problems of incidental capture of marine mammals in fisheries.

Using the Marine Mammal Commission's guidelines, the NMFS developed a proposal that drew upon its internal expertise and a series of hearings around the country. In May 1991, the agency released its draft proposal. The most innovative feature of the proposal was a requirement that the agency estimate the number of animals that could be removed from a population of marine mammals without reducing the population below its optimum sustainable population (OSP) level or hindering its recovery.[1] This allowable biological removal (or ABR) would set a benchmark for determining whether a fishery should be allowed to capture individual animals of a population. If a fishery were likely to capture fewer animals than the ABR, it would be allowed to do so, even if the population had been listed as "depleted" under the MMPA. Fisheries that were capturing marine mammals at a rate higher than the ABR for the different species would have to reduce their captures. At last, the NMFS would be implementing the precautionary approach incorporated in the MMPA of 1972.

This feature and others in the proposal from the NMFS generated controversy among environmental groups and the fishing industry. Environmental groups believed that the proposal would allow the number of captures to increase as marine mammal populations increased rather than reduce captures to "insignificant levels approaching zero," as the act had mandated from the beginning. Fishing groups, on the other hand, thought that the formula for determining the ABR included too many precautionary elements, which would lead to excessively low levels of allowable capture.

The objections were not fatal to the proposal. In 1993, environmental and animal welfare groups, some fishing groups, and Alaska natives launched a series of negotiations to produce an alternative to the agency's proposal. In some important respects, the agreement that emerged from these negotiations tracked closely with the proposal of the NMFS.

"An important element was that you had to know the status of the animal and whether it was increasing or decreasing in numbers," says Iudicello. "You had to know the amount of take and whether that had been increasing or decreasing over time, and that there were measures to reduce it. There was a hierarchy of concern that was linked to the status of the animal. That was taken primarily from the proposal that the agency had put on the table and taken to Congress. The terminology was a little different, but the heart of the NMFS proposal was there."

In other important respects, the negotiated agreement differed from the agency's proposal. "The operational element of this was the idea that the people who are really going to know how to reduce interactions with marine mammals are the people who are running the boats," says Iudicello. "If you don't talk to fishermen and get their ideas about how to avoid takes, you're not going to get their views by publishing stuff in the Federal Register. It's just not going to work. So we came up with this idea of incidental take teams." Composed of independent and agency scientists, fishermen, and environmentalists, these teams were to develop plans for reducing the capture of marine mammals in fisheries in which it was a significant problem. The NMFS then would review and implement the plans if the plans met the standards of the MMPA.[2]

Fish Are Wildlife, Too

In 1991, the politics surrounding the management of fisheries for Atlantic bluefin tuna by the International Commission for the Conservation of Atlantic Tunas (ICCAT) shifted suddenly. Then, the National Audubon Society formally proposed that trade in Atlantic bluefin tuna be halted, under the authority of the Convention for International Trade in Endangered Species of Fauna and Flora (CITES). Under the CITES, an international treaty that been negotiated at the same time that the U.S. Congress was finalizing passage of the Endangered Species Act (ESA) in 1973, international trade in species that were found to be in danger of extinction was banned, with few exceptions. The Audubon petition proposed to classify western Atlantic bluefin tuna as in danger of extinction and to end the small, but very lucrative fishery for Atlantic bluefin tuna in the western Atlantic that supplied Japanese markets.

"I was an angry sports fisherman and a dismayed scientist," says Carl Safina, founder of the National Audubon Society's Living Oceans Campaign and author of the petition to enlist the CITES in protecting Atlantic bluefin tuna. "When I started looking into the existing scientific literature, I was just appalled, really appalled. I found that a lot was known, that people were making livings and careers ostensibly off management. It was a complete farce and total failure."

The government and the commercial fishing industry were stunned by the Audubon proposal to use the CITES to address their concerns about the bluefin tuna fisheries rather than working through the established ICCAT process. Soon, the owners of the purse seine fleet, who had given generously to the Bush election campaign, were using their political connections at the highest levels of the Bush administration to attack the CITES petition and proposals to reduce ICCAT quotas by 50%.

As the NMFS and the U.S. Fish and Wildlife Service reviewed the Audubon petition and developed U.S. positions for the 1991 meeting of the CITES, White House advisors asked for regular briefings on the growing controversy. Organized demonstrations by fishermen in New England encouraged the New England congressional delegation to pressure the federal agencies to reject the Audubon petition. Longtime players in ICCAT decisions, both inside and outside government, argued that the management of Atlantic bluefin tuna fisheries should be left in the hands of the ICCAT and not handed over to the CITES.

When the commercial fishing industry as well as the Canadian and Japanese governments succeeded in convincing the United States not to submit the Audubon proposal to the CITES countries, the World Wildlife Fund convinced the government of Sweden to sponsor the proposal. Mike Sutton, the World Wildlife Fund's Endangered Seas campaign coordinator at the time, said: "We couldn't believe that bluefin tuna were so depleted, that that situation had been allowed to develop. We decided that some kind of dramatic intervention was needed, so we launched the effort to get Atlantic bluefin tuna on the CITES list, as a kind of electric shock treatment."

"We thought that the biggest problem wasn't any lack of scientific information, but a lack of political will to put to work what was known," says Sutton. "Scientists at NMFS told us that they needed us involved, that their scientific advice was being ignored and bad decisions were being made. We thought of ourselves as the white knights and [that] the other scientists were the forces of evil, always trying to maximize uncertainty to keep quotas high."

In the end, the campaign by the Swedish government and conservation organizations was met by an equally organized campaign by several governments, led by Canada and Japan, to squelch consideration of the proposal in committee. Under strict orders from the White House, the U.S. delegation accepted a proposal from Sweden that the ICCAT adopt several measures, including reductions in quotas on bluefin tuna, once Sweden withdrew its CITES proposal.

Although defeated, the proposal to list Atlantic bluefin tuna on the CITES list shifted the politics of U.S. policy on Atlantic bluefin tuna fisheries, and other fisheries. Using their own political connections, conservationists succeeded in convincing the Bush administration to pursue a 50% reduction in western Atlantic bluefin tuna quotas at the 1991 meeting of the ICCAT. This initiative was somewhat successful as the ICCAT reduced quotas slightly, but the quota reductions were short-lived. The commercial fishing industry and its allies in the New England congressional delegation soon succeeded in pressuring the NMFS into sponsoring a National Academy of Sciences's review of the science underlying the reduced quotas. While the study eventually confirmed that the adult population of Atlantic bluefin tuna in the western Atlantic had declined by 80% since 1975, it cast doubt on a fundamental assumption of past ICCAT decisions: that bluefin tuna in the western Atlantic were members of a population separate from bluefin tuna in the eastern Atlantic.

The doubt was sufficient grounds for the NMFS to change its policy from pressing for quota reductions in the western Atlantic to insisting that European countries bring their much larger fishery under control first. The CITES proposal also led to the U.S. delegation pressing the ICCAT to use trade measures in encouraging observance of their decisions by nonmember countries. By the end of the 1990s, however, evidence of progress in reversing the decline of western Atlantic bluefin tuna was scant. In its 2000 report to Congress on the status of U.S. fisheries, NMFS scientists concluded not only that Atlantic bluefin tuna remained overfished, but that overfishing continued.

The Rise of Precaution in International Fisheries

Reflecting the precautionary standards of the MMPA, the Marine Mammal Commission began urging the NMFS and the State Department in the 1980s to assess the impact of drift net fishing on high seas ecosystems. Besides the salmon drift net fishery, the commission was concerned about high seas drift netting for squid and tuna, which had been pioneered by Japanese fishermen in the 1970s. Like most other fisheries, the drift net fishery for squid and tuna had grown rapidly, with little assessment of its sustainability or its impacts on other species. By the mid-1980s, more than 800 vessels from Japan, Taiwan, and South Korea were deploying 25,000 miles of net in the surface waters of the Pacific Ocean each night of the fishing season. No one knew what impact such intense fishing might be having on squid and tunas, much less other finfish, sharks, seabirds, turtles, and marine mammals that became entangled and died in the nets. Unlike high seas fisheries for salmon that had spawned in North American streams, management of high seas fisheries for squid and tuna were beyond the reach of international law or direct influence by the United States and other countries in the region.

In 1987, the Alaska congressional delegation and a coalition of conservation and fishing groups succeeded in convincing Congress to direct the Department of Commerce to negotiate agreements with Japan, South Korea, and Taiwan to monitor these fisheries. The agreements were to authorize observers on enough fishing vessels to allow the collection of information on bycatch that would enable statistically sound estimates of total bycatch.

"The Alaska delegation brought up the drift netting issue for years until suddenly it caught the attention of the environmental community," says Rod Moore, who served as staff to Alaska Congressman Don Young when he was ranking minority member of the House Subcommittee on Fisheries and Wildlife Conservation and the Environment in the late 1970s and 1980s. "As long as it was an issue of some poor, dumb Eskimo fishermen on the fringes of Alaska versus international negotiations with the Japanese on this, that, and the other thing, it never got any attention given to it. It was only when it became a major environmental issue that it mushroomed from there."

U.S. negotiators began their negotiations with the Japanese, believing that Taiwan and South Korea would follow Japan's lead. In 1989, Japan agreed to accept some U.S. observers on its drift net fleet, and expanded the program in 1990. At the same time, both Taiwan and South Korea began accepting an increasing number of observers on their vessels.

While observers collected data, political momentum built toward ending fishing with large drift nets altogether. In the South Pacific, a consortium of nations, including the United States, was concerned about the damage that might be done to albacore populations by expanding drift net fishing for tunas. In November 1989, these countries adopted the Wellington Convention, which effectively banned the use of drift nets in most of the western and South Pacific.

As international and U.S. conservation organizations increased their attacks on high seas drift net fishing, the Bush administration seized on the issue with unusual fervor. The State Department's unusually strong stand owed itself to a number of things. Within the federal government, the State Department was under pressure from the Marine Mammal Commission, the U.S. Fish and Wildlife Service, and the NMFS, which had recently adopted a strategic plan that called for reducing bycatch and using a precautionary approach in the management of fisheries. In February 1990, President Bush appointed Curtis Bohlen as assistant secretary of state for Oceans and International Environmental and Scientific Affairs. In the decade before the appointment, Bohlen had served as a senior vice president at the World Wildlife Fund—one of the organizations pressing for a moratorium on drift net fishing on the high seas. Finally, the proponents of ending high seas drift netting included in their number the influential Alaska delegation. "The State Department was finally paying attention to the fact that their clients were U.S. citizens—not the Japanese, or the Koreans, or the Taiwanese," says Rod Moore.

Since there was no international treaty organization specifically charged with management of these high seas fisheries, critics of high seas drift net fishing took their case to the United Nations. The Bush administration and other advocates for a moratorium on high seas drift net fishing argued that the burden of proof rested with the Japanese to demonstrate that their fishery had no great impact or to develop alternatives if fishing were to continue. The Japanese argued that opponents of drift net fishing could not cite evidence of the scale or impact of bycatch in the fisheries and urged further study of impacts and alternatives while fishing continued. Other critics of the proposed moratorium argued that damage to marine wildlife from drift net fishing was remote and that shifting the burden of proof to fishing interests would prevent the development of new fisheries, since the costs of gathering necessary information would be prohibitive.

In December 1989, the United Nations General Assembly sided with advocates of a moratorium by passing Resolution 44/255, which called for a review of information on the fisheries and a suspension of drift net fishing by June

1992, unless agreements were reached that avoided damage to marine wildlife. With this resolution, the General Assembly shifted the burden of proof to those who wished to continue drift net fishing.

In June 1991, scientists from the United States, Canada, and the drift netting nations gathered in Sidney, British Columbia, to review data on bycatch collected by observers on drift net vessels in the first full year of the monitoring agreements. Based on these data, scientists estimated that in 1990 the Japanese squid drift net fleet alone caught millions of fish, hundreds of thousands of seabirds, thousands of marine mammals, and hundreds of sea turtles. Nearly all of the bycatch was discarded dead or dying. Generally, scientists could not say if these catches were damaging particular wildlife populations.

In the fall of 1991, the political battle over drift net fishing intensified when the General Assembly of the United Nations began its own review of information from the observer program. Predictably, the Japanese delegation argued that the data collected by observers did not demonstrate significant harm to wildlife populations or that measures could not be developed that would reduce bycatch. The U.S. delegation presented its views in a paper that had been developed by an interagency working group involving members of Congress as well as fishing, environmental, and animal welfare organizations. The overriding principle of the paper was that fishing carried a responsibility to protect ecosystems so that they were not irreversibly damaged, management options were preserved, and both consumptive and nonconsumptive values could be optimized.

Most UN members were swayed by the evidence from the observers and by the intense lobbying by conservation organizations and the U.S. government in particular. "You had the Japanese seeing the writing on the wall, and cutting loose their own drift net fleet, which left the Koreans and Taiwanese out to dry," says Moore.

The denouement of the drift net drama at the United Nations was swift. On November 26, 1991, the Japanese government announced that it would cease drift net fishing on the high seas by the end of 1992. The United States then announced that it had agreed to support the moratorium announced by Japan. Just before the New Year, the General Assembly adopted a resolution calling upon all countries to cease fishing on the high seas with large drift nets by the end of 1992.

Although scattered outlaw fishing with large drift nets continued after the deadline, hundreds of drift net vessels from Japan, South Korea, and Taiwan stopped their fishing before the deadline. The government of Japan compensated fishermen for their loss of income and for the disposal of fishing vessels and gear. The Republic of Korea funded the scrapping of some drift net vessels and the refitting of others. The government of Taiwan bought some vessels and issued low-interest loans for refitting other vessels.

The United Nations's decision to end high seas drift netting only reflected a precautionary approach. The articulation of the precautionary approach in international fisheries law awaited the negotiation of a new treaty on fisheries.

The Precautionary Approach Expanded

At the same time as UN delegates were debating restrictions on drift net fishing, the shortcomings of existing international law on fisheries were coming under attack in preparatory meetings for the United Nations Conference on Environment and Development, or UNCED. The decline of major fisheries such as the cod fisheries in the United States and Canada, as well as increasing conflicts between developing countries and distant water fishing fleets from Japan, South Korea, Taiwan, and Spain, added to the concerns raised by the high seas drift net fishing.

When delegates from around the world met in Rio de Janeiro in June 1992 to attend UNCED, fisheries conservation had become a second tier, if not a first tier, issue. Conservationists and some governments urged that the delegates adopt the precautionary principle in guidelines for fisheries that were to be included in Agenda 21, the summary document for the UN conference. When it concluded in June 1992, the conference not only called for the use of a precautionary approach in fisheries, but also for a new treaty to address growing conflicts over fish that cross international boundaries.

When negotiations regarding the new treaty began in 1993, the United States found itself between two warring camps. On one side were countries, including Canada and tiny island states in the South Pacific, which were intent on bringing distant water fleets under control. Other countries such as Japan, South Korea, and Spain were as intent on protecting their access to tunas and other species on which their distant water fleets depended.

The U.S. delegation itself was in the familiar position of having to answer to U.S. fishermen who fished in distant waters and those who fished in U.S. coastal waters. What was new was that negotiators were exposed to a well-organized effort by conservation organizations, who had demonstrated their influence in the United Nations adoption of the moratorium on drift net fishing on the high seas. Nonetheless, the negotiations soon reached a stalemate between distant water fishing nations and coastal nations. Negotiations regained momentum in 1994, when the United States announced that it was committed to fashioning a binding agreement that incorporated the precautionary approach as well as other provisions, such as strong enforcement provisions and requirements for data collection.

On March 9, 1995, the stakes in the negotiations were made plain when Canadian patrol boats seized the Spanish trawler *Estai* as it was fishing for turbot (*Reinhardtius hippoglossoides*) on the Grand Banks just beyond Canada's exclusive economic zone (EEZ). The Canadian government, which had severely cut quotas for its own fishermen within its EEZ in 1991, claimed that it was protecting its interests in a population of fish that straddled the high seas and Canada's EEZ. The Spanish government accused the Canadian government of piracy, claiming that its vessels were legally fishing in the area. Earlier in the year, the European Union had heeded the urgings of the governments of Spain and Portugal and objected to the allocation of turbot they had received from the North Atlantic Fisheries Organization, the successor to the ICNAF. Rather than accepting the allocation of 3,200 metric tons, the European Union set itself a target of 19,000 metric tons.

Although the European Union had international law on its side, the behavior of the Spanish fleet fed criticism of other distant water fishing fleets. Within six months, negotiators settled upon a final text for the United Nations Agreement on the Management of Straddling Fish Stocks and Highly Migratory Fish Stocks. The agreement included not only general language on the precautionary approach, but also an annex on applying the approach that had been prepared by a committee led by NMFS scientist Andrew Rosenberg. The precautionary approach in the UN agreement was not as strong as the standard in the MMPA, in which the default position generally was to prohibit exploitation unless it could be demonstrated to cause no significant harm. Still, the UN agreement did include constraints on fisheries that were strong enough to provoke intense opposition.

Optimism, however, that the new treaty would usher in a dramatically new era of international fisheries management soon cooled. Although several countries, including the United States, quickly ratified the treaty, such major fishing countries as Japan and those in the European Union delayed their consideration of the treaty. By 1999, treaty supporters still lacked 6 of the 30 ratifications needed for the treaty to become effective, and many of the world's leading fishing countries had yet to ratify. Even so, several regional organizations, such as the North Atlantic Fisheries Organization, began applying the precautionary standards of the new treaty. The UN agreement also spurred the development of a new arrangement to manage tuna fisheries in the western and central Pacific Ocean.

The negotiations that led to the UN agreement also influenced growing domestic discussions about reform of U.S. fisheries policy. During the negotiations, the U.S. delegation had kept in mind that the Senate had to ratify any agreement if the United States were to become a full participant. With this in mind, the State Department had kept members of Congress briefed on the progress of the negotiations. This strategy was partly responsible for the United States being among the first countries to ratify the final agreement. The strategy also encouraged a review of U.S. fisheries policy that reflected international experience and new thinking about what makes for effective fisheries conservation.

The End of Abundance

Peter Fricke is one of a handful of social scientists and economists in the NMFS. As a group and individually, they have enjoyed even less support than biologists have. In the 1990s, however, the economic and social disruption caused by declining fisheries and increasing management restrictions generated greater political interest in the social and economic dimensions of fisheries. "I keep telling people that we have gone back to 1870 when there was a tremendous interest in what was happening in fishing communities," says Fricke. "We are just beginning to recapture this."

The federal government had long carried out economic research that directly or indirectly benefited the fishing industry. During World War II, the Bureau of Fisheries had analyzed labor markets to anticipate wage and hour demands. In later years, the Bureau of Commercial Fisheries (BCF) evaluated the feasibility of different types of transport for fishery products, designed incentive programs for encouraging new fisheries, intervened in government hearings on freight rates, and evaluated market demand for fishery products in individual fisheries as well as returns to capital and labor.

In the 1960s, economists began developing other models that aimed at estimating the right mix of catch quotas, labor, and investment for producing maximum economic yield and economic efficiency. Rather than simply seeking to explain human behavior or to measure economic inputs and outputs, economists also set about trying to design fisheries. By the 1970s, however, overfishing and increasing regulation of fisheries generated demands for analyses of the economic impacts of different types of management measures. The continued poor economic performance of several U.S. fisheries, such as the New England trawl fishery, also prompted repeated research on causes and remedies.

"As our fisheries were fully Americanized, there was a realization in the 1980s that we were now in the business of allocation," said Fricke. "Some people had been talking about this for a long time, but the science side was not listening. They still believed that you could build a perfect bio-model that would describe a fishery."

The social and political fallout from the collapse of New England ground-fish fisheries in the late 1980s encouraged some policy makers to look to the social sciences for explanations and ways of resolving the crisis. Why had fish populations in New England declined so catastrophically when their biology had been so thoroughly studied and analyzed? And what would be the social and cultural effects of restrictions on the very fishery that had enriched the country in its youth?

Increasing restrictions in the New England groundfish fishery, in particular, provoked outrage among fishermen and threats of intervention by members of Congress. Fishermen argued that the restrictions were unwarranted and would decimate coastal fishing communities. The protests of fishermen and the long historical link of New England with fisheries provided politically potent grounds for analyzing the impacts of management restrictions in New England, as nowhere else.

Social scientists argued that understanding the views of fishermen is crucial to implementing management plans. Little if any information on these aspects of fishing communities in the United States was collected for many years. One of the few efforts in the 1990s was a study of the New England groundfish fishery that was commissioned by the NMFS. Among other things, the study found several important shifts in the attitudes of fishermen in the New England ground-fish fishery. In the past, determining what to fish for, with what, and when depended upon understanding the biology of fish and market demand. By the 1990s, however, fishermen weighed possible outcomes from the political process of management as well as government enforcement capabilities. An activity that had been free of restriction for generations now had to be pursued in a welter of legal requirements and increasing competition with other fishermen.

Peter Fricke notes other, broader changes since the 1970s. "Three things have happened. First, the usual boom and bust in the fisheries cycle, which had been local, became regional. People suddenly began bumping into one another. Second, there was tremendous pressure for capital. Fishing vessels have become more complex; they're using more gear. The skill levels of fishermen in many cases have declined, because they didn't need the skills that had restricted fisheries in the past. Capital was being substituted for that."

"The third thing that changed was the notion that fisheries were open, were an inexhaustible resource," says Fricke. "Everyone recognized that this was now a finite resource and that fisheries were essentially closed. There is a generation, the changed generation between 1980 and 1995, that moved from the expectation that fisheries were open for the taking to the new generation that realized that it was finite."

Summary

Throughout the history of its involvement in marine fisheries, the federal government has provided scientific advice to states and international organizations regarding the management of fisheries. Passage of the Magnuson-Stevens Act increased the demand for scientific advice; however, the National Marine Fisheries Service (NMFS) and the fishery management councils often had to contend with inadequate scientific understanding. This inadequacy, together with the standards of the Magnuson-Stevens Act, contributed to setting unsustainable rates of exploitation.

In the late 1980s, management-oriented research began receiving additional support as the economic consequences of inadequate management information and precautionary reductions in quotas became apparent. Nonetheless, scientific surveys of fisheries remained rare.

In 1987, conservation organizations challenged the issuance of a permit that would have allowed Japanese salmon fishermen to incidentally capture marine mammals in the North Pacific. A federal court prohibited issuance of the permit because the NMFS was unable to determine that the captures would not harm marine mammal populations, as required by the Marine Mammal Protection Act (MMPA). If applied more generally, the ruling also would have closed many U.S. fisheries. Instead, conservation and fishermen's organization developed a legislative proposal, adopted by Congress in 1988, that suspended the MMPA's standard for five years while additional information was collected on marine mammal captures and an alternative regulatory scheme could be developed. In 1994, Congress adopted a new regulatory scheme that embodied a precautionary approach.

Reacting to the dramatic decline of bluefin tuna in the western Atlantic Ocean, the National Audubon Society petitioned to have trade in the species controlled by the Convention on International Trade in Endangered Species (CITES). Opponents in the fishing industry and in other nations that fished bluefin tuna successfully blocked the petition. Later, the International Commission for the Conservation of Atlantic Tunas (ICCAT) did adopt some additional conservation measures, but the western Atlantic population of bluefin tuna remained overfished in the year 2000.

In the 1980s, the Marine Mammal Commission began pressing for the application of the MMPA's precautionary standard to high seas drift net fishing for squid and tuna in the Pacific Ocean. The U.S. government, spurred on by conservation and fishermen's organizations, led successful efforts at the United Nations to end drift net fishing on the high seas, largely because it was having untold impacts on high seas ecosystems.

In the early 1990s, the United Nations also sponsored negotiations over an agreement to control the exploitation of fish that crossed international boundaries. The resulting treaty included precautionary standards and other features that marked a departure from past policy.

Socioeconomic research on marine fisheries by federal agencies varied in focus and in level over the years. The demand for such information outstripped its availability as management restrictions under the Magnuson-Stevens Act led to economic and social dislocation. Political controversy led to increased support for socioeconomic research in the 1990s. Among other things, surveys found widespread acceptance that fishing in the future would be limited far more than in the past.

Notes

1. As finally adopted, this measure, called potential biological removal, was derived by multiplying a population's minimum size estimate times 20% of its theoretical maximum net productivity times a recovery factor of 0.1 to 1.0.
2. By 2000, take reduction teams had been established to develop plans for Gulf of Maine harbor porpoise, mid-Atlantic harbor porpoise, Pacific offshore cetaceans, Atlantic offshore cetaceans, and Atlantic large whales. Take reduction plans had been developed and completely or partially approved for Pacific offshore cetaceans, Atlantic large whales, and harbor porpoise in the Gulf of Maine and mid-Atlantic.

2000   *For fiscal year 2000, Congress appropriated $421 million for National Marine Fisheries Service (NMFS) operations, including 35% for resource information, 18% for fishery management programs, 16% for protected species management, 12% for acquisition and dissemination of information, 7% for fishery industry information, 4% for enforcement and surveillance, 3% for financial assistance to states, 2% for habitat conservation, and 2% for fisheries development programs.*

The agency maintained 5 regional management offices, 5 regional science centers, 14 laboratories, and 5 field stations. Eight of 10 fisheries research vessels had been constructed before 1970. NMFS staffing stood at 2,607 employees. Of these, 13% were located at the agency's headquarters, 29% were assigned to regional offices, and 58% were at regional science centers and other science facilities.

In 2000, 40 fishery management plans were in effect, and an additional 8 were being developed. The NMFS published roughly 1,000 formal notices regarding domestic fishing.

Chapter 10 | Reinventing the Revolution

A week after the United Nations Earth Summit in Rio de Janeiro in June 1992, an article in *U.S. News & World Report* titled "The Rape of the Oceans" claimed that overfishing would likely replace the destruction of tropical rain forests as the next global ecology concern. The article was framed by the story of the collapse of a fishery, which was causing ecological, economic, cultural, and political upheaval—not in a distant developing country, but in New England.

Unlike previous times of troubles, the decline of the New England ground-fish fishery in the late 1980s engaged the political interests of more than the fishing industry itself and its government representatives. The exhaustion of the fishery was spectacular enough to spark the passions of an environmental community having interest in marine fisheries that had been confined to controversies over marine mammals or endangered species. Within four years, environmentalists successfully used their political skills and the financial support of charitable foundations to build a political coalition that turned fisheries politics on its head and led to the first major revision of the Magnuson-Stevens Fishery Conservation and Management Act in two decades.

While the social and cultural impact of New England's damaged groundfish fishery was especially gripping, other U.S. fisheries were showing problems also, including overfishing, bycatch, and overcapitalization. In one of its first systematic assessments in many years, the National Marine Fisheries Service (NMFS) found in 1992 that nearly half of U.S. fisheries were overfished. Another 37% were fished to their maximum level. Some fish populations were put at risk by incidental capture or bycatch in fisheries aimed at other species. After passage of the Magnuson-Stevens Act, fleets in some fisheries had grown so large that fishermen had to cope with shorter seasons or declining catches even if fish populations were healthy. By the late 1980s, so many fishermen had squeezed into Alaska's halibut fishery that fishing seasons in some areas fell from more than 150 days to two 24-hour seasons. The hyperdevelopment of fleets had other consequences.

Long before the crisis of the early 1990s, the concerns of biologists and economists about overfishing, bycatch, and overcapitalization had found their way into policies and reports issued by the NMFS. These concerns, however, were muted by the desires of other agency staff, the industry itself, and congressional patrons to promote and expand U.S. fleets and catches, particularly after the Magnuson-Stevens Act gave domestic fishermen preferred access to waters within 200 miles of U.S. shores.

As passed in 1976, the Magnuson-Stevens Act provided ample authority to address most of the problems that later burst onto the national scene in the early 1990s. For most fisheries, however, this authority was ignored in favor of expanding fishing, until a headline-grabbing crisis turned the New England groundfish fishery into a poster child for abused and mismanaged fisheries.

The End of an Era

The era of laissez-faire development of fisheries began closing in July 1989 when the NMFS issued revised guidelines for implementing the national standards of the Magnuson-Stevens Act. In the view of the agency's new director Bill Fox, the national standards contained the basis for a more precautionary approach to managing fisheries.

"Basically, the first national standard states that the secretary shall prevent overfishing, while allowing optimum sustainable yield," says Fox. "The only way you can prevent overfishing is to apply the precautionary approach. If you don't apply the precautionary approach, the probabilities are that you're going to overfish, and you're going to have to recover from it. And that's not preventing overfishing."

"The Magnuson Act also embodied the precautionary principle through the provision requiring that action shall be taken based on the best available scientific information," says Fox. "Again, there are several ways to read that. In the past, fishery management had proceeded on the basis of: 'Well, it looks like we might have a problem, but the science really is not that good. Let's study it for awhile and see if we really have to take this drastic action.' I interpret the Magnuson Act as saying that you shouldn't wait for better scientific information, that if the best available scientific information says that you've got a problem, you should be taking action, not waiting for the information to get better."

The most important revisions to NMFS policy on implementing the Magnuson-Stevens Act had to do with the so-called 602 guidelines that advised fishery management councils how to implement the national standard requiring the prevention of overfishing. The new guidelines mandated that fishery management plans include an "objective and measurable" definition of overfishing, and a recovery plan for overfished populations. By the end of the year, the New England fishery management council was compelled to admit openly what the agency's biologists had been saying for a long time: The New England fleet was overfishing haddock (*Melanogrammus aeglefinus*), cod (*Gadus morhua*), and yellowtail flounder (*Limanda ferruginea*) off much of New England.

Despite its admission of overfishing, the New England council continued dawdling with half measures and internal debates, as fishermen bitterly protested the slightest move toward restricting their freedom to fish as they wished. In June 1991, however, the forum for making decisions changed dramatically when the Conservation Law Foundation and the Massachusetts Audubon Society filed a lawsuit in federal court claiming that the secretary of commerce had violated the Magnuson-Stevens Act by allowing the overfishing of New England groundfish. The council found itself isolated and powerless as the NMFS entered into a consent decree, which survived court challenges by several fishing groups. Under the decree, the New England council was to submit a plan by September 1992 that would end overfishing within five to seven years. If the council did not meet the deadline, the secretary of commerce was to develop a plan by November 1992.

Congress quickly intervened. Within a month of the filing of the lawsuit, Congressman Gerry Studds of Massachusetts responded with a legislative proposal that also set a timetable for adopting a rebuilding plan for New England groundfish. The proposed legislation also called for job-training programs for fishermen and an ambitious program to buy out fishermen's permits and their vessels.

Although fishermen preferred the congressman's timetable for bringing the fishery under control to the schedule of the consent decree, their opposition to the means for funding the vessel buyout effectively scuttled the bill. Under the Studds proposal, the vessel buyout would be funded with tax revenues generated by repealing the fishing fleet's exemption from the diesel fuel tax of 15 cents per gallon. In later versions, Congressman Studds's bill dropped the buyout provisions entirely and lengthened the period within which a fishery management plan would have to rebuild depleted groundfish populations. Like its counterpart in the Senate, which was introduced by Massachusetts Senator John Kerry, the Studds bill was eventually reduced to fostering improved enforcement and promoting the marketing of fish species that New England fishermen either didn't catch or caught and threw back into the water, such as monkfish. Opposi-

tion from the New England groundfish fleet had effectively blunted Congressman Studds's effort to address the underlying problem of the fishing fleet's size.

As part of its court-ordered draft management plan released in March 1992,
the New England council proposed to limit future entry into the fishery and
reduce the number of days that fishermen could fish. As the September deadline for submission of a management plan to the NMFS approached, however,
the council's proposal was stalled by vehement opposition from the fishing fleet,
which had developed its own more relaxed proposal under the auspices of the
council. In December, the state directors from Rhode Island and Maine effectively killed the council's draft proposal by attacking the analysis of socioeconomic impacts and the intervention of the courts in the management of New
England's fisheries.

At the end of September 1993, a year after the deadline imposed by the consent decree, the New England council submitted its plan for rebuilding cod, haddock, and yellowtail flounder. Between 1989, when the council first acknowledged that groundfish were overfished, and the 1993 release of the draft plan,
landings of haddock from the Gulf of Maine had declined 96%. Despite the des-
perate state of haddock populations, the council doubled its proposed quota for
haddock landings and broadened the opportunity for fishing vessels from other
stressed fisheries to enter the groundfish fishery. After some haggling among the
NMFS, the New England council, and members of Congress, the haddock quota
was reduced tenfold from the level initially adopted by the council.

Scientists at NMFS's science center in Massachusetts soon reported even
bleaker news about groundfish off New England. Yellowtail flounder on Georges
Bank joined Gulf of Maine haddock as a commercially extinct population. Federal scientists concluded that Georges Bank cod would not recover for at least
15 years even if fishing ceased completely. The scientists' recommendation was
grim: Stop catching groundfish on Georges Bank, the former fish basket of the
North Atlantic.

The debacle in New England attracted the attention of several conservation
organizations besides the Conservation Law Foundation and the Massachusetts
Audubon Society. Representatives of the Center for Marine Conservation and
the Environmental Defense Fund began appearing at council meetings and generating broader media coverage. Prodded by the increased scrutiny and continuing reports of a historically low abundance of groundfish, the New England
council began considering another set of amendments to the fishery management
plan in 1994. Besides further restricting the number of days that fishermen
could fish, the amendments also closed large areas to fishing.

In February 1996, after 18 months of debates and public hearings, the council adopted Amendment 7 to the fishery management plan for groundfish and submitted it to the secretary of commerce for approval. The action triggered protests by fishermen's organizations and several members of Congress, including Senators Snowe and Cohen of Maine, who attacked the science as inadequate. Other members of the New England congressional delegation, including Massachusetts Congressman Gerry Studds and Senator John Kerry, supported the restrictions and sought continued funding for disaster relief to the New England groundfish fleet.

Although the New England debacle revealed a number of weaknesses in the Magnuson-Stevens Act's management system, none were more troubling than the ability of the New England Fishery Management Council to ignore scientific advice and to allow, even defend, overfishing in order to meet short-term economic and social demands. The council was able to do so partly because the Magnuson Act's definition of optimum yield allowed setting quotas above biologically safe levels in order to take socioeconomic factors into consideration. When Congress began considering amendments to the Magnuson-Stevens Act in 1994, closing this loophole became a major goal of reformers.

Americanizing the Fisheries

When the councils began preparing fishery management plans and the NMFS began reviewing them, the councils and the agency found that much of the federal research conducted over the previous several decades did not answer the kinds of questions that fisheries managers were confronting. Collecting and analyzing that kind of information was expensive and had to compete for funding against demands for industry assistance and regulatory tasks.

While managers within the NMFS struggled to reorient scientific programs toward management, with limited success, longstanding agency programs of industry assistance were expanding rapidly, with enthusiastic congressional and administration support. "There was a very small window in the last years of the Carter administration, when we were full bore on developing the nation's fisheries resources by government policy and new legislative mandates," says Bruce Morehead, who worked on the NMFS's industry services staff at the time. Whether the immediate aim was the expansion of an existing domestic fishery, as in the Gulf of Mexico shrimp fishery, or the Americanization of a foreign-dominated fishery, as off Alaska and the West Coast, development programs proceeded with little or no regard for the momentum toward overfishing that they were creating. Indeed, it was as if the NMFS were really two separate agencies: one that created fishing pressure through marketing, subsidies, and technical assistance, and another agency that tried to contain that pressure through regulations.

Already in 1985, some staff in the NMFS were warning that fleets were expanding to unsustainable levels. "Perhaps the most serious question to address in the future, in addition to further stock improvements, is how to balance fishing capacity with the size of the resource," wrote Robin Finch in a 1985 review about implementation of the Magnuson-Stevens Act. In his review, Finch identified 6 fleets in major fisheries such as Gulf of Mexico shrimp and New England groundfish as overdeveloped, and another 11 fully developed.

The most spectacular growth in vessel sizes and catches occurred in the fleets that worked the waters off Alaska. There, unlike New England, foreign and domestic fishing had not driven down most fish and shellfish populations. What was lacking for increased U.S. catches were vessels and processing facilities.

The Seattle-based fleet that fished in Alaska's waters expanded into the new opportunities, initially for snow (*Chionoecetes opilio*) and tanner crabs (*C. bairdi*), soon after passage of the Magnuson-Stevens Act in 1976. "The program that allowed you to put away your profits untaxed and reuse them for boat construction gave a lot of impetus to boat building at that time," says Lee Alverson, in describing the use of the Capital Construction Fund.[1] "Some of the early boats took advantage of the vessel subsidy. All of a sudden the boat length for crab boats jumped to 90 feet; then it jumped from there to more than a hundred feet. Then they went to 120 feet and that became fairly standard."

The offshore fleet of crab vessels did well until king crab populations fell precipitously in 1981. With state funds generated by the boom in North Slope oil, some vessel owners survived by converting their crab vessels to trawlers for catching groundfish, such as yellowfin sole, Pacific cod, and later, walleye or Alaska pollock.

The North Pacific Fishery Management Council took steps to avoid the kind of uncontrolled fishing that had marked the early implementation of the Magnuson-Stevens Act in New England. Relying heavily upon its science and statistical committee and biological analyses by the NMFS, the North Pacific council set quotas well below what was thought to be the maximum possible long-term levels. Through research cruises and other activities, the NMFS built upon data it had gathered from the Japanese and Soviet fleets to develop a better understanding of the enormous North Pacific fisheries.

In many ways, the management of the Bering Sea and Gulf of Alaska ground-fish fisheries became a showcase for the Magnuson-Stevens Act's potential. To a large extent, conservation and management measures kept pace with expansion of the domestic fleet and processing plants. In other ways, the fisheries exhibited the same problems found in many other fisheries around the country. Although the North Pacific council was among the first to address the problem of bycatch and discarding, trawl fisheries continued catching and discarding enormous amounts of fish, although the discards made up only a very small fraction of the total catch.[2] Nor did the North Pacific council avoid the over-capitalization of the offshore and inshore fleets as well as the processing plants that needed their catches.[3]

"Several of us at the University of Washington pointed out that when we booted the foreign vessels out of the Gulf of Alaska and Bering Sea fisheries, that we had a wonderful opportunity, with only a few large harvesting vessels and mother ships in operation, to control entry so that we could keep capacity down to something approximating the yield capacity of the stock," says Jim Crutchfield, who taught economics at the University of Washington from 1949 to 1982. "We didn't do it. So we ended up with 72 large processing ships and a season that lasted only two or three months. Absolutely asinine!"

By 1990, the fleets had grown to twice the size necessary to catch the available quota. As a result, the lengths of fishing seasons had to be cut drastically to remain within quotas.[4] In growing to catch and process more fish than any other U.S. fishery, the Alaska groundfish fleets and processors had become unprofitable.

"I was surprised, when I first got involved in fisheries, to see how difficult it was to convince people that the root of the difficulty lay in the common property problem," says Jim Crutchfield "We said that no matter what you did to improve the efficiency of fishing vessels or to expand the range of species or geographic range over which they could harvest, you would always end up with too many boats." The implications of this finding presented fishery managers with a politically daunting task that they largely avoided: to close access to fisheries before problems developed. This unwillingness persisted through the Americanization of fisheries during the 1970s and 1980s.

Although closing access to fisheries enjoyed wide support among economists and many fishery managers, it inspired fierce opposition from many fishermen and members of Congress. In the 1980s, Congress hamstrung the councils and the NMFS with special procedural requirements for adopting even modest limitations on access to federal fisheries. Some councils pressed ahead anyway.

For example, the Mid-Atlantic Fishery Management Council had imposed a moratorium on new entrants to the fishery for surf clams in 1977. The slow-growing clams were in danger of being fished out and the small fleet of vessels was hovering on bankruptcy. For the next ten years, the council struggled with developing a regime for allocating shares among participants in the fishery. Allocation of transferable shares, or individual transferable quotas (ITQs), was thought to be a promising means of ending the race for the fish, since a fisherman would be assured of having an exclusive right to a percentage share of the quota.

It helped that Lee Anderson, one of the council members, was an expert in natural resource economics. "I knew what the program should look like if it was to work in the simple way that an economist would tell you: that is, secure property rights, transferability," says Anderson. The council's consideration of ITQs in the surf clam fishery enjoyed the support of the NMFS, which had opposed ITQs in the past, but by the 1990s viewed controlled access as a key element in the agency's strategic plan for recovering U.S. fisheries.

Even so, there was plenty of controversy. While Anderson anticipated controversy over transferability of quotas among fishermen and others, fishermen were most concerned about the initial distribution of the shares: How many years would be used to determine the catch history of a vessel? Would quota shares become concentrated in the hands of a few powerful companies?

While this and later ITQ programs in the South Atlantic wreckfish fishery and the North Pacific halibut and sablefish fisheries performed more or less as anticipated, concerns about winners and losers under the new management regimes added to concerns about the effects of management restrictions on fishermen and fishing communities in other U.S. fisheries.

In the halibut fishery, in which conservative management by the International Pacific Halibut Commission had maintained catches, neither the U.S. nor the Canadian governments controlled the growth of their fleets after moving foreign fleets outside their 200-mile zones. The North Pacific council did include a proposal to limit future entry to the fishery when it released a draft management plan. As commonly occurs, however, the mere mention of limiting entry to a fishery itself triggered the entry of more fishermen, who hoped to qualify for inclusion in any limited entry program the council might adopt. By the late 1980s, the fleet of long-liners registered to fish for halibut had grown to nearly 4,000 vessels. The North Pacific council responded by reducing the length of the seasons. By 1990, thousands of fishermen were racing to get their gear in and out of the water within the 24 to 48 hours that each of three or four seasons lasted.[5] Facing a glut of halibut, processors paid fishermen little for their catch, consumers paid premium prices for frozen fish, and boats sat idle for months at a time.

Facing a similar situation in the related longline fishery for sablefish, the North Pacific council began formally considering alternative forms of management for both the sablefish and halibut fisheries in 1987. In 1991, the council decided to develop a proposal to manage the fisheries under individual fishing quotas, or IFQs. Under this system, fishermen would be allocated percentage shares of quotas that they would be able to use themselves, or rent, lease, or sell to other fishermen.

The proposal generated heated opposition from some fishermen and crew members especially, who believed that they would be unfairly excluded from the fishery.[6] Opponents raised the specters of corporate privatization of a public resource, of lost jobs, and of the transformation of a owner-operated fleet into a fleet of corporate employees. Although the council modified its plan to take into account some of these concerns, it had submitted the final plan in the midst of bitter controversy.

Part of that controversy was spillover from growing conflicts in the much larger groundfish fishery. There, competition between the Seattle trawler fleet and the Alaska nearshore fleet had become especially sharp as the restrictions forced by conservative quotas and overdeveloped fleets bit into profits. By the early 1990s, allocating quotas of groundfish between the offshore and onshore fleets and processors became so polarized that it regularly touched off battles between the Alaska and Washington State congressional delegations and grabbed the worried attention of the Bush and Clinton administrations. In the midst of this controversy, representatives of the offshore fleet began suggesting ITQs as a means of reducing the size of the groundfish fleets. Like some fishermen in the halibut fishery, smaller-scale Alaska groundfish fishermen characterized the proposal to convert the groundfish fishery to IFQs as a subterfuge for a corporate takeover of the entire fishery.

As the council's proposal for an IFQ program in the halibut and sablefish fisheries wound its way through the process of approval in the Department of Commerce, opponents enlisted members of Congress, particularly the Alaska delegation, in a campaign against ITQs generally.[7] As Congress began considering amendments to the Magnuson-Stevens Act in 1994, opponents of the ITQs escalated their campaign. Soon, the use of ITQs became so divisive an issue that it nearly scuttled passage of the Sustainable Fisheries Act (SFA) at the end of the 104th Congress in 1996.

The Birth of a Movement

In the early 1990s, events and the entrance of new players provoked a striking change in the politics and policy of fisheries management in the United States. The spectacular demise of the New England groundfish fishery, the hyperdevelopment of fishing fleets off Alaska, and the bycatch and discard of marine wildlife fueled much of the change and mobilized progressive groups of scientists, fishermen, environmentalists, and charitable foundations. Together, these new players took the fisheries establishment by surprise and accelerated changes in fisheries policy that had been caught in a standoff between regional fishery management councils, Congress, and the fishing industry on one hand and the NMFS on the other.

"The New England situation was the perfect example because foreign overfishing off New England was the impetus for the Magnuson-Stevens Act in the first place," says Ken Hinman, who joined the staff of the National Coalition for Marine Conservation soon after passage of the Magnuson-Stevens Act in 1976. "It's such a stark example of how we can destroy a once-abundant ecosystem, and take down with it whole fishing communities and jobs. The collapse of the New England groundfish fishery brought environmental organizations in, raised public awareness, and was the impetus for most of the recent changes in policy we've seen."

Until the early 1990s, few environmental organizations had involved themselves directly in the complex and intense business of fisheries management. The National Coalition for Marine Conservation had been involved since the 1970s, but because its founders were recreational fishermen, commercial fishing groups and their allies in the NMFS and in Congress dismissed its policy positions as veiled efforts to expand recreational fisheries at the expense of commercial fisheries. In the late 1980s, Greenpeace expanded its campaigns in Alaska, which had focused on incidental catch of marine mammals, to the impact of additional groundfish trawling on food sources for marine mammals. The Center for Marine Conservation launched a small fisheries conservation program in 1988, prompted by frustration with the refusal of the Gulf of Mexico Fishery Management Council to reduce the bycatch of sea turtles and finfish in the shrimp fishery.

The center, which had programs funded largely by mass-mail appeals to protect marine mammals and sea turtles, would not have been able to venture into the conservation of fisheries without the support of an entrepreneur within the charitable foundation community. "It's the empty room theory of investment, because you realize that that room has potential and no one else has seen it yet. That's what makes a classic good investment," says Wolcott Henry III, who managed the Curtis and Edith Munson Foundation in the 1980s and 1990s. "I didn't see anyone working on marine fisheries except the National Coalition for Marine Conservation."

Besides continuing its funding of the National Coalition and underwriting the development of a fisheries program at the Center for Marine Conservation, the Munson Foundation made a planning grant to the World Wildlife Fund for expanding its marine programs. More importantly, Henry began promoting marine fisheries conservation among other foundations. At meetings sponsored by the Environmental Grantmakers Association, the Consultative Group for Biological Diversity, and the National Fish and Wildlife Foundation, Henry organized presentations on marine fisheries.[8] "The first two or three years at the Environmental Grantmakers Association meetings, it was hard to get people," says Henry. "One year, we were up against spotted owls. We were a new issue, so we weren't given great slots."

Within several years, other foundations such as the David and Lucile Packard Foundation, the Rockefeller Brothers Fund, the Pew Charitable Trusts, and the Surdna Foundation, among others, began providing grants for marine fisheries conservation to progressive fishermen's organizations and to national and regional conservation organizations. By offering funds for fisheries conservation, foundations attracted greater interest among environmental organizations, which were reluctant to begin a new program on issues and animals that did not enjoy the public support that marine mammals or endangered species did. The growing controversy over high seas drift net fisheries in the Pacific Ocean and preparations for the United Nations Earth Summit in 1992 also attracted major national environmental organizations such as the Environmental Defense Fund and the Natural Resources Defense Council into discussions of fisheries policy generally.

After a tentative foray into fisheries policy making during the reauthorization of the Magnuson-Stevens Act by Congress in 1990, staff from the Center for Marine Conservation, the National Coalition for Marine Conservation, the National Audubon Society, the World Wildlife Fund, and Greenpeace began planning for reauthorization of the Magnuson-Stevens Act in 1992. In developing their plans, these organizations used tools that were foreign to fisheries policy making, such as opinion polls and focus groups. Eventually, these groups settled upon forming a broadly based coalition called the Marine Fish Conservation Network.

"The basic idea behind Marine Fish Conservation Network was to reform federal fisheries management," says Bill Mott, who served as executive director of the network from 1993 to 1996. "Several groups had addressed the issues individually in the past, but until then, there was no concerted effort to address the significant issues in American fisheries policy. So, those five groups came up with a national agenda, which became the platform for the fish network.[9]

"The agenda was primarily addressing overfishing, eliminating problems with bycatch, and addressing marine habitat protection issues. There were several other issues, such as reforming the councils. But as the campaign progressed, it really became those three issues—overfishing, bycatch, and habitat. That was our mantra."

The agenda adopted by the Marine Fish Conservation Network was similar to that presented at a 1989 congressional hearing by a group of scientists, most of whom were best known for their work with marine mammals. The testimony was presented by Bill Fox, who was serving as chairman of the Marine Mammal Commission at the time. This group of scientists recommended that four features of the Marine Mammal Protection Act (MMPA) be incorporated into the Magnuson-Stevens Act: adopting an ecosystem perspective, exercising conservative management under uncertainty, setting a threshold beyond which exploitation ceases, and establishing independent oversight of the act's implementation.

Within these broader themes, the scientists raised issues and principles that soon became part of the common parlance of debates over fisheries management. The scientists argued for an ecosystem perspective that included protection of essential fish habitat and the consideration of species that were affected by fishing though they were neither caught nor consumed. In order to reduce the risk of depletion due to uncertainty about the status of fish populations and the effectiveness of management, the scientists urged a conservation ethic that placed the burden of proof upon those who were fishing and emphasized long-term rather than short-term benefits over the prevailing exploitation ethic.

When Bill Fox was appointed director of the NMFS in January 1990, he attempted to apply these principles to the agency's implementation of the Magnuson-Stevens Act. Fox also had these principles incorporated in a strategic plan that circulated within the agency but was never formally adopted. The top priority of the plan was to rebuild overfished marine fisheries partly by requiring rebuilding plans. Agency scientists estimated that the dozens of overfished fisheries were costing fishermen about $1 billion annually—an economic argument that resonated within the Bush administration. The second of the plan's objectives emphasized maintaining currently productive fisheries by erring on the side of conservation when there was uncertainty. The plan also called for integrating fisheries and protected species conservation, and increasing the predictive capacity of fisheries models. Finally, the plan proposed addressing overcapitalization in fisheries by moving from open access to closed access through such measures as ITQs.[10]

Fox's efforts to reform fisheries management administratively met fierce resistance from commercial fishermen and their allies on Capitol Hill, who found Fox's approach confrontational. Soon after Bill Clinton entered the White House as president in 1993, Dr. Fox was replaced as director of the agency. Nonetheless, many of the principles he had advocated were adopted by later directors, the Marine Fish Conservation Network, and many members of Congress. "The network's agenda turned out to be not very different from the administration position when that was presented a couple of months later," says Suzanne Iudicello, one of the principals in the Marine Fish Conservation Network.

Although the administration and the network coalesced around similar goals for change in the Magnuson-Stevens Act, reformers faced enormous political obstacles. In order to elevate the importance of conservation over development in the Magnuson-Stevens Act, they would have to disrupt the entrenched politics of fisheries on Capitol Hill.

The Campaign Begins

"The fishing industry did not take seriously all of the public statements by the environmental community that we were in it, we were prepared, and we were going to go for it," says Iudicello, who served on the network's executive committee. "They went their own way. They just assumed it was going to be business as usual, with a few congressmen from the coast doing constituent casework and taking care of their people. They behaved the same way they always behave. They had one or two people they talked to and thought they were going to be taken care of."

Unlike the commercial fishing industry, which had never been able to organize itself nationally, the Marine Fish Conservation Network had more than 100 organizations supporting its agenda. "The industry was certainly surprised a couple of years down the road when the network not only stayed around, but grew much larger and much more powerful because of the different groups," says Bill Mott.

Most members of the network were conservation organizations, but it also included progressive fishermen's organizations. Among the commercial fishing organizations, individual organizations had their own agendas. The Alaska Longline Fishermen's Association, for example, was concerned with reducing bycatch in the Bering Sea pollock fishery, while the Lobsterman's Association pressed for habitat protection.

"When the media saw the diversity of groups—commercial, recreational, and environmental—all working together, it was very helpful," says Mott. "Everybody had their own private agenda, and the network had its own overarching agenda. When their individual agendas meshed with ours, they were effective in getting to their senators. In many cases, we set the agenda for the congressional debates, the policy discussions. The industry was always scrambling to catch up and to organize."

In building a power base, the network used other tactics and strategies that conservation groups had perfected in battles over endangered sea turtles and marine mammals. Greenpeace, for example, sent canvassers into key congressional districts to drum up support for the network's agenda. In the spring and summer of 1994, the network sent two grassroots educators on a 19,000-mile tour of 28 states, many of them inland states, where they presented the network's agenda for fisheries conservation to hundreds of people. "We went to the heartland," says Iudicello. "We went to places where there was no obvious self-interest. Our grassroots educators made the case that fish are like parks. They are like any public resource. They aren't just something for Boston or Alaska. That message, and the whimsical way we did it, brought in new voices, both grassroots and congressional."

The network took to the airwaves with television and radio advertisements featuring Katherine Hepburn and other celebrities. The network also placed advertisements in key newspapers in states from Louisiana to South Dakota, as well as at platforms in Washington, D.C.'s subway system. The network's media coordinator helped place dozens of articles and editorials in magazines and newspapers around the country. Fishermen and conservationists who belonged to the network flew into Washington, D.C., for days of intense lobbying of their congressional representatives, providing crucial political leverage to the Washington-based conservation groups.

Finally, the network searched for members of Congress who would champion their agenda. Rather than seek support among the traditional power brokers on Capitol Hill, such as leaders on key committees, the network looked for champions among new representatives. But while individual members of Congress were willing to take on single issues such as habitat protection, no one was willing to sponsor the network's entire agenda, until network leaders met with Congressman Wayne Gilchrest from Maryland's Eastern Shore. "We got really lucky with Congressman Gilchrest," says Mott. "He was a Republican who sat on the right committee and who showed from our first meeting with him on the Eastern Shore a sincere interest in doing the right thing, in conserving our fisheries."

Gilchrest, who had first been elected to Congress in 1990, drew upon his familiarity with the fisheries of the Chesapeake Bay, some of which had suffered dramatic declines due to overfishing and habitat degradation. Briefings by the network convinced him that the problems he had seen in the Chesapeake Bay were not unique. "Certainly, the decline of the New England groundfish fishery figured in my decision to become involved, but also problems such as bycatch of red snapper in the shrimp fishery in the Gulf of Mexico, the dead zone there as well," says Gilchrest.

"I was also concerned that the councils could ignore data collected by the National Marine Fisheries Service. I thought there needed to be a better structure," says Gilchrest. "We heard a lot of criticism of NMFS, from state fisheries people, that they don't have the right kind of data, that they're too cautious. And I said I would rather be too cautious than continue as is."

On May 12, 1994, Congressman Gilchrest introduced a bill, H.R. 4404, that was based largely on the network's agenda. Within months, the network gathered more than 100 cosponsors of the bill and seemed poised for a quick victory, when the congressional elections of November 1994 transformed the political landscape on Capitol Hill. The Republican victories in congressional races replaced the traditionally Democratic leadership of the House of Representatives with conservative Republicans, many of whom aimed to dismantle the programs of environmental protection established in the previous quarter-century of Democratic dominance. In the House of Representatives, Republicans disbanded the Merchant Marine and Fisheries Committee, where the Magnuson-Stevens Act and other coastal and ocean legislation had been formulated, and placed responsibility for these programs in the House Resources Committee. The new chairman of that committee, Congressman Don Young from Alaska, had a long record as an opponent of the kind of marine conservation being promoted by the network. Congressman Jim Saxton, a moderate from New Jersey, who held the chairmanship of the subcommittee that would deal with the Magnuson-Stevens Act, was sympathetic to the network's agenda, but found his influence over the legislation circumscribed by the chairman's interest.

In May 1995, the House Resources Committee approved H.R. 39, Congressman Young's bill reauthorizing the Magnuson-Stevens Act. The committee rejected an amendment on overfishing by Congressman Gilchrest that would have closed the loophole in the definition of optimum yield that allowed quotas to be set above biologically sound levels for economic or social purposes. In other ways, the committee's bill appeared to address the network's agenda, but as a matter of fact, reflected the regional interests of committee members. For example, the committee included provisions on reducing bycatch that were aimed principally at the Seattle-based fleet of factory trawlers, which competed for pollock against the Alaska fleet of trawlers that supplied processors based onshore. At the same time, the committee exempted the Gulf of Mexico shrimp fleet from reducing its massive bycatch by approving an amendment offered by Congressman Billy Tauzin of Louisiana, who had led the battle against turtle excluder devices (TEDs) a few years before.

Having lost in the committee, the network prepared to fight for its agenda on the House floor when H.R. 39 came up for a vote. While the network built support in the hinterlands, Congressman Gilchrest sought support from other members of Congress. "I talked to nearly every member of the House," says Gilchrest. "Members from Nebraska, Utah, and Colorado were fascinated by the issue. No one had ever approached them about it before. They were easy to convince: 'If you want fish on your plate, we had better manage fisheries appropriately.' It was a little more difficult to talk with someone like Barney Frank from Massachusetts. He said, 'If you can come up with enough money to subsidize the fishermen, then come back and we can talk.'"

As the summer passed, the Republican assault on the environment began wearing thin with the public and with some members of Congress. "Moderate Republicans were getting sick of getting beat up by their constituents and the media on gutting the Clean Water Act, gutting the Clean Air Act, gutting the Safe Drinking Water Act," says Iudicello. "They were looking for a green vote. And we characterized fisheries management as a conservation issue, as an environmental issue."

On October 18, 1995, the House of Representatives began debating H.R. 39, the Fishery Conservation and Management Act amendments of 1995. The network had worked with members of Congress in gaining support for amendments to the committee bill. Congressman Farr from California sponsored an amendment to strengthen the protection of essential fisheries habitat from damaging activities, including fishing. Congressman Goss from Florida and Congresswoman Furse from Oregon offered an amendment on bycatch that closed the loophole for bycatch in the Gulf of Mexico shrimp fishery. Finally, Congressman Gilchrest was prepared to offer his amendment on overfishing and the definition of optimum yield.

Perhaps sensing that he was holding a losing hand and that the Senate might yet resist reform, Congressman Young did not actively seek support for H.R. 39; nor did he lobby members to oppose the amendments. The continued decline of the New England groundfish fishery and the political, economic, social, and cultural costs associated with it remained a grim warning about the future if conservation continued to be sacrificed to short term gain. In supporting Congressman Gilchrest's amendment on optimum yield, Congressman Gerry Studds from Massachusetts spoke from experience in warning his colleagues: "I would really ask that all Members look carefully at what we have just gone through and are still going through and will be going through, unfortunately, for a good many years to come in New England. I think we are paying a heavy price for having allowed ourselves the luxury of modifying that yield for economic and social reasons."

By a vote of 304 to 113, the House of Representatives approved the Gilchrest amendment. By smaller, but still large margins, the House also approved the other two amendments.[11] On a vote of 384 to 30, the House sent the bill to the Senate.

Early in 1996, the Senate Committee on Commerce, Science, and Transportation, chaired by powerful Alaska Senator Ted Stevens, took up the reauthorization of the Magnuson-Stevens Act. Rather than building upon the House bill, the Senators focused upon S. 39, the Sustainable Fisheries Act that Senator Stevens had introduced. Although reformers were unable to use many of the tactics that had proved successful in the House of Representatives, they did campaign to preserve the House amendments they had won and to prevent any weakening amendments in the Senate bill. Indeed, the SFA came to resemble the House bill in many respects.

In May, the Senate Commerce Committee reported its bill to the floor of the Senate for action. The bill resolved most issues within the Senate and with the House of Representatives, with the exception of the use of ITQs in managing fisheries. Although fishermen, conservationists, and members of Congress from other parts of the country hotly disputed whether there should be a moratorium on ITQ programs, the principal dispute involved Senator Stevens and Senator Slade Gorton from Washington. Both senators sought to protect their own fishermen as the Alaska groundfish fishery became less and less economical due largely to overdevelopment of the fishing fleets. Senator Stevens's supporters feared that an ITQ program in the groundfish fishery would favor the Seattle-based fleet, while Senator Gorton's supporters feared insolvency if the fishery remained open access. More generally, opponents argued (among other things) that ITQs privatized a public resource without compensating the public and would lead to corporate takeovers of small-scale fisheries. The Marine Fish Conservation Network was so split over the issue that it remained silent in the debate although some of its members did not.

By August 1996, the dispute over ITQs was resolved with an agreement on a four-year moratorium on new ITQ programs and a thorough study of ITQs by the National Academy of Sciences. The agreement held together even through threats of a filibuster by the senators from Washington and through two days of sometimes bitter debate on the floor of the Senate in September. On September 19, the Senate passed the SFA by a unanimous vote and sent its bill to the House for concurrence.

Although House leaders expressed dismay that they had no opportunity to revise the bill, the House passed S. 39 by a vote of 384 to 30. On October 11, President Clinton signed the SFA into law, "delighted that the legislation addresse[d] many of the conservation and management issues identified by my Administration's proposal of 1994."[12]

The Sustainable Fisheries Act of 1996

Passage of the SFA marked a major shift in emphasis within federal fisheries management. This shift was most evident in the revised definition of optimum yield (OY), which stipulated that social, economic, or ecological factors might be used to set OY at lower but not at higher levels than maximum sustainable yield (MSY). The new definition also required that OY must allow for rebuilding overfished populations to levels consistent with MSY. This language effectively closed a major loophole that had contributed greatly to the hyperdevelopment of many fisheries after initial passage of the Magnuson-Stevens Act in 1976.

Other provisions reinforced this shift in policy.[13] For example, the SFA required that fishery management plans include standards for identifying when a particular fishery should be considered overfished. Using these standards, the NMFS was to annually identify fisheries that were overfished or were approaching that condition. Fishery management councils had to adopt or amend fishery management plans to end overfishing and to rebuild overfished fisheries as quickly as possibly, generally within ten years.

The SFA also took some tentative steps toward reducing the bycatch and discard of marine fish. As so often happens in setting standards for reducing environmental problems, Congress hedged by limiting the reduction of bycatch "to the extent practicable." Also, while requiring councils to develop standardized methods for reporting bycatch in fisheries, Congress did not require reporting itself. In addition, Congress intervened in the reduction of bycatch in two fisheries of interest to influential members of Congress. The SFA required the North Pacific Fishery Management Council to lower the discard of fish and shellfish caught and discarded because they were undesirable for one reason or another. Congress authorized the council to use a system of fines and other methods in doing so. Congress intervened once again in the Gulf of Mexico shrimp fishery by deferring requirements that shrimp fishermen use bycatch reduction devices. Instead, Congress required yet another program to develop technology for reducing bycatch and to provide a report to Congress on economic impacts, benefits, and other aspects of the problem.

The SFA also attempted to increase the influence of fisheries managers over activities that damage fisheries habitat. The provisions on habitat required that fishery management councils amend their fishery management plans to identify essential fish habitat (EFH) for individual fisheries, reduce damage to EFH from fishing, as practicable, and develop measures to conserve and enhance EFH.[14] If another federal agency were involved in an activity that might damage EFH, it was required to consult with the NMFS and take any recommended actions to reduce that damage or explain why it was not doing so. With vigorous application, these procedural requirements could significantly increase the consideration given fisheries habitat in the myriad projects that alter coastal lands and waters each year.

The act's amendments to the financial assistance programs of the NMFS also reflected the shift from development toward conservation and restoration noted elsewhere. Besides prohibiting the use of loan guarantees for the construction of new vessels until October 2001 if it would increase the fishing capacity of fleets, the act authorized the use of funds from the newly renamed Fisheries Finance Program for underwriting the reduction of fleets.

The shift in the politics of fisheries was as important as the shift in the policies of fisheries. For decades, the fishing industry and its allies in the federal government were unchallenged in setting national policy on fisheries. In policy, and even more in practice, the principal aim of industry and government was the expansion of fishing rather than the stewardship of living marine resources. Although scientists and policy makers within the NMFS sometimes argued for restraint and a more cautious approach, they were no match for the political support that the expansion of fisheries enjoyed elsewhere in federal, state, and local levels of government.

In the campaign that led to passage of the SFA, conservation groups especially shifted the emphasis from development to conservation and from regional and special-interest agendas to national policy. They did so by injecting values and principles from more protective legislation on marine mammals and endangered species and by applying grassroots campaign strategies that undercut the power and influence of entrenched interests in Congress.

Although the campaign for reform of fisheries legislation was difficult, it was just the first step in the reform of federal fisheries management in the United States. The efficacy of the legislation would be judged in its implementation by the NMFS and each of the eight fishery management councils. Reformers no longer would enjoy the strategic advantage of having Congress as a single focus for attention. Instead, the future of reform would depend upon overcoming entrenched interests in the regional councils. At the same time, reformers would have to compete with industry interests in influencing implementation by the NMFS as it struggled with its divided roles as protector of the public trust and promoter of the fishing industry.

Summary

In the late 1980s, a new interpretation of the Magnuson-Stevens Act initiated the first significant tightening of the act's conservation standard since 1976. A lawsuit filed by the Conservation Law Foundation later led to a protracted but dramatic revision of the fishery management plan for the New England groundfish fishery. The revision provoked protests from fishermen and their congressional representatives.

Unlike the New England Fishery Management Council, the North Pacific council had managed to restrain catches in the country's largest fishery. The North Pacific council, however, was no more successful than the New England council in coping with the rapid expansion of fishing fleets that was supported and encouraged by the NMFS and fueled to a large extent by private funding.

Councils in other regions faced similar threats to fisheries from the hyperdevelopment of fleets after passage of the Magnuson-Stevens Act. In the mid-Atlantic, after a decade of discussion, the council adopted an individual transferable quota (ITQ) program for the surf clam and ocean quahog fishery—the first in the country. The program was aimed principally at bringing the fishing fleet into balance with the fishery it depended upon. Several years later, the North Pacific council adopted a similar program for the halibut and sablefish fisheries, in which fishing seasons had been reduced to several days each year. This ITQ program

generated enormous controversy that spilled over into congressional consideration of amendments to the Magnuson-Stevens Act in the mid-1990s.

In the early 1990s, the decline of the New England groundfish fishery and
other fisheries around the United States attracted the attention of conservation
organizations and charitable foundations. At the same time, government and
independent scientists were raising concerns about traditional management approaches and proposing the adoption of a precautionary approach to fishing.

In 1993, conservation organizations and several fishing groups formed a network to promote reform of the Magnuson-Stevens Act. The network relied on
techniques that conservation organizations had used successfully in campaigns
for marine mammal and endangered species conservation. The entry of this
network of organizations fundamentally changed the politics of setting national
policy on fisheries.

In 1996, Congress passed the Sustainable Fisheries Act (SFA), which included
major amendments to the Magnuson-Stevens Act. Besides requiring plans for
rebuilding depleted fish populations, the SFA closed a loophole in the definition of optimum yield that had allowed quotas to be set at levels that were biologically unsustainable. The SFA also called for reducing bycatch in fisheries
and for protecting essential fish habitat from any destructive effects of fishing
or other activities. The SFA also completed the redirection of fisheries financial
assistance programs away from expansion of fishing fleets.

Notes

1. Alverson, Dayton Lee. Interview on June 25, 2000.
2. The fisheries for pollock in the Bering Sea and around the Aleutian Islands, which
   landed about 1.3 million metric tons of pollock in 1992, also caught and discarded
   more than 204,000 metric tons of pollock, Pacific cod, flounders, and other fish in
   that same year.
3. Overcapitalization exists when more capital than is needed is used to produce the
   optimal level of a good. In open-access fisheries, this usually refers to the excessive
   number and size of vessels, as well as the amount of gear, used to harvest fish.
4. Between 1988 and 1993, fishing seasons in the Bering Sea and Aleutian Islands were
   reduced from 12 to 6 months. In some areas, seasons shrank to less than 100 days.
   In the Gulf of Alaska, the fleets were able to catch entire annual quotas within a
   month in some areas.
5. In a related fishery using longlines to catch sablefish, the number of vessels longer
   than 50 feet grew tenfold between 1981 and 1988, and the number of smaller vessels grew at an even faster rate.

6. As finally adopted, quota shares were allocated to vessel owners whose ships had landed halibut or sablefish at least once during 1988–1990. The amount of shares was based on the catch history of the vessel.

7. When it became effective in 1995, this ITQ program was the largest of three that had been adopted under the Magnuson-Stevens Act. The first ITQ program approved under the Magnuson-Stevens Act was developed by the mid-Atlantic council for the surf clam and ocean quahog fisheries. The second ITQ program was developed by the South Atlantic council for the wreckfish fishery. For a more extensive discussion of these fisheries, see *Fish, Markets, and Fishermen* by Iudicello, Weber, and Wieland, published by Island Press in 1999.

8. The Environmental Grantmakers Association grew out of, and is still a part of, the Environmental Grantmakers Affinity Group of the Council on Foundations. In 1987, a group of environmental grantmakers met in Washington, D.C., to discuss common interests and to learn about each other's specific programs. (http://www.ega.org)

   The Consultative Group on Biological Diversity (CGBD) is a grantmakers forum that seeks to focus attention on issues and program opportunities related to the conservation and restoration of biological resources. Established in 1987, the CGBD was comprised of 46 foundations and the U.S. Agency for International Development in 2000. The CGBD is funded by program grants from its members. (http://www.cgbd.org)

   Congress created the National Fish and Wildlife Foundation in 1984 to benefit the conservation of fish, wildlife, and plants, and the habitat on which they depend. The foundation does not support lobbying, political advocacy, or litigation. The foundation fosters partnerships among federal, state, and local governments, corporations, private foundations, individuals, and nonprofit organizations. By 2000, the foundation had made more than 3,850 grants, committing over $150 million in federal funds, matched with nonfederal dollars, delivering more than $490 million for conservation. (http://www.nfwf.org)

9. In its first newsletter published in 1993, the Marine Fish Conservation Network presented a broader set of issues for reform than the three that became the focus of the network's campaign. These were the following:
   - eliminating overfishing and rebuilding of depleted fish populations;
   - adopting a precautionary, risk-averse approach to fisheries management;
   - reducing the conflicts of interest on fishery management councils;
   - improving conservation of large pelagic fishes;
   - minimizing bycatch;
   - protecting marine fish habitats;
   - enhancing monitoring and enforcement; and
   - providing adequate funding for fisheries research and enforcement.

10. "Our Living Oceans," a periodic national assessment of marine fisheries launched during Fox's tenure, became a staple of discussions and debates about the status of U.S. fisheries.

Several shorter analyses of the problems in marine fisheries domestically and globally also contributed to the foundations of reform. These included a 1993 article in *Fisheries* by Drs. Michael P. Sissenwine and Andrew A. Rosenberg, two senior scientists at the NMFS. An article by Dr. Carl Safina of the National Audubon Society in *Scientific American* broadened awareness of fisheries problems within the scientific community and the general public.

11. The Farr amendment on habitat passed by a vote of 294 to 129. The Goss/Furse amendment on bycatch passed by a vote of 251 to 162.

12. White House Press Release, October 11, 1996.

13. For a thorough review of the act's provisions, see Bean and Rowland (1997), as well as reports and newsletters maintained on the web page of the NMFS. (http://www.nmfs.noaa.gov)

14. The Sustainable Fisheries Act defined essential fish habitat as "those waters and substrate necessary to fish for spawning, breeding, feeding or growth to maturity."

Conclusion

In 1999, after seven years of discussion, the New England Fishery Management Council adopted a fishery management plan for monkfish. In trying to manage this rapidly growing and diverse fishery, the New England council adopted a complex set of regulations that attempted to dole out small amounts of monkfish to different types of fishermen, from scallop draggers to gill-netters. Although the plan did not cut catches in half as had been proposed in the draft plan, the restrictions did not sit well with many fishermen. Some fishermen formed the Monkfish Defense Fund and unsuccessfully challenged the regulations in federal court.

However onerous the regulations may have been, fishermen landed 55 million pounds of monkfish in 1999—9 million more pounds than were landed in 1992, when the fishery management plan process began, and just 6 million pounds less than the peak catch in 1997. The high catches obscured the deteriorating condition of monkfish populations off New England. In its congressionally mandated report on the status of U.S. fisheries in 2000, the National Marine Fisheries Service (NMFS) reported that monkfish in southern and northern New England waters were overfished. Indeed, the catch of monkfish in government surveys had fallen by more than two-thirds in the last two decades and was at near-record lows.

In 2000, the Monkfish Defense Fund took a different tack in its campaign to relax the restrictions of the fishery management plan. Insisting that government assessments and surveys overlooked concentrations of monkfish known to commercial fishermen, the Monkfish Defense Fund collaborated with government scientists in using the knowledge and know-how of commercial fishermen in conducting surveys for monkfish. The pilot surveys proved workable and led to an expanded program of surveys in 2001.

In its own way, this industry program hinted at one of the most profound changes in federal fisheries policy during the last century. Until 1996, an ideology of abundance had prevailed. The biological sustainability of fishing was presumed, and the goal of management was to ensure maximum use. In this atmosphere, fisheries developed with no idea of how large or productive fish populations were, and generally faced restrictions only when problems became inescapable. The development of the monkfish fishery in the early 1990s, as described in the introduction, is one of many examples.

In the early 1990s, however, the rise of the precautionary approach in fisheries management began shifting the burden of proof toward having to demonstrate sustainability of fishing rather than the need for management restrictions. Whereas the shortcomings of science and surveys had been used to rationalize high levels of exploitation in the past, those shortcomings constrained catches in many fisheries by the late 1990s. The Pacific Fishery Management Council, for example, reduced optimum yield in its fisheries by 25 to 75%, depending upon the degree of ignorance about fish populations. In the Atlantic monkfish fishery, fishermen who hoped to relax restrictions on fishing saw an advantage in sponsoring surveys, hoping to find information that government surveys had not gathered.

Whatever scientific shortcomings the collaborative surveys of monkfish might have had, they also represented a potentially beneficial shift in the relationship between scientists and fishermen. With any luck and some hard work, such research in other fisheries could begin bridging the gulf in views concerning the status of marine wildlife populations. With few exceptions, distrust had pervaded the relationship between scientists and fishermen. The possibility that research would lead to restrictions accounted partly for the distrust, as did the independence from short-term concerns that sound scientific research requires. The frequent unwillingness of fishermen to accept the results of scientific calculations frustrated scientists, and the reluctance of scientists to use anecdotal observations frustrated fishermen. Designing a research survey collaboratively could reduce distrust and yield information that enjoys greater credibility.

Such collaborative research could also fill a growing gap in fisheries information created by the exclusion of foreign fishing vessels from U.S. waters and the decline in federal funding for such research. Until the mid-1980s when foreign fishing in U.S. waters all but ceased, observers on foreign fishing vessels provided U.S. scientists with valuable information on catches, bycatches, and other matters. The Magnuson-Stevens Act, however, did not require observers on the U.S. vessels that filled the gap left by foreign vessels after their exclusion. As U.S. catches rose, information declined.

A decrease in funding for fisheries research further reduced information necessary for conservation and management. Lack of funding for replacement vessels during the 1980s and 1990s led to a federal research fleet in which many vessels were well beyond their useful lives, and few fully incorporated new technologies. Only in the late 1990s was any significant new funding for research vessels appropriated by Congress. Funding for research surveys also fell during the 1980s, then grew in the late 1990s, as the lack of survey information led to restrictions in fisheries. By the end of the decade, however, overall fisheries research funding had not regained the ground it had lost in the previous decades. In this situation, exploring new vehicles for gathering information, such as collaborative surveys, made sense.

Experience suggested, however, that more information alone would not eliminate the resistance to reductions in fishing that force fishermen to find different jobs while fish populations recover. Despite a wealth of information regarding monkfish, reining in the fishery to sustainable levels proved elusive. In its report to Congress for 2000, the NMFS concluded that monkfish were still suffering from overfishing.

The Rise of Conservation

In the 1960s, the seemingly rapacious efficiency of foreign fleets provided fodder for the revolution in fisheries management that passage of the Magnuson-Stevens Act in 1976 represented. Much of the rhetoric of the time pinned the hopes of the U.S. fishing industry and the conservation of U.S. fisheries on excluding foreign fleets. Although the Magnuson-Stevens Act reflected many of the progressive fisheries management principles of the early 1970s, the institutional challenges of managing regional fisheries and the very objectives of the Magnuson-Stevens Act itself impeded the imposition of timely conservation measures in many fisheries.

The institutional challenges had partly to do with the poorly defined relationship between the NMFS and the regional fisheries management councils and partly to do with the nature of each of these institutions. While the NMFS was responsible for reviewing, approving or disapproving, and implementing fishery management plans, it was the councils that developed the plans themselves. NMFS staff, especially those who had had some experience in managing fisheries under treaties, found their role as reviewers frustrating, particularly when councils did not adopt strong enough conservation measures. The councils, in turn, found the NMFS meddlesome, and complained that the agency was preempting the authority that Congress had invested in the councils.

These institutions' conflicting missions presented obstacles to proactive conservation as well. The councils, in which membership was dominated by fishermen, were responsible not simply for conservation of fisheries in their regions but for ensuring that the fisheries generated maximum economic benefit. The emphasis of the Magnuson-Stevens Act upon development generally discouraged councils from restraining fisheries until clear problems arose. Fishermen and state fisheries officials on the councils found themselves having to consider long-term conservation at the same time that they confronted the short-term needs of fishermen to continue fishing in order to make a living.

Similarly, the NMFS had far more experience in developing fisheries than in conserving them. Before the Magnuson-Stevens Act, the agency's involvement with restricting fisheries had been confined to the incidental catch of marine mammals and endangered species or to domestic fisheries that operated under an international treaty. The NMFS's primary activities had been scientific research, much of it in support of the fishing industry, and direct assistance to the fishing industry through marketing, grants, and loan programs. The act's goal of expanding U.S. fishing reinforced the development role of the NMFS, which was carried out independently of the agency's conservation role until the 1990s.

The conservation standard of the Magnuson-Stevens Act itself was an obstacle to conservation. By allowing optimum yield (OY) to be adjusted for social or economic reasons, the Magnuson-Stevens Act created an enormous loophole in the weak restraint on catches represented by maximum sustainable yield (MSY)—the basis for (OY). Since it was highly unlikely that social and economic factors would lead to tighter restrictions, this language served largely to incorporate political concerns into the evaluation of conservation measures. Arguments for deferring strict management measures due to their socioeconomic effects were rarely scrutinized with the same degree of scepticism as were warnings by biologists that fishing rates were too high. Yet, hard data on the social and economic aspects were even scarcer than biological data on most fisheries.

Further complicating conservation, Congress continued to play an active role in fisheries management, often in ways that undermined implementation of the Magnuson-Stevens Act. In the past, Congress had attempted to assist industry, if only very modestly, by funding various forms of direct and indirect technical and financial assistance. Indeed, this pattern continued in the early years after passage of the Magnuson-Stevens Act, as the U.S. industry grew into the fisheries that had been the domain of foreign fleets. Increasingly, however, Congress attempted to influence implementation of the Act's conservation objectives through legislation on particular fisheries. Congressional members and delegations also attempted to influence or overturn decisions by the NMFS and the councils by intervening at higher levels of the executive branch, sometimes involving the White House directly.

By the late 1980s, the shortcomings of the Magnuson-Stevens Act had become quite clear as the decline of flagship fisheries, such as the New England groundfish fishery, attracted public attention. Little might have come of the increased scrutiny were it not for the entry of conservation organizations into the growing debate over the direction of federal fisheries management.

The agendas of these organizations reflected two fundamental shifts in attitudes about marine wildlife. First, as the result of the campaigns by some of these organizations in the late 1960s and early 1970s, some groups of marine wildlife that had been regarded solely as commodities were recognized for their aesthetic and ecological values. This shift was embodied most clearly in the Marine Mammal Protection Act (MMPA), which placed a moratorium not only on killing, but also on harming marine mammals. Within a short time, the U.S. government ended its sponsorship and management of hunts for great whales, northern fur seals, and other marine mammals.

This shift in values was accompanied by shifts in scientific views about the productivity of marine ecosystems as well as the capacity of science to predict how marine ecosystems respond to exploitation. Predictions in the 1960s and 1970s that the oceans could yield 400–500 million metric tons annually were abandoned as more conservative estimates were confirmed by much lower maximum global catches of 90 million metric tons. Rather than cogs in a machine that scientists could manipulate to produce maximum output for society, marine wildlife came to be seen as an ensemble of players in a complex drama in which the script was constantly being rewritten. As a result of the uncertainty arising from the complexity and dynamism of wildlife communities, scientific estimates of sustainable fishing levels were fraught with uncertainty, in this view. Failing to incorporate this uncertainty into the management would contribute to the depletion of wildlife populations as it had in the past.

Buoyed by widespread public support for protecting marine mammals, these shifts in scientific understanding found their first expression in the MMPA of 1972. Unlike prevailing fisheries management policy and practice, the MMPA did not generally assume that marine mammal populations could withstand direct exploitation or harm. If anything, the MMPA presumed the opposite: that an activity would harm a population of marine mammals.

For more than two decades, these shifts in public policy regarding marine mammals were not reflected in public policy on fisheries. Rather, the pent-up desires of government and industry to restore U.S. fisheries to world leadership encouraged high expectations for catches in individual fisheries, particularly during the expansion of domestic fishing effort between 1976 and 1986. As fisheries expanded, fishery management councils often interpreted the scientific uncertainty about the productivity of fish populations as a justification for allowing high levels of fishing in order to meet the apparent needs of commercial and recreational fishing fleets. By the late 1980s, the consequences of this approach became evident as fishery after fishery declined, and the need for restraint became inescapable. Conservation organizations for which initial concerns had been the depletion of the great whales and the drowning of dolphins in tuna nets saw parallels in the wasteful bycatch and overfishing that seemed to characterize many fisheries: Exploitation had proceeded, sometimes without and sometimes despite, scientific understanding of the limits of wild populations. At the same time, a cadre of scientists expanded the critique of traditional management beyond marine mammals to fisheries.

In the early 1990s, many conservationists and some scientists drew upon their experience with the MMPA in their analyses and prescriptions for a reformation of federal fisheries management policy. A chief target was the definition of OY that allowed limits on fishing to be set above MSY for social or economic reasons. Reformers were intent on ending the use of uncertainty in estimating sustainable fishing levels to meet short-term demands for increasing or maintaining fishing levels. Using campaign methods that were foreign to congressional debates over marine fisheries, conservation organizations succeeded in closing this loophole when Congress passed the Sustainable Fisheries Act (SFA) of 1996.

The coalition of conservation organizations, scientists, and fishermen also succeeded in requiring that fishery management councils bring an end to overfishing and begin rebuilding depleted fisheries. Under the Magnuson-Stevens Act, fishery management councils had been able to avoid formally acknowledging that fishing levels were unsustainable or that a fishery was depleted. In the early 1990s, NMFS leaders attempted to require councils to adopt rebuilding plans for fisheries in which fishing levels were unsustainable, but these attempts were successfully resisted. When Congress later took the matter up during its review of the Magnuson-Stevens Act, the reform coalition succeeded in overcoming this resistance. The SFA of 1996 explicitly required the councils to define overfishing in individual fisheries. Based on those definitions, the NMFS was required to identify where overfishing was occurring. The councils then had to develop plans for rebuilding overfished fisheries or ending overfishing.

Although the SFA did not go as far as the MMPA in shifting the burden of proof, it did end the presumption that fish populations could bear the risks associated with uncertainty in scientific understanding. The effects of the new law were dramatic. Reductions in fishing that had seemed beyond reach were soon adopted in many fisheries. Arguments over whether a fishery needed to be restored gave way to arguments over how quickly it should be restored.

The new scheme, however, suffered from one critical weakness. The SFA took only very tentative and contradictory steps toward reducing the fleets that had grown dramatically in size and sophistication after passage of the Magnuson-Stevens Act in 1976.

International Trade and Conservation

In the last two decades of the twentieth century, the use of economic sanctions by the U.S. government to encourage compliance with its conservation policy both changed and grew. Until the mid-1980s, the U.S. government confined its use of economic sanctions in marine conservation to encouraging observance of measures adopted by treaty organizations such as the International Whaling Commission (IWC). In 1984, however, Congress dramatically broadened the use of sanctions to include implementation of domestic conservation law. The immediate object of these sanctions was the drowning of dolphins in tuna nets in the eastern tropical Pacific Ocean. Until the early 1980s, the U.S. fleet so dominated the tuna fishery that reducing dolphin deaths in purse seine nets was a matter of implementing the MMPA of 1972. Between 1976 and 1982, required use of new fishing gear and practices reduced the U.S. fleet's dolphin kill from 108,740 to 23,267.

As the U.S. tuna fleet began leaving the eastern tropical Pacific for the western Pacific in the early 1980s, Latin American fleets expanded to fill the vacuum. Neither the countries themselves nor the Inter-American Tropical Tuna Commission, which oversaw the fishery, required that these fleets take steps to reduce dolphin captures, such as American fishermen had in the 1970s. The dolphin kill in the eastern tropical Pacific yellowfin tuna fishery grew rapidly once again and reached a peak of 112,482 dolphins in 1986.

The increased dolphin deaths attracted renewed attention from conservationists and from the San Diego tuna fleet, which now was competing with the Latin American fleets for a share of the U.S. canned tuna market. In 1984, Congress approved amendments to the MMPA requiring the embargo of tuna imported from countries with tuna vessels having a higher average rate of dolphin kills than the U.S. fleet. Like later requirements for comparability in the foreign catch of sea turtles in shrimp trawls, the 1984 marine mammal provisions were meant not only to promote conservation but also to ensure that U.S. fishermen did not fish at a disadvantage to foreign fishermen by taking additional measures to protect dolphins.

Fearful of provoking a diplomatic fight with Mexico and other countries with growing tuna fleets, the Reagan administration delayed implementing the amendments. The controversy erupted again in 1988, however, when a biologist and former fisherman by the name of Sam LaBudde showed members of Congress film footage that he had shot on a Panamanian tuna vessel off Costa Rica. Images of hundreds of dolphins drowning, being crushed as they were dragged through pulleys, or being tossed lifeless across the fishing deck, shocked many people. Congress reacted by tightening the requirements for foreign fleets. The 1988 amendments to the MMPA also expanded the embargo to so-called intermediary nations, which simply traded in tuna, if they too did not embargo tuna from countries in which tuna fishing failed to meet U.S. standards.

Erratic implementation of the 1988 amendments by the Reagan and Bush administrations attracted a flurry of lawsuits by Earth Island Institute, founded by the legendary environmentalist David Brower in 1982. Generally, the courts upheld the complaints of Earth Island Institute, provoking a series of on-again, off-again embargoes on imports of tuna from a constantly changing list of countries.

In 1990, the conflict between the United States and South American fishing countries reached a turning point. Under court order, Commerce Secretary Robert Mosbacher determined that Mexico's tuna fleet had failed to meet U.S. standards. Mexico reacted to the embargo by lodging a formal complaint with a special panel convened under the General Agreement on Tariffs and Trade, or GATT. Besides establishing a general framework for international trade, the GATT also provided for the resolution of trade disputes through consultation or through submission to a dispute panel. The GATT panel that convened to hear the appeal of Mexico upheld the challenge, largely because the U.S. embargo had been unilateral. Rather than pursue retaliatory trade actions, however, Mexico entered into negotiations with the United States.

Concerned about gaining congressional support for its free trade policy, the Bush administration worked to overcome the flaws that the GATT panel had found in the tuna embargoes. In 1990 and 1991, the U.S. government met

with representatives of the major tuna-fishing nations, under the auspices of
the Inter-American Tropical Tuna Commission. By 1992, negotiators had developed the La Jolla Agreement, which created the International Dolphin Conservation Program. Among other things, the new program set voluntary declining limits on the number of dolphins killed in purse seine nets in the yellowfin
tuna fishery of the eastern tropical Pacific.

While the multilateral La Jolla Agreement seemed to solve the GATT panel's
objection to unilateral imposition of U.S. standards abroad, it did not overcome a new obstacle to the enormous U.S. market. After secret negotiations
with a small group of environmental and animal rights organizations led by the
Earth Island Institute and the Humane Society of the United States, the H. J.
Heinz Company, owner of Starkist Seafood, announced that it would no longer
purchase tuna caught by encircling dolphins. Immediately, the two other major
U.S. tuna canners followed with similar commitments. The announcements
effectively closed the U.S. market to tuna from the eastern tropical Pacific.

In 1992, Congress incorporated the new definition of "dolphin safe" tuna,
and incorporated it into the International Dolphin Conservation Act of 1992.
When the new definition took effect in June 1994, tuna could no longer be imported into the United States if it had been captured on a trip in which dolphins
had been encircled. The tightening of U.S. requirements angered Latin American countries; their fleets had already reduced the number of dolphins killed in
their purse seines by more than 90% between 1990 and 1994. These countries
were not appeased by provisions committing the United States to lifting embargoes if they committed to a five-year moratorium on encircling dolphins.

Fearing the collapse of the International Dolphin Conservation Program
and a return of massive drowning of dolphins, several conservation organizations began negotiating in 1995, not with tuna canners but with representatives of Latin American governments led by Mexico. These organizations, like
officials at the Departments of Commerce and State, also believed that the World
Trade Organization (WTO), successor to GATT, would reject economic sanctions that were not based upon a multilateral agreement.[1]

By October 1995, when negotiators completed their deliberations, 12 nations signed the Declaration of Panama. The new agreement called for further
negotiations to make the International Dolphin Conservation Program binding, if the United States redefined "dolphin safe" tuna to include tuna caught
by encircling tunas if no dolphins were killed. At first, opponents succeeded
in blocking legislation to implement the agreement, but in August 1997, Con-

gress adopted the International Dolphin Conservation Program Act. The legislation, which went into effect after a binding international agreement itself took effect in February 1999, lifted the import ban on tuna.

The use of economic sanctions to support international and national conservation measures was uniquely American. Although their effectiveness varied over the years, conservation embargoes did contribute to achieving such U.S. policy goals as ends to both commercial whaling and the drowning of dolphins and sea turtles in fishing nets of foreign fishermen. The use of economic sanctions also highlighted key weaknesses in international environmental law and in organizations as different as the IWC and the WTO. Facing repeated rejection of conservation embargoes by the WTO, the Clinton administration and Congress effectively abandoned the use of unilateral sanctions and domestic standards to encourage conservation of marine wildlife abroad. Instead, the administration began promoting the economic sanctions as a tool that international organizations could use in ensuring observance of their conservation measures. In 1995, after an intense campaign by the U.S. government and conservation organizations, the International Commission for the Conservation of Atlantic Tunas (ICCAT) took the unprecedented step of identifying several nonmember countries as diminishing the effectiveness of the Commission's conservation program for Atlantic bluefin tuna (*Thunnus thynnus*). When vessels flying the flags of Belize, Honduras, and Panama continued catching Atlantic bluefin tuna during closed seasons in closed areas without a quota, the ICCAT adopted a resolution calling upon its members to prohibit the import of Atlantic bluefin tuna from these countries.

It remains to be seen if multilateral sanctions will succeed in curing the problem of noncompliance that plagues international conservation regimes, or if the WTO will give meaning to its rhetoric of caring for the environmental effects of free trade; however, the growing influence of intergovernmental and nongovernmental organizations in environmental governance, and fisheries management in particular, represents a crucial new opportunity for—and potential constraint on—the nation's ability to protect its marine resources.

From Abundance to Scarcity

From its early involvement in marine fisheries, the federal government viewed assistance to the fishing industry as an essential part of its mission. The federal government promoted the growth and economic well-being of the fishing industry through small financial aid programs, marketing, product development, and biological and gear research. With the election of Ronald Reagan as president in 1980, however, support within the federal government for assistance to the fishing industry weakened greatly, as questions were raised about the proper use of tax dollars and as the ideology of free markets took hold. Industry and congressional supporters of assistance to the fishing industry had to focus their efforts on protecting rather than increasing these programs. In the mid-1980s, as Congress sought to support the Americanization of fisheries in U.S. waters, many of these programs enjoyed their last burst of support. By the late 1990s, however, programs for marketing and product development, for example, were all but eliminated, although they persisted with devastating effect as the story of the monkfish fishery showed.

The other major way in which the federal government sought to assist the fishing industry was financial support for the construction of fishing vessels. For several decades after World War II, government policy makers and the fishing industry argued that the number, size, and sophistication of U.S. fishing vessels were major obstacles to the growth of the industry. For a variety of reasons, including ambivalence about using tax dollars for such purposes, the federal government's support for the construction of fishing vessels never matched the levels provided by many other governments. Direct and indirect financial support through grants, loans, and tax incentives, however, did contribute to the expansion of some fishing fleets.

Changes in markets and the pro-growth rhetoric that accompanied passage of the Magnuson-Stevens Act fueled the expansion of fleets in many parts of the country. By the mid-1980s, the balance between the productivity of marine wildlife populations and the capacity of fishing fleets to exploit them had shifted: Fleets in many fisheries were two to three times the size that fish populations could sustain. By the 1990s, the imbalance between fish and fleets could no longer be ignored, as fisheries managers tightened restrictions in many fisheries. Commercial fishermen especially faced not only economic hardship, but also increasing conflicts with other commercial fishermen, recreational fishermen, and conservationists. In the United States, as elsewhere around the world, overcapitalization of fleets became synonymous with overfishing and economic dislocation. Reducing fleets rose to the top of the agendas of government agencies, fishermen, and conservationists.

As in the past, those regions of the country with influential congressional delegations set policy for the entire country in reducing the size of fishing fleets. In New England, Congress funded an experimental vessel buyback program as part of a package of disaster relief that came on the heels of the first meaning-ful restrictions on the groundfish fleet's activities in many years. Using $24.4 million in specially appropriated funds, the NMFS working with fishermen of the region in designing a buyback program that eventually bought 79 ves-sels and fishing permits, out of a total of 1,763 permits.

The actual reduction in the fishing power of the New England groundfish fleet was ephemeral, for several reasons. The buyback program allowed a fish-erman to use the proceeds from the sale of a vessel or permit to purchase an-other vessel and to enter the groundfish fishery once again. According to the General Accounting Office, at least eight fishermen who participated in the buyback program not only reentered the fishery but also nearly doubled their landings in 1998. Other fishermen who participated in the buyback program moved to other fisheries. The General Accounting Office found that at least nine fishermen had moved to the American lobster fishery, which already was classified as overfished. In focusing on removing vessels with a history of high catches, the program neglected the potential for hundreds of permit holders with previously low catches to increase their catches. This "latent capacity" posed a very real threat of overwhelming whatever actual reductions in fishing the buyback program might achieve. In the end, the buyback program in New Eng-land had little effect on the fishing capacity of the New England groundfish fleet. The program did demonstrate some of the difficulties in designing effec-tive buyback programs, including securing adequate funding.

Elsewhere, fishermen pursued similar approaches to reducing fleets, but did not receive the kind of congressional support that the New England fleet did. Along the Pacific coast, groundfish fleets also had expanded rapidly after 1976. By the early 1980s, the fleets were large enough that they soon reduced rela-tively abundant groundfish populations to levels that could not support the fleets. Restrictions imposed by the Pacific Fishery Management Council seemed to slow the decline of groundfish populations, although scientists were unable to determine the status of 80% of the species caught in the fishery. The fish-ery seemed manageable, if not financially optimal.

Soon after passage of the SFA in 1996, the council learned that scientists' ear-lier estimates of the productivity of rockfish had been too generous. Reflecting the new precautionary approach of the act, the council responded by reducing quotas for some species to their lowest levels ever. Comprehensive assessments also found that unfavorable oceanographic conditions and heavy fishing had re-duced populations of several key species to such low levels that they were declared

overfished. In order to implement the requirements of the SFA, the council eliminated all but incidental catches as a first step in rebuilding these populations.

Reducing the Pacific groundfish fleet had long been desirable, but became
critical as the council slashed quotas. A council working group concluded that
the future of the fishery depended upon cutting the fleet by half. Among the
means for reducing the fleet, the council included both a buyback of permits
and an individual transferable quota (ITQ) program. In the end, the poor financial condition of the fleet made a buyback program improbable without
some direct government funding, but Congress provided none. Furthermore,
the moratorium on new ITQ programs that Congress imposed in 1996 prevented the council from seriously considering such a program. The inability
to reduce the fleet made the additional cuts in quotas even harder to bear and
encouraged fishermen to enter other fisheries. Some of these fisheries were also
at or beyond their biological limits.

In contrast, the influential Alaska delegation succeeded in persuading Congress to adopt and finance an industry plan to rationalize the Bering Sea pollock fleet. In growing to fill the gap left after the Magnuson-Stevens Act by foreign fleets, the Alaska and Seattle-based fleets had grown far too large. As a result,
fishing days for the large offshore catcher–processor vessels from Seattle fell
from 148 days to 29 days between 1991 and 1994. The fleet of smaller vessels
that delivered to shoreside processors in Alaska filled their quotas in 41 days
in 1994 compared to 148 days in 1991.

Declining profits fueled efforts by some members of the Bering Sea fishery
to reduce the size of the fleet. Internal industry negotiations produced a plan
that Alaska Senator Ted Stevens introduced as the American Fisheries Act. In
1998, Congress passed the bill, which effectively closed the Bering Sea pollock
fishery to new entrants, allocated catches to different fleets within the fishery,
and used $15 million in public money to match $75 million in government
loans to buy out 9 of the 30 catcher–processor vessels from Seattle. Besides scrapping 8 of the 9 catcher–processors, the act prohibited the remaining vessels from
increasing their catches in other fisheries or entering other U.S. fisheries without the permission of the regional fishery management council. By prohibiting
new entrants in the fishery, the act avoided the return of vessels to the fishery,
as had occurred in the New England groundfish fishery.

The act also allowed the formation of cooperatives among fishermen and
processors. The fleet of 21 catcher–processors was the first to form a cooperative, which allocated the cooperative's total quota among its members. Like fish-

ermen in the halibut–sablefish ITQ program, fishermen in the offshore groundfish cooperative were able to slow the fishery down, reduce bycatch, and increase
the quality of the fish that they delivered.

Owners and operators of the smaller vessels in Alaska, whose running battle with Seattle fishermen had stoked the controversy over factory trawlers and
ITQs, found themselves blocked from selling to whichever shoreside processor
they might choose. Instead, the act required them to form cooperatives with
the processors to whom they had delivered pollock in the past—probably reducing the fishermen's bargaining power with the processors.

In 2000, Alaska fleets gained additional help from their delegation when
Congress authorized an even more generous program to rationalize the Alaska
crab fleet, for which hyperdevelopment was described in chapter 10. Some members of the crab fleet had earlier developed a proposal for an industry-funded
buyback of crab vessels, but saw their plan founder as crab catches and income
fell. Using his influence again as chairman of the Senate Appropriations Committee, Senator Stevens succeeded in convincing Congress to authorize a vote
by boat owners on the buyback plan developed by the industry. The legislation
required that bought-out boats be scrapped or used for a purpose other than
fishing. The legislation also authorized financing the vessel buyback program
with up to $50 million in government grants and $50 million in government
loans to the remaining boat owners.

While the benefits of reducing the Bering Sea pollock and Alaska crab fleets
might prove to be considerable, these programs were no more than regional fixes
for a problem that demanded a national policy. In this aspect, these programs
followed a long-established pattern of congressional "constituent casework" sub-
stituting for national fisheries policy. Whether or not the congressional delegations of other regions resisted making these tools available to their own fishery
management councils, these tools ended up benefiting only Alaska fisheries.

Bringing fishing fleets back into balance with the wildlife populations they
depend upon will require tools other than public funding. As the New England
buyback program showed, the benefits of buyback programs are easily dissi-
pated if vessels are allowed to continue entering a fishery or shift to another
fishery. Yet, even if a fishery is closed to new vessels, the race for the fish can
continue as fishermen seek to gain advantage by increasing the catching power
of their vessels. Mechanisms such as ITQs or the cooperatives authorized for
the Bering Sea pollock fishery are critical to preventing the socially irrational
outcomes that arise from individually rational decisions to increase fishing power.

The ecological, economic, and social dislocation caused by the hyperdevelopment of fisheries in the last quarter of the twentieth century itself has forced a shift in attitudes. National policy on marine fisheries moved from an ideology of abundance to a recognition of scarcity. The SFA of 1996 recognized as much, by requiring rebuilding plans for overfished populations and by eliminating the loophole that allowed fisheries managers to loosen biologically sound limits on fishing in the name of short-term social and economic demands. Yet, the success of those changes in policy hinged upon reducing the enormous inertia of the country's overbuilt fishing fleets toward unsustainable fishing. At the beginning of the twenty-first century, reducing fleets in a humane but resolute manner, remained the great unfinished business of reformers.

Notes

1. In 1996, the WTO ruled in favor of several countries contesting U.S. legislation that placed an embargo on shrimp from countries not requiring their fishermen to reduce the capture of sea turtles in their nets, as U.S. fishermen were required to do beginning in 1989.

Sources

Introduction

Alliance for the Chesapeake Bay. *Bay Journal.* October 1993.

Alverson, Dayton Lee. 1978. "Commercial Fishing." In *Wildlife in America.* Howard P. Brokaw (Ed.). Council on Environmental Quality, Washington, D.C. Pages 67–85.

Barlow, J. P., P. S. Hill, K. A. Forney, and D. P. DeMaster. 1998. U.S. Pacific marine mammal stock assessments: 1998. U.S. Dep. Commer., NOAA Tech. Memo., NOAA-TM-NMFS-SWFSC-258, 41 p. NTIS No. PB99-152837. (http://swfsc.nmfs.noaa.gov/publications/swfsc98.htm)

Bean, Michael J., and Melanie J. Rowland. 1997. *The Evolution of National Wildlife Law, Third Edition.* Praeger, Westport, CT.

Cart, T. W. 1968. "The Federal Fisheries Service, 1871–1940." A thesis submitted to the faculty of the University of North Carolina at Chapel Hill in partial fulfillment of the requirements for the degree of Master of Arts in the Department of History.

Child, Julia. 1979. *Julia Child & More Company.* Alfred A. Knopf, New York, NY.

Commission on Marine Science, Engineering, and Resources. 1969. *Our Nation and the Sea.* U.S. Government Printing Office, Washington, D.C.

Conservation Law Foundation. December 1996. *New England Fisheries News.*

———. February 1997. *New England Fisheries News.*

Crestin, David. Telephone conversation on February 4, 1999.

Dewar, M. E. 1983. *Industry in Trouble: The Federal Government and the New Enland Fisheries.* Temple University Press, Philadelphia, PA.

Hobart, W. L. December 1995. *Baird's Legacy: The History and Accomplishments of NOAA's National Marine Fisheries Service, 1871–1996.* NOAA Tech. Memo. NMFS-F/SPO-18. Seattle, WA.

Iudicello, Suzanne. 1996. "Overfishing Lures Legislative Reforms." *Forum for Applied Research and Public Policy.* Vol. 11, No. 2. Pages 19–23.

Kendall, J., and B. Stevenson. 1999. "New England Region." In *Report of the Task Force on the Federal Investment in Marine Fisheries.* Atlantic States Marine Fisheries Commission, Washington, D.C.

National Marine Fisheries Service. 1996. "Our Living Oceans." *Report on the Status of*

U.S. Living Marine Resources, 1995. U.S. Department of Commerce, NOAA Tech. Memo. NMFS0F/SPO-19. Silver Spring, MD.

———. 1998. *Status of the Fishery Resources off the Northeastern United States.* (http://www.wh.whoi.edu/sos)

———. 1999. *Commercial Fisheries: Landings Background Information.* Office of Science & Technology. (http://www.st.nmfs.gov)

———. January 2001. *Status of Fisheries of the United States, 2000.*(http://www.nmfs.gov)

New England Fishery Management Council (NEFMC) and Mid-Atlantic Fishery Management Councils. September 1998. *Monkfish Fishery Management Plan.* Vol. 1. NEFMC, Saugus, MA.

Ross, Bob. Telephone conversation on March 9, 1999.

Thomas, Jack. April 9, 1997. "Julia: With Whisk in Hand, Child Won America's Hearts." *Seattle Post-Intelligencer.*

U.N. Food and Agriculture Organization (FAO). 1993. *Marine Fisheries and the Law of the Sea: A Decade of Change.* FAO, Rome, Italy.

———. 1998. *FISHSTAT PC.* Two diskette database. FAO, Rome, Italy.

U.S. Department of the Interior. Various years. *Annual Report of the Department of the Interior.* U.S. Government Printing Office, Washington, D.C.

Weber, Michael L. 1986. "Federal Marine Fisheries Management." In *Audubon Wildlife Report: 1986.* Roger L. DiSilvestro (Ed.). National Audubon Society, New York, NY. Pages 267–344.

Weber, Michael L., and Judith G. Gradwohl. 1995. *The Wealth of Oceans: Environment and Development on Our Ocean Planet.* W. W. Norton, New York, NY.

Wenk, Edward, Jr. 1972. *The Politics of the Ocean.* University of Washington Press, Seattle, WA.

Chapter 1. The Sciences

Alaska Fisheries Science Center. 1999. *National Marine Fisheries Service.* (http://www.afsc.noaa.gov)

Alverson, Dayton Lee 1978. "Commercial Fishing." In *Wildlife in America.* Howard P. Brokaw (Ed.). Council on Environmental Quality, Washington, D.C. Pages 67–85.

———. Telephone interview on February 9, 1999.

———. Telephone interview on March 9, 1999.

———. Interview on June 25, 2000.

Bean, Michael J., and Melanie J. Rowland. 1997. *The Evolution of National Wildlife Law, Third Edition.* Praeger, Westport, CT.

Brown, Sandra, and Ariel E. Lugo. 1981. *Management and Status of U.S. Commercial Marine Fisheries.* Council on Environmental Quality, Washington, D.C.

Bureau of Commercial Fisheries. 1966. *Report of the Bureau of Commercial Fisheries for the Calendar Year 1964.* U.S. Government Printing Office, Washington, D.C.

Cart, T. W. 1968. "The Federal Fisheries Service, 1871–1940." A thesis submitted to the faculty of the University of North Carolina at Chapel Hill in partial fulfillment of the requirements for the degree of Master of Arts in the Department of History. 87 pages.

Commission on Marine Science, Engineering, and Resources. 1969. *Our Nation and the Sea.* U.S. Government Printing Office, Washington, D.C.

Fogarty, Michael J., Andrew A. Rosenberg, and Michael P. Sissenwine. Undated. *Uncertainty and Risk in an Exploited Ecosystem: A Case Study of Georges Bank.* NMFS, Woods Hole, MA.

Hobart, W. L. December 1995. *Baird's Legacy: The History and Accomplishments of NOAA's National Marine Fisheries Service, 1871–1996.* NOAA Tech. Memo. NMFS-F/SPO-18. Seattle, WA.

Holt, Sidney J. 1998. "Fifty Years On." Reviews in *Fish Biology and Fisheries.* Vol. 8. Pages 357–366.

Holt, Sidney J., and Lee M. Talbot. 1978. *New Principles for the Conservation of Wild Living Resources.* The Wildlife Society, Washington, D.C.

McGoodwin, James R. 1990. *Crisis in the World's Fisheries.* Stanford University Press, Stanford, CA.

National Marine Fisheries Service. 1991. *Strategic Plan of the National Marine Fisheries Service: Goals and Objectives.* NMFS, Silver Spring, MD.

————. 1998. *Status of Fisheries of the United States.* (http://www.nmfs.gov)

————. 1999. *Commercial Fisheries: Landings Background Information.* Office of Science & Technology. (http://www.st.nmfs.gov/stl/commercial)

National Research Council, Committee on Fish Stocks Assessment Methods. 1998. National Academy Press, Washington, D.C. (http://romulus.nap.edu/readingroom/books/fish)

Northeast Fisheries Science Center. 1999. *National Marine Fisheries Service.* (http://www.wh.whoi.edu)

Power, E. A. 1968. *Highlights in the Collection, Tabulation, and Publication of Fisheries Statistics, 1880–1967.* Division of Economics, Bureau of Commercial Fisheries, Washington, D.C.

Roe, Richard. Telephone interview on February 25, 1999.

Schlee, Susan. 1973. *The Edge of an Unfamiliar World: A History of Oceanography.* E. P. Dutton & Co., New York, NY.

Schlesinger, J. (Assistant Director, Bureau of the Budget). Letter to Walter J. Hickel, secretary of the interior. October 22, 1969.

U.S. Commission of Fish and Fisheries. 1884–1887. *The Fisheries and Fishing Industries of the United States.* U.S. Government Printing Office, Washington, D.C.

U.S. Department of Commerce. 1976. *A Marine Fisheries Program for the Nation.* U.S. Government Printing Office, Washington, D.C.

U.S. Department of the Interior. 1965. *Quest for Quality: U.S. Department of the Interior Conservation Yearbook.* U.S. Government Printing Office, Washington, D.C.

———. 1970. *River of Life, Water: The Environmental Challenge.* U.S. Government Printing Office, Washington, D.C.

———. Various years. *Annual Report of the Department of the Interior.* U.S. Government Printing Office, Washington, D.C.

Weber, Michael L. 1986. "Federal Marine Fisheries Management." In *Audubon Wildlife Report: 1986.* Roger L. DiSilvestro (Ed.). National Audubon Society, New York, NY.

Weber, Michael L., and Judith Gradwohl. 1995. *The Wealth of Oceans: Environment and Development on Our Ocean Planet.* W.W. Norton, New York, NY.

Wenk, Edward, Jr. 1972. *The Politics of the Ocean.* University of Washington Press, Seattle, WA.

Chapter 2. Industry's Partner

Alverson, Dayton Lee. 1978. "Commercial Fishing." In *Wildlife in America.* Howard P. Brokaw (Ed.). Council on Environmental Quality, Washington, D.C. Pages 67–85.

———. 1985. "The Evolution of the National Fisheries Policy." Presented at the Alaska Management Conference. Anchorage, AK.

Anonymous. 1972. "The Role of Marketing in Resource Research, Utilization and Management." NMFS Mimeographed report. 30 pages.

———. July 1999. *Federal Fisheries Investment Task Force: Report to Congress.* Atlantic States Marine Fisheries Commission, Washington, D.C.

Bureau of Commercial Fisheries. Various years. *Report of the Bureau of Commercial Fisheries for the Calendar Year.* U.S. Government Printing Office, Washington, D.C.

Cart, T. W. 1968. "The Federal Fisheries Service, 1871–1940." A thesis submitted to the faculty of the University of North Carolina at Chapel Hill in partial fulfillment of the requirements for the degree of Master of Arts in the Department of History.

Chandler, Alfred D. 1988. "The National Marine Fisheries Service." In *Audubon Wildlife Report: 1988/1989.* Academic Press, New York, NY. Pages 3–98.

Commission on Marine Science, Engineering, and Resources. 1969. *Our Nation and the Sea.* U.S. Government Printing Office, Washington, D.C.

Crestin, David. Telephone interview on February 4, 1999.

Crutchfield, James. Telephone interview on February 7, 1999.

Dewar, M. E. 1983. *Industry in Trouble: The Federal Government and the New England Fisheries.* Temple University Press, Philadelphia, PA.

Eshbach, Charles. 1966. "Report to the Bureau of Commercial Fisheries on the Branch of Marketing." Mimeographed report. 81 pages.

Famighetti, Robert (Ed). 1998. *The World Almanac and Book of Facts.* Primedia Reference, Mahwah, NJ.

Finch, Roland. May 1977. "Whatever Happened to Fish Protein Concentrate?" *Food Technology.* Pages 44–53.

———. Telephone interview on February 12, 1999.

———. 1999. Draft of *"Fish Protein Concentrate." The Marine and Freshwater Natural Products Handbook.* Aspen Publishers, New York, NY.

Food and Agriculture Organization of the United Nations (FAO). 1998. *FISHSTAT PC.* Two diskette database. FAO, Rome, Italy.

Frye, John. August 1970. "Fishing Subsidies' History, Outlook Bleak." *National Fishermen.* Page 10b.

Garrett, Spencer. Telephone conversation on February 23, 1999.

Gordon, William G. Telephone interview on February 15, 2000.

Hobart, W. L. December 1995. *Baird's Legacy: The History and Accomplishments of NOAA's National Marine Fisheries Service, 1871–1996.* NOAA Tech. Memo. NMFS-F/SPO-18. Seattle, WA.

Jones, Bob. Telephone interview on February 5, 1999.

Morehead, Bruce. Telephone conversation on February 18, 1999.

National Marine Fisheries Service. 1996. "Fisheries of the United States, 1995." *Current Fisheries Statistics No. 9500.* U.S. Government Printing Office, Washington, D.C.

———. 1999. *Commercial Fisheries: Landings Background Information.* Office of Science & Technology. (http://www.st.nmfs.gov)

———. July 2, 1999. Office of Industry and Trade. (http://www.nmfs.gov/trade)

National Oceanic and Atmospheric Administration. 1978. *U.S. Ocean Policy in the 1970s: Status and Issues.* U.S. Department of Commerce, Washington, D.C.

Paradis, Paul. Telephone conversation on April 2, 1999.

Schlesinger, J. (Assistant Director, Bureau of the Budget). Letter to Walter J. Hickel, secretary of the interior. October 22, 1969.

Trager, James. 1992. *The People's Chronology: A Year-by-Year Record of Human Events from Prehistory to the Present.* Henry Holt & Company, New York, NY.

U.S. Department of Agriculture. July 1999. *Seafood Purchases by the U.S. Department of Agriculture.* (http://www.ams.usda.gov/icp)

U.S. Department of Commerce. 1976. *A Marine Fisheries Program for the Nation.* U.S. Government Printing Office, Washington, D.C.

U.S. Department of the Interior. Various years. *Annual Report of the Department of the Interior.* United States Government Printing Office, Washington, D.C.

Weber, Michael L. 1986. "Federal Marine Fisheries Management." In *Audubon Wildlife Report: 1986.* Roger L. DiSilvestro (Ed.). National Audubon Society, New York, NY. Pages 267–344.

Weber, Michael L., and Judith Gradwohl. 1995. *The Wealth of Oceans: Environment and*

Development on Our Ocean Planet. W. W. Norton, New York, NY.

Wenk, Edward, Jr. 1972. *The Politics of the Ocean.* University of Washington Press, Seattle, WA.

Wise, J. A. 1991. *Federal Conservation and Management of Marine Fisheries in the United States.* Center for Marine Conservation, Washington, D.C.

Chapter 3. Manufacturing Fish

Ausman, Lynn. June 23; 1999. "Statement of Lynn Ausman, Washington Association of Wheat Growers and the Washington Barley Commission," before the Senate Committee on Environment and Public Works Subcommittee on Fisheries, Wildlife, and Drinking Water.

Barton, Katherine. 1987. "Federal Wetlands Protection Programs." In *Audubon Wildlife Report: 1986.* Roger L. DiSilvestro (Ed.). Academic Press, Orlando, FL. Pages 179–198.

Bean, Michael J., and Melanie J. Rowland. 1997. *The Evolution of National Wildlife Law, Third Edition.* Praeger, Westport, CT.

Bonneville Power Administration. 1987. *Backgrounder: The World's Biggest Fish Story: The Columbia River's Salmon.* BPA, Portland, OR.

Brouha, Paul. November 1999. *The NMFS Habitat Protection Program: Lost in the Bureaucracy.* (http://www.nmfs.gov/habitat)

Bureau of Commercial Fisheries. Various years. *Report of the Bureau of Commercial Fisheries for the Calendar Year.* U.S. Government Printing Office, Washington, D.C.

Cart, T. W. 1968. "The Federal Fisheries Service, 1871–1940." A thesis submitted to the faculty of the University of North Carolina at Chapel Hill in partial fulfillment of the requirements for the degree of Master of Arts in the Department of History. 87 pages.

Chandler, Alfred D. 1988. "The National Marine Fisheries Service." In *Audubon Wildlife Report: 1988/1989.* Academic Press, New York, NY. Pages 3–98.

Chandler, William J. 1985. "Inland Fisheries Management." In *Audubon Wildlife Report: 1985.* Roger L. Di Silvestro (Ed.). The National Audubon Society, New York, NY.

Culliton, Thomas J. 1998. "Population Distribution, Density, and Growth." *NOAA's State of the Coast Report.* Silver Spring, MD. (http://state_of_coast.noaa.gov/ bulletins)

Eley, Thomas J., and T. H. Watkins. Fall 1991. "In a Sea of Trouble: The Uncertain Fate of the Pacific Salmon." *Wilderness.* Pages 19–26.

Lichatowich, Jim. 1999. *Salmon without Rivers: A History of the Pacific Salmon Crisis.* Island Press, Washington, D.C.

Mager, Andy. 2000. Telephone interview on February 23, 2000.

National Marine Fisheries Service. Various years. *Report of the National Marine Fisheries Service.* NMFS, Seattle, WA.

National Oceanic and Atmospheric Administration. 1978. *U.S. Ocean Policy in the 1970s: Status and Issues.* U.S. Department of Commerce, Washington, D.C.

————. February 1, 1999. *NOAA FY2000 Budget Request.* (http://www.noaa.gov)

————. November 1999. *Conservation of Columbia Basin Fish: Building a Conceptual Recovery Plan with the Four Hs.* Working Paper. (http://www.bpa.gov/Power/PL/federalcaucas/Conservation.pdf)

————. November 17, 1999. "Federal Government Proposes Endangered Species Listing for Atlantic Salmon in Maine." Press release (http://www.noaanews.noaa.gov/stories/s323.htm).

————. November 16, 1999. Press release: Federal Agencies Release Four-H "Working Paper" on Salmon Recovery in Pacific Northwest.

Nehlsen, Willa, Jack E. Williams, and James A. Lichatowich. 1991. "Pacific Salmon at the Crossroads: Stocks at Risk from California, Oregon, Idaho, and Washington." *Fisheries.* Vol. 16, No. 2. Pages 4–21.

Norris, Ruth. 1987. "Water Projects and Wildlife." In *Audubon Wildlife Report: 1986.* Roger L. DiSilvestro (Ed.). Academic Press, Orlando, FL. Pages 201–221.

Northwest Fisheries Science Center. 1999. *National Marine Fisheries Service.* (http://www.nwfsc.noaa.gov)

Office of Habitat Conservation. August 8, 1996. *A Plan to Strengthen the National Marine Fisheries Service's National Habitat Program.* NOAA, Silver Spring, MD. (http://www.nmfs.gov/habitat/publications/plan)

Phinney, Lloyd A. 1986. "Chinook Salmon of the Columbia River Basin." In *Audubon Wildlife Report: 1986.* Roger L. DiSilvestro (Ed.). National Audubon Society, New York, NY. Pages 715–741.

Resource Writers. 1991. *The Columbia River System: The Inside Story.* U.S. Bureau of Reclamation, U.S. Army Corps of Engineers, and Bonneville Power Administra- tion, Portland, OR.

U.S. Department of Commerce. 1976. *A Marine Fisheries Program for the Nation.* U.S. Government Printing Office, Washington, D.C.

U.S. Department of the Interior. 1963. *The Third Wave . . . America's New Conservation.* U.S. Government Printing Office, Washington, D.C.

————. 1971. *River of Life, Water: The Environmental Challenge.* U.S. Government Printing Office, Washington, D.C.

————. 1972. *Our Living Land.* U.S. Department of the Interior Environmental Report. U.S. Government Printing Office, Washington, D.C.

————. 1994. *The Impact of Federal Programs on Wetlands.* Vol. II. A Report to Congress by the Secretary of the Interior. DOI, Washington, D.C.

————. Various years. *Annual Report of the Department of the Interior.* U.S. Government Printing Office, Washington, D.C.

Weber, Michael L. 1987. "Federal Marine Fisheries Management." In *Audubon Wildlife Report: 1986.* Roger L. DiSilvestro (Ed.). Academic Press, Orlando, FL. Pages 131–146.

Wenk, Edward, Jr. 1972. *The Politics of the Ocean.* University of Washington Press, Seattle, WA.

Chapter 4. International Affairs

Alverson, Dayton Lee. 1978. "Commercial Fishing." In *Wildlife in America*. Howard
P. Brokaw (Ed.). Council on Environmental Quality, Washington, D.C. Pages 67–85.

Bean, Michael J., and Melanie J. Rowland. 1997. *The Evolution of National Wildlife
Law, Third Edition*. Praeger, Westport, CT.

Beasley, Henry. Telephone interview on February 9, 1999.

Buck, Eugene H. March 8, 1995. *Atlantic Bluefin Tuna: International Management of a
Shared Resource*. 95-367 ENR. Congressional Research Service, Washington, D.C.

———. Various years. *Report of the Bureau of Commercial Fisheries for the Calendar Year*.
U.S. Government Printing Office, Washington, D.C.

Bureau of Commercial Fisheries. 1970. "Background for International Fisheries Affairs."
Office of the Assistant Director for International Affairs. Mimeographed document.

Cart, T. W. 1968. "The Federal Fisheries Service, 1871–1940." A thesis submitted to
the faculty of the University of North Carolina at Chapel Hill in partial fulfillment of
the requirements for the degree of Master of Arts in the Department of History. 87
pages.

Dewar, M. E. 1983. *Industry in Trouble: The Federal Government and the New England
Fisheries*. Temple University Press, Philadelphia, PA.

Food and Agriculture Organization of the United Nations (FAO). 1998. *FISHSTATPC*.
FAO, Rome, Italy.

Gordon, William G. Telephone interview on February 15, 2000.

Graham, Herbert W. 1970. "Management of the Groundfish Fisheries of the Northwest Atlantic." In *A Century of Fisheries in North America*. American Fisheries Society, Washington, D.C.

Hobart, W. L. December 1995. *Baird's Legacy: The History and Accomplishments of
NOAA's National Marine Fisheries Service, 1871–1996*. NOAA Tech. Memo. NMFS-
F/SPO-18. Seattle, WA.

International Fisheries Division. 1998. *International Agreements Concerning Living Marine Resources of Interest to NOAA Fisheries.*(http://www.nmfs.gov/oneagree.html)

Jones, Bob. Telephone interview on February 5, 1999.

Larkin, P. A. 1970. "Management of Pacific Salmon of North America." In *A Century
of Fisheries in North America*. Norman G. Benson (Ed.). Special Publication No. 7.
American Fisheries Society, Washington, D.C. Pages 223–236.

Marine Mammal Commission. Various years. *Annual Report to Congress: 1995*. MMC,
Washington, D.C.

McGoodwin, James R. 1990. *Crisis in the World's Fisheries*. Stanford University Press,
Stanford, CA.

National Marine Fisheries Service. 1999. *Commercial Fisheries: Landings Background Information*. Office of Science & Technology. (http://www.st.nmfs.gov)

Power, E. A., and W. L. Peck. 1971. "The National Picture." In *Our Changing Fisheries*.

S. Shapiro (Ed.). U.S. Government Printing Office, Washington, D.C. Pages 1–18.

Safina, Carl. 1997. *Song for the Blue Ocean.* Henry Holt & Company, New York, NY.

Trager, James. 1992. *The People's Chronology: A Year-by-Year Record of Human Events from Prehistory to the Present.* Henry Holt & Company, New York, NY.

U.S. Department of the Interior. 1944. *Annual Report of the Secretary of the Interior: Fiscal Year Ended June 30, 1944.* U.S. Government Printing Office, Washington, D.C.

Warner, William W. 1983. *Distant Water.* Little, Brown, & Company, Boston, MA.

Weber, Michael L. 1986. "Federal Marine Fisheries Management." In *Audubon Wildlife Report: 1986.* Roger L. DiSilvestro (Ed.). National Audubon Society, New York, NY. Pages 267–344.

———. August 1990. *A Preliminary Study of International Trade in Western Atlantic Bluefin Tuna: A Report to the Sport Fishing Institute.* Washington, D.C.

Weber, Michael L., and Judith Gradwohl. 1995. *The Wealth of Oceans: Environment and Development on Our Ocean Planet.* W. W. Norton, New York, NY.

Weber, Michael L., and Frances Spivy-Weber. 1995. *Proposed Elements for International Regimes to Conserve Living Marine Resources.* Report in fulfillment of Marine Mammal Commission Contract No. T30916119. National Technical Information Service, Springfield, VA.

Wise, J. A. 1991. *Federal Conservation and Management of Marine Fisheries in the United States.* Center for Marine Conservation, Washington, D.C.

Chapter 5. A Revolution in Management

Alverson, Dayton Lee. Telephone interview on February 9, 1999.

———. Telephone interview on March 9, 1999.

———. Interview on June 25, 2000.

Anonymous. 1977. *Eastland Fisheries Survey: A Report to the Congress.* Atlantic States, Gulf States, and Pacific Marine Fisheries Commissions. Washington, D.C.

Bean, Michael J., and Melanie J. Rowland. 1997. *The Evolution of National Wildlife Law, Third Edition.* Praeger, Westport, CT.

Bell, Thelma I., and Donald S. FitzGibbon (Eds.). 1980. "Fishery Statistics of the United States, 1976." *Statistical Digest No. 70.* NMFS, Washington, D.C.

Bureau of Commercial Fisheries. Various years. *Report of the Bureau of Commercial Fisheries for the Calendar Year.* U.S. Government Printing Office, Washington, D.C.

Cart, T. W. 1968. "The Federal Fisheries Service, 1871–1940." A thesis submitted to the faculty of the University of North Carolina at Chapel Hill in partial fulfillment of the requirements for the degree of Master of Arts in the Department of History. 87 pages.

Commission on Marine Science, Engineering, and Resources. 1969. *Our Nation and the Sea.* U.S. Government Printing Office, Washington, D.C.

Crestin, David. Telephone interview on February 4, 1999.

Crutchfield, James. Telephone interview on February 7, 1999.

Dewar, M. E. 1983. *Industry in Trouble: The Federal Government and the New England Fisheries.* Temple University Press, Philadelphia, PA.

FAQALASKA Project. 2000. *Frequently Asked Questions about Alaska.* Fairbanks North Star Borough Public Library for the Alaska State Library. (http://sled.alaska.edu/akfaq)

Finch, Roland. 1985. "Fishery Management under the Magnuson Act." *Marine Policy.* Vol. 9, No. 3. Pages 170–179.

———. Telephone interview on February 12, 1999.

Fisheries Statistics Division. 1997. "Fisheries of the United States, 1996." *Current Fisheries Statistics No. 9600.* NMFS, Silver Spring, MD.

Fordham, Sonja V. 1996. *New England Groundfish: From Glory to Grief.* Center for Marine Conservation, Washington, D.C.

General Accounting Office. 2000. *Fishery Management: Problems Remain with National Marine Fishery Service's Implementation of the Magnuson-Stevens Act.* GAO-01-204. General Accounting Office, Washington, D.C.

Gordon, William G. Telephone interview on February 15, 2000.

Greenberg, Eldon. Telephone conversation on April 17, 2000.

National Marine Fisheries Service. 1999. *Commercial Fisheries: Landings Background Information.* Office of Science & Technology. (http://www.st.nmfs.gov)

———. 1999. *Report on the Status of U.S. Living Marine Resources. 1999.* U.S. Department of Commerce, NOAA Tech. Memo. NMFS-F/SPO-41. Silver Spring, MD.

———. Various years. *Annual Report of the National Marine Fisheries Service.* NMFS, Seattle, WA.

National Oceanic and Atmospheric Administration. 1978. *U.S. Ocean Policy in the 1970s: Status and Issues.* U.S. Department of Commerce, Washington, D.C.

National Research Council, Committee on Fisheries. 1994. *Improving the Management of U.S. Marine Fisheries.* National Academy Press, Washington, D.C.

O'Bannon, Barbara (Ed.). 1988. "Fisheries of the United States, 1987." *Current Fisheries Statistics No. 8700.* U.S. Government Printing Office, Washington, D.C.

Power, E. A., and W. L. Peck. 1971. "The National Picture." In *Our Changing Fisheries.* S. Shapiro (Ed.). U.S. Government Printing Office, Washington, D.C. Pages 1–18.

Roe, Richard. Telephone interview on February 25, 1999.

Royce, W. F. 1985. "The Historical Development of Fisheries Science and Management." Taken from a lecture given at the Fisheries Centennial Celebration. Woods Hole Oceanographic Institution, Woods Hole, MA.

Talbot, Lee M. September 1993. Draft of *Prelminary Report on Consultations: Principles for Living Resource Conservation.* Marine Mammal Commission. 42 pages. Fairfax, VA.

Thompson, B. G. 1986. "Fishery Statistics of the United States, 1985." *Current Fishery Statistics No. 8368.* NMFS, Washington, D.C.

Trager, James. 1992. *The People's Chronology: A Year-by-Year Record of Human Events from Prehistory to the Present.* Henry Holt & Company, New York, NY.

U.S. Department of Commerce. 1976. *A Marine Fisheries Program for the Nation.* U.S. Government Printing Office, Washington, D.C.

U.S. Department of the Interior. Various years. *Annual Report of the Secretary of the Interior.* U.S. Government Printing Office, Washington, D.C.

Weber, Michael L., and Judith Gradwohl. 1995. *The Wealth of Oceans: Environment and Development on Our Ocean Planet.* W. W. Norton, New York, NY.

Wise, J. A. 1991. *Federal Conservation and Management of Marine Fisheries in the United States.* Center for Marine Conservation, Washington, D.C.

Wise, John P. Telephone interview on February 3, 1999.

Chapter 6. Precautionary Science and the ESA

Allen, K. Radway. 1980. *Conservation and Management of Whales.* University of Washington Press, Seattle, WA.

Bean, Michael J., and Melanie J. Rowland. 1997. *The Evolution of National Wildlife Law, Third Edition.* Praeger, Westport, CT.

Bohlen, Curtis. Telephone conversation on March 30, 2000.

Bureau of Commercial Fisheries. 1970. "Background for International Fisheries Affairs." Office of the Assistant Director for International Affairs. Mimeographed document.

Bureau of Commercial Fisheries. Various years. *Report of the Bureau of Commercial Fisheries for the Calendar Year.* U.S. Government Printing Office, Washington, D.C.

Carson, Rachel. 1962. *Silent Spring.* Houghton Mifflin Company, Boston Massachusetts.

Cart, T. W. 1968. "The Federal Fisheries Service, 1871–1940." A thesis submitted to the faculty of the University of North Carolina at Chapel Hill in partial fulfillment of the requirements for the degree of Master of Arts in the Department of History. 87 pages.

Cohn, Jeffrey P. Winter 1997/1998. "How the Endangered Species Act Was Born." *Defenders.* Pages 6–13.

Environmental Defense Fund. August 1970. "Whales and Interior's Endangered Species List." *EDF Newsletter.* Vol. 1, No. 4. (http://www.edf.org/pubs/newsletter)

Garrett, Spencer. Telephone conversation on February 23, 1999.

Grandy, John. Telephone interview on April 10, 2000.

Holt, Sidney J., and Lee M. Talbot. 1978. *New Principles for the Conservation of Wild Living Resources.* The Wildlife Society, Washington, D.C.

International Fisheries Division. 2000. *International Agreements Concerning Living Marine Resources of Interest to NOAA Fisheries.* (http://www.nmfs.gov/oneagree.html)

Lyles, Charles H. 1967. "Fishery Statistics of the United States, 1965." *Statistical Digest No. 57.* Bureau of Commercial Fisheries, Washington, D.C.

———. 1968. "Fishery Statistics of the United States, 1966." *Statistical Digest No. 60.* Bureau of Commercial Fisheries, Washington, D.C.

———. 1969. "Fishery Statistics of the United States, 1967." *Statistical Digest No. 61.* Bureau of Commercial Fisheries, Washington, D.C.

National Marine Fisheries Service. Various years. *Annual Report of the National Marine Fisheries Service.* NMFS, Seattle, WA.

Norris, K. 1978. "Marine Mammals and Man." In *Wildlife and America.* Howard P. Brokaw (Ed.). Council on Environmental Quality, Washington, D.C.

Potter, Frank. Telephone interview on April 3, 2000.

Power, E. A. 1958. *Fishery Statistics of the United States, 1956.* U.S. Government Printing Office, Washington, D.C.

———. 1960. *Fishery Statistics of the United States, 1957.* U.S. Government Printing Office, Washington, D.C.

———. 1961. *Fishery Statistics of the United States, 1959.* U.S. Government Printing Office, Washington, D.C.

———. 1963. *Fishery Statistics of the United States, 1961.* U.S. Government Printing Office, Washington, D.C.

Power, E. A., and C. H. Lyles. 1964. *Fishery Statistics of the United States, 1962.* U.S. Government Printing Office, Washington, D.C.

Ray, G. Carleton. Telephone interview on April 11, 2000.

Regenstein, Lewis G. December 1974. "A History of the Endangered Species Act of 1973, and an Analysis of its History; Strengths and Weaknesses; Administration; and Probable Future Effectiveness." Master's Thesis. Emory University, Atlanta, GA.

———. 1975. *The Politics of Extinction.* Macmillan, New York, NY.

———. Telephone conversation on March 30, 2000.

Small, George L. 1971. *The Blue Whale.* Columbia University Press, New York, NY.

Spence, B. 1980. *Harpooned: The Story of Whaling.* Crescent Books, New York, NY.

Talbot, Lee M. 1974. "The Great Whales and the International Whaling Commission." In *Mind in the Waters.* Joan McIntyre (Ed.). Charles Scribner's Sons, New York, NY.

———. August 8, 1974. Testimony before the House Subcommittee on Fisheries and Wildlife Conservation and the Environment.

———. Telephone interview on April 3, 2000.

Thompson, B. G. 1974. "Fishery Statistics of the United States, 1971." *Statistical Digest No. 65.* NMFS, Washington, D.C.

Twiss, John R., Jr., and Randall R. Reeves (Eds.). 1999. *Conservation and Management of Marine Mammals.* Smithsonian Institution Press, Washington, D.C.

Weber, Michael L. 1985. "Marine Mammal Protection." In *Audubon Wildlife Report: 1985.* Roger L. DiSilvestro (Ed.). National Audubon Society, New York, NY.

Wheeland, Hoyt A. 1972. "Fishery Statistics of the United States, 1969." *Statistical Digest No. 63.* NMFS, Washington, D.C.

Chapter 7. New Values, New Roles

Anonymous. July 1971. "NFI Weighs Crippling Contamination Crisis." *National Fisherman*. Page 20A.

———. 1998. *Clean Water Action Plan: Restoring and Protecting America's Waters*. U.S. Environmental Protection Agency and U.S. Department of Agriculture, Washington, D.C.

Bean, Michael J., and Melanie J. Rowland. 1997. *The Evolution of National Wildlife Law, Third Edition*. Praeger, Westport, CT.

Bohlen, Curtis. Telephone conversation on March 30, 2000.

Bureau of Commercial Fisheries. Various years. *Report of the Bureau of Commercial Fisheries for the Calendar Year*. U.S. Government Printing Office, Washington, D.C.

Cart, T. W. 1968. "The Federal Fisheries Service, 1871–1940." A thesis submitted to the faculty of the University of North Carolina at Chapel Hill in partial fulfillment of the requirements for the degree of Master of Arts in the Department of History. 87 pages.

Coffey, Burton T. June 1971. "Metal Pollution Casting A Long Shadow." *National Fisherman*. Page 3A.

Commission on Marine Science, Engineering, and Resources. 1969. *Our Nation and the Sea*. U.S. Government Printing Office, Washington, D.C. 305 pages.

Fox, William W., Jr. Telephone conversation on February 17, 1999.

Grandy, John. Telephone interview on April 10, 2000.

McIntyre, Joan (Ed.). 1974. *Mind in the Waters*. Charles Scribner's Sons, New York, NY.

Millhouser, William C., John McDonough, John Paul Tolson, and David Slade. 1998. "Managing Coastal Resources." *NOAA's State of the Coast Report*. NOAA, Silver Spring, MD. (http://state_of_coast.noaa.gov/bulletins)

Minasian, Stanley M. (Producer). 1975. *The Last Days of the Dolphins?* Save the Dolphin and Environmental Defense Fund. Film. San Francisco, CA.

———. 1990. *Where Have All the Dolphins Gone?* Marine Mammal Fund and American Society for the Prevention of Cruelty to Animals. Film (48 minutes). San Francisco, CA.

National Marine Fisheries Service. 1978. *The Marine Mammal Protection Act of 1972 Annual Report, April 1, 1977, to March 31, 1978*. NMFS, Washington, D.C.

———. 1982. *The Marine Mammal Protection Act of 1972 Annual Report, April 1, 1981, to March 31, 1982*. NMFS, Washington, D.C.

———. 1984. *The Marine Mammal Protection Act of 1972 Annual Report, April 1, 1983, to March 31, 1984*. NMFS, Washington, D.C.

———. 1985. *The Marine Mammal Protection Act of 1972 Annual Report, April 1, 1984, to March 31, 1985*. NMFS, Washington, D.C.

———. 1988. *The Marine Mammal Protection Act of 1972 Annual Report, April 1, 1987, to March 31, 1988*. NMFS, Washington, D.C.

————. Various years. *Annual Report of the National Marine Fisheries.* NMFS, Seattle, WA.

National Oceanic and Atmospheric Administration. 1978. *U.S. Ocean Policy in the 1970s: Status and Issues.* U.S. Department of Commerce, Washington, D.C.

Norris, K. 1978. "Marine Mammals and Man." In *Wildlife and America.* Howard P. Brokaw (Ed.). Council on Environmental Quality, Washington, D.C.

Potter, Frank. Telephone interview on April 3, 2000.

Power, E. A. 1961. *Fishery Statistics of the United States, 1959.* U.S. Government Printing Office, Washington, D.C.

Power, E. A., and C. H. Lyles. 1964. *Fishery Statistics of the United States, 1962.* U.S. Government Printing Office, Washington, D.C.

Rabalais, Nancy N. 1998. "Oxygen Depletion in Coastal Waters." *NOAA's State of the Coast Report.* NOAA, Silver Spring, MD. (http://state_of_coast.noaa.gov/bulletins)

Ray, G. Carleton. Telephone interview on April 11, 2000.

Regenstein, Lewis G. December 1974. "A History of the Endangered Species Act of 1973, and an Analysis of its History; Strengths and Weaknesses; Administration; and Probable Future Effectiveness." Master's Thesis. Emory University. Atlanta, GA.

————. 1975. *The Politics of Extinction.* Macmillan, New York, NY.

Talbot, Lee. M. Telephone interview on April 3, 2000.

Trager, James. 1992. *The People's Chronology: A Year-by-Year Record of Human Events from Prehistory to the Present.* Henry Holt & Company, New York, NY.

Twiss, John R., Jr., and Randall R. Reeves (Eds.). 1999. *Conservation and Management of Marine Mammals.* Smithsonian Institution Press, Washington, D.C.

U.S. Department of the Interior. 1971. "Our Living Land." *U.S. Department of the Interior Environmental Report.* U.S. Government Printing Office, Washington, D.C.

————. 1972. *River of Life, Water: The Environmental Challenge.* U.S. Government Printing Office, Washington, D.C.

————. Various years. *Annual Report of the Secretary of the Interior.* U.S. Government Printing Office, Washington, D.C.

Weber, Michael L. 1985. "Marine Mammal Protection." In *Audubon Wildlife Report: 1985.* Roger L. DiSilvestro (Ed.). National Audubon Society, New York, NY.

————. 1987. "Marine Mammal Protection." In *Audubon Wildlife Report: 1986.* Roger L. DiSilvestro (Ed.). Academic Press, Orlando, FL.

Wenk, Edward, Jr. 1972. *The Politics of the Ocean.* University of Washington Press, Seattle, WA.

Wheeland, Hoyt A. 1972. "Fishery Statistics of the United States, 1969." *Statistical Digest No. 63.* NMFS, Washington, D.C.

Chapter 8. Agency Resistance

Anonymous. July 20, 21, and 22, 1997. "Opinion Pages." *The Idaho Statesman.*

Bean, Michael J., and Melanie J. Rowland. 1997. *The Evolution of National Wildlife Law, Third Edition.* Praeger, Westport, CT.

Chandler, Alfred D. 1988. "The National Marine Fisheries Service." In *Audubon Wildlife Report: 1988/1989*. Academic Press, New York, NY. Pages 3–98.

Cohn, Jeffrey P. Winter 1997/1998. "How the Endangered Species Act Was Born." *Defenders*. Pages 6–13.

Eley, Thomas J., and T. H. Watkins. Fall 1991. "In a Sea of Trouble: The Uncertain Fate of the Pacific Salmon." *Wilderness*. Pages 19–26.

Environmental Defense Fund. March 1975. "EDF Enters Suit to Save Thousands of Porpoises." *EDF Letter*. Vol. 6, No. 2. (http://www.edf.org/pubs/newsletter)

———. May 1976. "Porpoise Victory Threatened by Legislation." *EDF Letter*. Vol. 7, No. 3. (http://www.edf.org/pubs/newsletter)

———. November 1977. "Final 1978–1980 Tuna Fishing Regulations Hailed as Significant Victory." *EDF Letter*. Vol. 8, No. 6. (http://www.edf.org/pubs/newsletter)

Fowle, Suzanne, and Rose Bierce (Eds.). 1991. *Proceedings of the Shrimp Trawl Bycatch Workshop*. Center for Marine Conservation, Washington, D.C.

Gambell, Ray. 1999. "The International Whaling Commission and the Contemporary Whaling Debate." In *Conservation and Management of Marine Mammals*. John R. Twiss Jr. and Randall R. Reeves (Eds.). Smithsonian Institution Press, Washington, D.C.

Gosliner, Michael L. 1999. "The Tuna–Dolphin Controversy." In *Conservation and Management of Marine Mammals*. John R. Twiss Jr. and Randall R. Reeves (Eds.). Smithsonian Institution Press, Washington, D.C.

Grandy, John. Telephone interview on April 10, 2000.

Greenberg, Eldon. Telephone conversation on April 17, 2000.

Hill, P. S., and D. P. DeMaster. 1999. *Alaska Marine Mammal Stock Assessments*. National Marine Mammal Laboratory, Seattle, WA.

Marine Mammal Commission. Various years. *Annual Report to Congress*. MMC, Washington, D.C.

McManus, Roger. Telephone conversation on March 30, 1999.

Minasian, Stanley M. (Producer). 1975. *The Last Days of the Dolphins?* Save the Dolphin and Environmental Defense Fund. Film. San Francisco, CA.

National Marine Fisheries Service. 1984. *The Marine Mammal Protection Act of 1972 Annual Report, April 1, 1983, to March 31, 1984*. NMFS, Washington, D.C.

———. 1999. *MMPA Bulletin*. 1st Quarter 1999, Issue No. 14.

———. 1999. *Commercial Fisheries: Landings Background Information*. Office of Science & Technology. (http://www.st.nmfs.gov)

———. Various years. *Annual Report of the National Marine Fisheries Service*. NMFS, Seattle, WA.

National Oceanic and Atmospheric Administration. 1978. *U.S. Ocean Policy in the 1970s: Status and Issues*. U.S. Department of Commerce, Washington, D.C. 328 pages.

National Research Council. 1990. *Decline of the Sea Turtles: Causes and Prevention*. National Academy Press, Washington, D.C.

Regenstein, Lewis G. December 1974. "A History of the Endangered Species Act of 1973, and an Analysis of its History; Strengths and Weaknesses; Administration; and Probable Future Effectiveness." Master's Thesis. Emory University. Atlanta, GA.

Reeves, Randall R., Brent S. Stewart, and Stephen Leatherwood. 1992. *The Sierra Club Handbook of Seals and Sirenians.* Sierra Club Books, San Francisco, CA.

Roe, Richard. Telephone interview on February 25, 1999.

Twiss, John R., Jr. Telephone conversation on March 30, 2000.

Twiss, John R., Jr., and Randall R., Reeves (Ed.). 1999. *Conservation and Management of Marine Mammals.* Smithsonian Institution Press, Washington, D.C.

Upton, Harold F., Peter Hoar, and Melissa Upton. 1992. *The Gulf of Mexico Shrimp Fishery: Profile of a Valuable Resource.* Center for Marine Conservation, Washington, D.C.

Weber, Michael L. Fall 1979. "Bowhead Whale: A U.S. Dilemma." *Whale Center Newsletter.* Pages 3–4.

―――. 1985. "Marine Mammal Protection." In *Audubon Wildlife Report: 1985.* Roger L. DiSilvestro (Ed.). National Audubon Society, New York, NY.

―――. 1986. "Federal Marine Fisheries Management." In *Audubon Wildlife Report: 1986.* Roger L. DiSilvestro (Ed.). National Audubon Society, New York, NY.

―――. 1987. "Marine Mammal Protection." In *Audubon Wildlife Report: 1986.* Roger L. DiSilvestro (Ed.). Academic Press, Orlando, FL. Pages 163–168.

Weber, Michael L., Deborah Crouse, Robert Irvin, and Suzanne Iudicello. 1995. *Delay and Denial: A Political History of Sea Turtles and Shrimp Fishing.* Center for Marine Conservation, Washington, D.C.

Chapter 9. Science, Uncertainty, and the Politics of Scarcity

Bean, Michael J., and Melanie J. Rowland. 1997. *The Evolution of National Wildlife Law, Third Edition.* Praeger, Westport, CT.

Blough, Heather. September 21–22, 2000. "The U.S. Pacific Groundfish Fishery off the Coasts of Washington, Oregon, and California." A case study prepared for a workshop on Pacific fisheries at risk sponsored by the David and Lucile Packard Foundation, Monterey, CA.

Buck, Eugene H. March 8, 1995. *Atlantic Bluefin Tuna: International Management of a Shared Resource.* 95-367 ENR. Congressional Research Service, Washington, D.C.

Crutchfield, James. Telephone interview on February 7, 1999.

Fricke, Peter. Telephone conversation on February 24, 1999.

Gordon, William G. Telephone interview on February 15, 2000.

Iudicello, Suzanne. Telephone conversation on February 23, 1999.

Iudicello, S., and M. Lytle. Winter 1994. "Marine Biodiversity and International Law: Instruments and Institutions that Can Be Used to Conserve Marine Biological Diversity Internationally." *Tulane Environmental Law Journal.*

Marine Mammal Commission. Various years. *Annual Report to Congress.* MMC, Washington, DC.

Moore, Rod. Telephone interview on February 12, 1999.

National Fish and Wildlife Foundation. 1995. *Needs Assessment of the National Marine Fisheries Service, 1996.* NFWF, Washington, D.C.

National Marine Fisheries Service. 1991. *Strategic Plan of the National Marine Fisheries Service: Goals and Objectives.* NMFS, Silver Spring, MD.

———. 1999. *Commercial Fisheries: Landings Background Information.* Office of Science & Technology. (http://www.st.nmfs.gov)

———. January. 2001. *Report to Congress: Status of Fisheries of the United States.* NMFS, Silver Spring, MD.

Rosenberg, Andrew. April 6, 2000. "Testimony before the House Committee on Resources Subcommittee On Fisheries Conservation, Wildlife, and Oceans." (http://www.legislative.noaa.gov)

Safina, Carl. 1997. *Song for the Blue Ocean.* Henry Holt & Company, New York, NY.

———. Telephone conversation on March 3, 1999.

Sutton, Michael. Telephone conversation on March 31, 1999.

U.S. Department of the Interior. Various years. *Annual Report of the Department of the Interior.* U.S. Government Printing Office, Washington, D.C.

Weber, Michael L. August 1990. A *Preliminary Study of International Trade in Western Atlantic Bluefin Tuna: A Report to the Sport Fishing Institute.* Sport Fishing Institute, Washington, D.C.

Weber, Michael L., and Sonja V. Fordham. 1996. *Managing the World's Shark Fisheries: Opportunities for International Conservation.* International Union for the Conservation of Nature and the Center for Marine Conservation, Washington, D.C.

Young, N. M., and S. Iudicello. 1997. "Blueprint for Whale Conservation: Implementing the Marine Mammal Protection Act." *Ocean and Coastal Law Journal.* Vol. 3, Nos. 1 & 2. Pages 149–216.

Chapter 10. Reinventing the Revolution

Alverson, Dayton Lee. Telephone interview on February 9, 1999.

———. Telephone interview on March 9, 1999.

———. Interview on June 25, 2000.

Alverson, Dayton L. Mark H. Freeberg, Steven A. Murawski, and J.B. Pope. 1994. *A Global Assessment of Fisheries Bycatch and Discards.* FAO, Rome, Italy.

Anderson, Lee G. Telephone interview on February 10, 1999.

Bean, Michael J., and Melanie J. Rowland. 1997. *The Evolution of National Wildlife Law, Third Edition.* Praeger, Westport, CT.

Congressional Record, 104th Congress, 2d session. 1996. October 18, 1995. H10235.

Crutchfield, James. Telephone interview on February 7, 1999.

Finch, R. 1985. "Fishery Management under the Magnuson Act." *Marine Policy.* Vol. 9, No. 3. Pages 170–179.

Fordham, Sonja V. 1996. *New England Groundfish: From Glory to Grief.* Center for Marine Conservation, Washington, D.C.

Fox, William W., Jr. Telephone conversation on February 17, 1999.

Fox, William W., Jr. et al. June 1989. *Statement of Concerned Scientists on the Reauthorization of the Magnuson Fishery Conservation and Management Act.* 6 pages.

Gilchrest, Wayne. Telephone conversation on September 28, 2000.

Henry, Wolcott, III. Telephone conversation on February 23, 1999.

Hinman, Ken. Telephone conversation on February 15, 1999.

———. Telephone conversation on March 12, 1999.

Iudicello, Suzanne. Telephone conversation on February 23, 1999.

Iudicello, Suzanne, Michael Weber, and Robert Wieland. 1999. *Fish, Markets, and Fishermen: The Economics of Overfishing.* Island Press, Washington, D.C.

Moore, Rod. Telephone interview on February 12, 1999.

Morehead, Bruce. Telephone conversation on February 18, 1999.

Mott, Bill. Telephone conversation on February 22, 1999.

National Fisheries Statistics Program. 1984. "Fishery Statistics of the United States, 1977." *Statistical Digest No. 71.* NMFS, Washington, D.C.

National Marine Fisheries Service. 1991. *Strategic Plan of the National Marine Fisheries Service: Goals and Objectives.* NMFS, Silver Spring, MD.

———. 1992. "Our Living Oceans." *Report on the Status of U.S. Living Marine Resources, 1992.* U.S. Department of Commerce, Washington, D.C.

———. 1996. "Our Living Oceans." *Report on the Status of U.S. Living Marine Resources, 1995.* U.S. Department of Commerce, NOAA Tech. Memo. NMFS- F/SPO-19. Silver Spring, MD.

National Oceanic and Atmospheric Administration. February 1, 2001. *NOAA FY2001 Budget Request.*(http://www.legislative.noaa.gov/budgetFy2001rev.html)

National Research Council, Committee on Fisheries. 1994. *Improving the Management of U.S. Marine Fisheries.* National Academy Press, Washington, D.C.

National Research Council, Committee on Fish Stocks Assessment Methods. 1998. National Academy Press, Washington, DC. (http://romulus.nap.edu/readingroom/books/fish)

Resource Statistics Division. 1981. "Fisheries of the United States, 1980." *Current Fishery Statistics No. 8100.* NMFS, Washington, D.C.

Safina, Carl. November 1995. "The World's Imperiled Fish." *Scientific American.* Pages 46–53.

Satchell, Michael. June 22, 1992. "The Rape of the Oceans." *U.S. News & World Report.* Pages 64–75.

Sissenwine, Michael P., and Andrew A. Rosenberg. 1993. "Marine Fisheries at a Critical Juncture." *Fisheries.* Vol. 18, No. 10. Pages 6–14.

Weber, Michael L. 1986. "Federal Marine Fisheries Management." In *Audubon Wildlife Report: 1986.* Roger L. DiSilvestro (Ed.). National Audubon Society, New York, NY. Office of the Press Secretary. October 11, 1996. Statement by the President. Washington, D.C.

Conclusion

Ad-Hoc Pacific Groundfish Fishery Strategic Plan Development Committee. 2000. *Transition to Sustainability: Pacific Fishery Management Council Groundfish Fishery Strategic Plan.* Pacific Fishery Management Council, Portland, OR.

Anonymous. July 1999. *Federal Fisheries Investment Task Force: Report to Congress.* Atlantic States Marine Fisheries Commission, Washington, D.C.

———. 2001. Monkfish Defense Fund Update, December 2000. (http://fish.org)

Bean, Michael J., and Melanie J. Rowland. 1997. *The Evolution of National Wildlife Law, Third Edition.* Praeger, Westport, CT.

Blough, Heather. September 21–22, 2000. "The U.S. Pacific Groundfish Fishery off the Coasts of Washington, Oregon, and California." A case study prepared for a workshop on Pacific fisheries at risk sponsored by the David and Lucile Packard Foundation. Monterey, CA.

Congressional Research Service. July 26, 1999. *Issue Brief 98011: Dolphin Protection and Tuna Seining.* (http://www.netpets.org/fish/reference/conservation/96011_3.html)

Crouse, Deborah. 1999. "Guest Editorial: The WTO Shrimp/Turtle Case." *Marine Turtle Newsletter.* No. 83. Pages 1–3.

Gay, Joel. February 2001. "Crab Rationalization Takes a Step Forward." *Pacific Fishing.* Page 34.

General Accounting Office. 2000. *Entry of Fishermen Limits Benefits of Buyback Programs.* GAO/RCED-00-120. General Accounting Office, Washington, D.C.

International Fisheries Division. 2000. *International Agreements Concerning Living Marine Resources of Interest to NOAA Fisheries.* (http://www.nmfs.gov/ oneagree.html)

Iudicello, Suzanne. September 21–22, 2000. "Case Study: The Pollock Trawl Fishery of the Eastern Bering Sea." A case study prepared for a workshop on Pacific fisheries at risk sponsored by the David and Lucile Packard Foundation. Monterey, CA.

Marine Mammal Commission. Various years. *Annual Report to Congress.* MMC, Washington, D.C.

National Marine Fisheries Service. January 29, 2001. "Press Release: Commercial Fishermen and NOAA Fisheries to Conduct Joint Monkfish Survey." Woods Hole, MA.

National Marine Fisheries Service. January 2001. *Report to Congress: Status of Fisheries of the United States.* NMFS, Silver Spring, MD.

Index